Philosophy
Journals
and
Serials

Philosophy
Journals
and
Serials

An Analytical Guide

Compiled by
DOUGLAS H. RUBEN

Annotated Bibliographies of Serials: A Subject Approach, Number 2

Greenwood Press
Westport, Connecticut • London, England

Library of Congress Cataloging in Publication Data
Ruben, Douglas H.
  Philosophy journals and serials.

  (Annotated bibliographies of serials: A subject
approach, ISSN 0748-5190; no. 2)
  Bibliography: p.
  Includes index.
  1. Philosophy—Periodicals—Bibliography.   I. Title.
II. Series: Annotated bibliographies of serials ; no. 2.
Z7127.R83   1985   [B72]   016.105   84-29021
ISBN 0-313-23958-4 (lib. bdg.)

Library of Congress Catalog Card Number: 84-29021
ISBN: 0-313-23958-4
ISSN: 0748-5190

First published in 1985

Greenwood Press
A division of Congressional Information Service, Inc.
88 Post Road West, Westport, Connecticut 06881

Printed in the United States of America

10 9 8 7 6 5 4 3 2 1

To my parents,

Belle and Chuck

*Philosophy recovers itself when it
ceases to be the device for dealing
with the problems of philosophers
and becomes the method, cultivated
by the philosophers, for dealing
with the problems of men.*

John Dewey

CONTENTS

SERIES FOREWORD

The effects of the "information explosion" have been pronounced in the area of serial publishing. Encouraged by the availability of word processing and computer printing, masses of journals have been flowing from the presses. Many of the new journals and serials have proved to be ephemeral, ceasing publication as a result of financial difficulties, mergers, or loss of interest by the editorial staff. However, a large number of useful new publications remains, augmenting older titles, which have undergone important editorial changes. On-line bibliographic databases and electronic publishing have also affected the direction of serial publishing. Despite modern technology, as the amount and type of material in most disciplines have proliferated, subscription prices have been maintaining a steady upward trend while library budgets generally have been declining.

The intent of the ANNOTATED BIBLIOGRAPHIES OF SERIALS: A SUBJECT APPROACH series is to make the task of serial selection and use more systematic through identifying, collecting, annotating, and indexing currently published English-language serials in the major fields of knowledge: social, natural, and applied sciences; humanities; medicine, and business. The scope of the series is worldwide. Serials cited are from the countries where English is a primary or important language, notably the United States, Canada, the United Kingdom, Ireland, Australia, New Zealand, South Africa, Nigeria, India, Pakistan, and Israel. It is worth noting that journals of international importance from areas of the world where the national language is not widely understood outside the country are often published wholly or in part in English.

Each series volume provides comprehensive coverage of the English-language serials in one subject area with extensively annotated entries for each serial. Titles are included if their primary focus is on the discipline of the particular volume. Many fields overlap, and it is sometimes difficult to decide where the dividing line should be. Occasionally, the same serial will appear in more than one volume, with the annotation pointing to its applicability to the subject area in question. The comprehensiveness of coverage and informative annotations, both exceeding that of other guides to the serial literature, will aid librarians in deciding whether a particular title is appropriate for their collections and aid scholars in determining whether the title will be useful for their research.

For the purposes of this series, "serial" is applied to periodicals having a frequency of issue of at least one per year.   This includes journals, publications of professional associations, magazines, selected newsletters, almanacs, and conference proceedings.   Newsletters are included only if they publish significant articles or have unique features. The newsletter literature is voluminous and in many disciplines would provide enough material for a separate volume.   The same can be said for government documents. Only the most important government publications are included in these serial volumes.

The serial entries are culled from extensive searches of manual and computerized information resources. Basic indexing and abstracting services, thorough searches of the most important resource collections, contacts with library associations and other professional associations: all have been utilized by the volume editors.   Wherever possible, volume editors have personally examined representative issues of each serial and have acquired information directly from publishers.

Frontmatter contains appropriate material, including a "How to Use this Book" section; a table of abstracts and indexes, a table of abbreviations, and a directory of microform and reprint publishers. Depending on the subject matter, some volumes are divided into chapters according to classified subdisciplines, while others are arranged in one unclassified sequence. Entries are alphabetical by title.   Geographic, subject, and, usually, title indexes round out each volume.

It is hoped that the information provided by ANNOTATED BIBLI-OGRAPHIES OF SERIALS will facilitate access to and help strengthen bibliographic control of the rapidly growing body of serial titles.

Norman Frankel

Series Editor

PREFACE

Philosophy is unique in that its progress can be measured by the kind of questions it asks rather than by the success of its answers. However, if we look merely at the answers, we are confronted by a bewildering variety of theories with so little common agreement. How is philosophy generally understood today? Do all these theories help define its aims and goals? For Bertrand Russell, modern philosophy is neither metaphysical nor subjective: rather, it aims only at clarifying the fundamental ideas of the sciences, and synthesizing the different sciences in a single comprehensive view. Broadly speaking, the historical emergence of philosophy as a recognized discipline is itself a synthesis of many naturalistic disciplines. Perhaps this explains why current philosophers think differently and why new trends begin.

One particular trend is to view philosophers either as <u>scholars</u> or <u>technicians</u>. Both scholars and technicians engage in free <u>intellectual</u> <u>inquiry</u>. Both seek in their respective realms the common task of exploring the unknown. But they tend to pull apart, the scholar drifting from immediate relevancies, and the technician defining problems too narrowly in terms of the environment of the moment. The strains of this divergence cause one to question the present-day role of philosophers.

Traditionally, scholars are viewed as "ivory tower" conservatives, alienated from the natural sources of philosophical events in the world. So headlong and pervasive is change today that the scholar's historical methods are decreasingly relevant as present guidelines. The scholar is in acute danger of being caught, in the words of one of Auden's poems, "Lecturing on navigation while the ship is going down." The technician, by contrast, works by the immediate relevance of his burgeoning twentieth-century world, which views all time as moving within a system of progress. Together, scholars and technicians try to make common sense a rational solution to radically new thinking. Such solutions currently take the form of the printed words in professional journals for philosophers. Journals from all over the world relate the analysis of intuition to the analysis of naturalistic events. The lines of connection may be illogical, and schools of philosophy may interact in functionally clumsy ways, but interact they do.

Thus, philosophy in the modern era paves the frontier for exciting new ideas and advances in both scholarly and technical domains. This rapid development accounts for a proliferation of journals in such specialty areas as children and education, biomedical ethics, business, medieval sciences, language, and artificial intelligence. As published papers abound in subspecialities, philosophy acquires important status in the humanities and natural sciences, a status that is highly attractive to a growing interdisciplinary readership.

Journals and Serials

Traditionally, philosophy comprises five general fields of study: logic, aesthetics, ethics, politics, and metaphysics. In all five fields is represented the continuum from historical to modern contemporary evolutions in philosophical criticism. This book surveys mainly the twentieth-century evolutions of philosophy in an analytic review of English-language serials published all over the world. To accomplish this goal, over 450 questionnaire surveys were sent to publishers and editors of philosophy journals listed in Ulrich's International Periodical Directory. An accompanying letter explained briefly the purpose of this study and requested a specimen copy of the journal for a fuller review. Over the past year seventy-four percent of the original sample returned questionnaires spanning the globe from such diverse countries as Japan and the Soviet Union to, of course, the United States.

The bibliography of 335 entries that follows includes newsletters, bulletins, and serials. Three basic criteria determined their selection. First, did the serial have a regular frequency of publication? Irregularity of distribution poses a problem because readers want a continuous flow of information. Second, did the serial contain articles, summaries, reviews, or some section in the English-language? Publications in Poland, France, Italy, and Israel, for instance, may circulate to English-speaking subscribers without ever or only rarely printing English articles or translations. But these were excluded from the survey. Finally, did the serial serve as a critical forum for discussion within the five traditional fields of philosophy? Ideally, the content of journals determines the appropriate field. But in practice even the most specialized journal in, say, aesthetics, may accept articles outside of the field proper, thereby creating an overlap. One alternative to reduce overlap was to expand beyond the five subfields to the following list: aesthetics, epistemology, ethics, morality, philosophy of religion, metaphysics (cosmology), philosophy of anthropology, philosophy of education, philosophy of history, philosophy of politics (law), philosophy of social sciences, semantics (language), logic, and general issues. Further divisions of philosophy covered in the journals may be found through the Subject Index.

As a reference tool, this analytical guide offers distinct advantages over the few directories of philosophical journals in print. First, evaluative comments strip away the artificial distinctions some professionals believe exist between "true" (hard) and "popularized" (soft) philosophy. Some argue, for instance, that Ayn Rand's creation of The Objectivist Forum is for the popular press rather than for a legitimate philosophy. Another artificial distinction exists between scholarly journals and journals predominately edited by graduate students. Such journals as Auslegung, Dialogue, Gnosis, and Kinesis receive subordinate billing in the international spotlight by virtue of assumptions about their lower caliber expositions.   Granted, articles in these journals are written by young or recently tenured philosophers, some even by undergraduates. But age alone can be a seriously irrelevant index of integrity for even the most complex theoretical paper.

A second major advantage of this analytical guide is that annotations may help guide librarians in making journal acquisitions and steer scholars to appropriate publication outlets. Each entry applies the same criteria for an objective evaluation of content, theme, and editorial policy.   Data on price, coverage of material, scholarship, and paid circulation simplify the purchase or submission decision.   Narratives seek to assess the authority of writers and the quality and extent of the material   suitable for the different branches of philosophy. Often an evaluation implies a recommendation for or against a purchase, which readers should assess in terms of their needs.

ACKNOWLEDGMENTS

Nearly two years ago the original concept for an analytical bibliography of philosophy serials and periodicals was brought to my attention by the series editor, Norman Frankel. During these past years, Norman's editorial advice on a number of spontaneous questions arising from the project greatly calmed my fears and confusion about the format and preferred analytical approach. Other colleagues to whom I owe a debt of appreciation participated in the preparatory and interpretation phases of research. Jeffrey Pack, from Adelphi University, a close friend, helped with the French-English translations on several foreign questionnaires. Marjorie Ho, head of the Cataloging Department at Western Michigan University, translated questionnaires in Chinese and other Oriental languages. Editorial representatives at Greenwood Press kept me abreast of productions of similar bibliographic sources and provided guidance regarding the stylistic logistics in the series. I especially acknowledge my wife, Marilyn, for her patience and diligence in proof-reading the manuscript. In the final analysis, however, the most important contribution to the completion of this book were the support and cooperation of publishers, editors, and professional organizations, who promptly returned their questionnaires with enlightening information about their serials.

HOW TO USE THIS BOOK

Today's burgeoning disciplines within philosophy make it nearly impossible to draw mutually exclusive divisions among schools of thought and applied research. Consequently, and also to avoid potential overlap among topics, the serials are arranged by entry number and alphabetically by title. Philosophical and broad areas represented by each journal, however, do appear in the Subject Index. Also provided is a Geographical Index, in which journals are arranged according to major country, state, or province of their circulation. While many serials enjoy an international circulation, concentrated areas for the target audience usually correspond to the geographic location of the publisher. This is particularly true for Polish, British, and Indian journals.

Entries in this analytical guide conform to a standard format used by each book in the series. A single entry usually contains two basic parts: preface and narrative. The preface documents the answers provided on the questionnaire regarding bibliographic information about the serial. Following this, a narrative section overviews such important considerations as the serial's scope, purpose and editorial policy, and a comparison to related serials. Narrative also describes the organization and special features of the content of appreciable interest to students and other potential readers. In cases where the questionnaire was returned but neither a reference nor a publisher copy of the journal was available, the narrative was omitted.

The descriptors in the preface divide that section into twenty discrete categories of information presented in the order below:

ENTRY NUMBER AND TITLE. DATE FOUNDED. TITLE CHANGES. FREQUENCY. PRICE. PUBLISHER. EDITOR. ILLUSTRATIONS. INDEX. ADVERTISEMENTS. CIRCULATION. MANUSCRIPT SELECTION. MICROFORMS. REPRINTS. BOOK REVIEWS. SPECIAL ISSUES. INDEXED/ABSTRACTED. TARGET AUDIENCE. SAMPLE COPIES. ACCEPTANCE RATE.

Where the category applies, it is noted followed by the appropriate information. The descriptors ILLUSTRATIONS, INDEX, and ADVERTISE-MENTS stand alone to indicate inclusion in the journal; by the same token, if the answer to a descriptor is not available, the descriptor is omitted. An explanation of each descriptor appears below:

ENTRY NUMBER AND TITLE: The correct formal title, preceded by an entry number.

TITLE CHANGES: Former title names and date changed.

DATE FOUNDED: Date of origin of the journal (not the organization).

FREQUENCY: Regularity of publication. *

PRICE: Subscription price to individuals (personal) and institutions.

PUBLISHER: Name and address as provided or found in reference works.

EDITOR: Editor-in-chief, individual(s) or institutional body.

ILLUSTRATIONS: Are there illustrations (graphs, figures, etc.)?

INDEX: Is there an index (yearly, monthly, etc.)?

ADVERTISEMENTS: Are paid or exchange advertisements included?

CIRCULATION: Regular paid circulation.

MANUSCRIPT SELECTION: Who decides what articles are accepted (refereed, editor)?

MICROFORMS: Are back issues available on microform? If so, from what source? ***

REPRINTS: Are reprints available? If so, from what source (authors, publishers, etc.)? ***

BOOK REVIEWS: Is there a book review section? What is the average number of reviews per issue? What is the average length of the review. Are the reviews signed?

SPECIAL ISSUES: Does the serial publish special issues or supplements? How frequently?

INDEXED/ABSTRACTED: Where is the serial primarily indexed or abstracted? **

TARGET AUDIENCE: Who is the intended readership (academic, general public, etc.)? *

SAMPLE COPIES: Are sample copies available to libraries, individuals?

ACCEPTANCE RATE: What is the average <u>percentage</u> of articles accepted for publication?

*   See Table of Abbreviations

**   See Table of Abstracts and Indexes

*** See Directory of Microform and Reprint Publishers

ABBREVIATIONS

Frequency of Publication

a	annual
bm	bimonthly (every two months)
bw	biweekly (every two weeks)
m	monthly
q	quarterly
sa	semiannual (twice per year)
sm	semimonthly (twice per month)
w	weekly
3/yr.	three issues per year
5/yr.	five issues per year
6/yr.	six issues per year
7/yr.	seven issues per year

Target Audience

AC	academic
GP	general public
HS	high school
SP	specialist

ABSTRACTS AND INDEXES

AbAn	Abstracts in Anthropology
ABC	ABC Political Science
AbEnSt	Abstracts of English Studies
AbSocW	Abstracts for Social Workers
AmerH	America: History and Life
AP	L'Anee Philoogique
API	Alternative Press Index
ArtHumCitI	Arts and Humanities Citation Index
BibFE	Bibliografia Filosofica Espanola
BIHEP	Bibliographic Index to Health Education Periodicals
BioAb	Biological Abstracts
BoA	Books Abroad
BPI	Business Periodicals Index
BRI	Book Review Index
BritHumI	British Humanities Index
BulSig	Bulletin Signaletique
CA	Computer Abstracts
CathI	Catholic Periodical Index
ChemAb	Chemical Abstracts
ChildDevAb	Child Development Abstracts
ChiPerI	Chicano Periodical Index
CIJE	Current Index to Journals in Education
CommAb	Communication Abstracts
CommDevAb	Community Development Abstracts
CPA	Criminology and Penology Abstracts
CurrConSocBS	Current Contents: Social and Behavioral Sciences
CurrContAH	Current Contents: Arts and Humanities
EcolAb	Ecology Abstracts
EdI	Education Index
EI	Engineering Index
EM	Excerpta Medica
EnInAb	Energy Information Abstracts

ERIC   Educational Resources Information Center

FamAb   Family Abstracts

HistAb   Historical Abstracts
HumI   Humanities Index

IMed   Index Medicus
InAmPerV   Index to American Periodical Verse
Infor   Infodex
InPhil   Informationsdienst fur Philosophie
IntBibZeit   Internationale Bibliographe der Zeitschriftenliteratue
IntPolSc   International Political Science Abstracts
IntZeitBibGren   Internationale Zeitschriftenshau fur Bibleweissenschrift
                        un Grenzgebiete

JProCIn   Journal Processing Citation Index

LLBA   Language and Language Behavior Abstracts

MathR   Mathematical Reviews
MC   Management Contents
MedL   Mediovo Latino
MHRA   MHRA Bibliography
MPerIn   Monthly Periodical Index
MusicArtG   Music Articles Guide

NewTAb   New Testament Abstracts

OldTAb   Old Testament Abstracts

PAIS   Public Affairs Information Service
PenAb   Penology Abstracts
PhilosI   Philosopher's Index
PolAb   Pollution Abstracts
PSA   Police Sciences Abstracts
PsyAb   Psychological Abstracts
PsyRG   Psychological Reader's Guide
PubAdAb   Public Administration Abstracts

RBibPhil   Repertoire Bibliographique de la Philosophie
RedG   Redation des Gnomon
RelAb   Religion and Theological Abstracts
RelPerI   Religious Periodical Index
RG   Reader's Guide to Periodical Literature

RIE	Resources in Education
RZ	Referativnyi Zhurnal
SafSciAb	Safety Science Abstracts
SCI	Science Citation Index
SciHu	Sciences Humaines
SLPrW	Stamm-Leitfaden durch Presse und Werbung
SocAb	Sociological Abstracts
SocEdAb	Sociology of Education Abstracts
SSCI	Social Science Citation Index
SSI	Social Science Index
URS	Universal Reference System
UrStAb	Urban Studies Abstracts
USSRAcScAbJ	USSR Academy of Science Abstracts Journal
VerZ	Verlagsgruppe Zeller
ZentMath	Zentralblatt fur Mathematik

DIRECTORY OF MICROFORM AND REPRINT PUBLISHERS

AMS

AMS Reprint Company
56 East 13th Street
New York, New York 10003

BaBPub

Basil Blackwell Publishers
108 Cowley Road
Oxford
England OX4 1JF

BHW

Bell & Howell
Microphoto Division
Old Mansfield Road
Wooster, Ohio 44691

EPML

E.P. Microform, Limited
East Ardsley, Wafefield
West Yorkshire
England WF3 2JN

GryEdL

Gryphon Editions, Limited
P.O. Box 76108
Birmingham, Alabama 35223

ISI

Institute for Scientific Information
3501 Market Street
University City Science Center
Philadelphia, Pennsylvania 19104

KR

Kraus Reprints
Route 100
Millwood, New York 10546

MIC

Micromedia Limited
P.O. Box 502, Station S
Toronto M5J 2L7, Canada

UMI   University Microfilms International
                             300 North Zeeb Road
                             Ann Arbor, Michigan 48106

Philosophy
Journals
and
Serials

BIBLIOGRAPHY

1. Accent. DATE FOUNDED: 1965. TITLE CHANGES: Good Templar (1965-1979), Reformation (1980-1981). FREQUENCY: q. PRICE: 35 Swiss Francs/yr. member, 59 Swiss Francs/yr. nonmember. PUBLISHER: Swedish Good Templar Youth Association, Bolidenvagen 14, S-121, 63 Johanneshov, Sweden. EDITOR: Hakan Olsson. ILLUSTRATIONS. ADVERTISEMENTS. MANUSCRIPT SELECTION: Editor (and occasionally editorial board). REPRINTS: authors. BOOK REVIEWS: 10-15 reviews, 1-2 pp., signed. TARGET AUDIENCE: GP, HS. SAMPLE COPIES: Individuals.

Accent is one of the few Scandinavian journals internationally known for consumerism news about drug abuse and policy structure. Local information on activities of the Swedish Good Templar Youth Association combines with an appraisal of governmental issues. Reviews of books, films and theatre focus on the preservation of human peace. The majority of articles by members of the Association discuss the Temperance movement and are against such rehabilitative moral philosophies as appear in Public Policy, Human Rights, and Ethics.
  A typical issue contains three to four short articles followed by reviews, announcements of the Association's events, and international Templar groups. Reviewers selected by the editorial board are specialists in world affairs and on Swedish drug enforcement laws.

2. Acta Philosophica Fennica. DATE FOUNDED: 1935. FREQUENCY: 3/yr. PRICE: $25/yr. institutions, $10/yr. personal. PUBLISHER: The Philosophical Society of Finland, 4 Laivurinkatu, Helsinki, 15, Finland. EDITOR: Ilkka Niiniluoto. ILLUSTRATIONS. ADVERTISEMENTS. CIRCULATION: 500. MANUSCRIPT SELECTION: Refereed, editorial board. REPRINTS: authors. INDEXED/ABSTRACTED: PhilosI. TARGET AUDIENCE: AC. SAMPLE COPIES: Libraries.

This journal addresses the work of Finnish philosophers in such traditional branches as epistemology, ethics, religion, metaphysics, law and logic. APF recognizes the contemporary need for eclecticism in the resolution of problems in scholarly inquiry. Academic contributors project this integrative position onto articles with the same clarity as in the Philosophical Review, American Philosophical Quarterly, and International Philosophical Review.

Each volume contains a collection of monographs or articles published as a book series on a special theme. Themes on Finnish philosophy draw noteworthy contrasts between American liberalism and European conservatism in the practice and theory of philosophical disciplines.

3.   Afro-American Journal of Philosophy.   DATE FOUNDED: 1977. FREQUENCY: q.   PRICE: $7.50/yr. personal, free to members. PUBLISHER: Afro-American Philosophy Association, Incorporated, P.O. Box 2121, New York, New York 10116.   EDITOR: Percy E. Johnston. ILLUSTRATIONS.   INDEX.   ADVERTISEMENTS.   CIRCULATION: 1,500. MANUSCRIPT SELECTION: Refereed, editorial board. REPRINTS: authors. BOOK REVIEWS: 2 reviews, 2 pp., signed.   TARGET AUDIENCE: AC. SAMPLE COPIES: Libraries.

AAJP is the official publication of the Afro-American Philosophy Association (AAPS), an organization whose primary aim is the promotion of scholarship among Black Americans.   Solicited essays on general topics of aesthetics, epistemology, history, education, cybernetics and Oriental and African cultures shape the genre of discussion toward advancements in thought. Articles strongly reflect the antithesis of historical perspectives about prejudice and racism. Much like Secular Subjects and American Atheist, this journal views itself as pragmatic for Blacks in philosophy.
   A typical issue offers two articles, announcements, and a list of forth-coming articles.   The style of typeset reflects a low budget, but this in no way detracts from the philosophical acumen in the arguments of each article.

4.   Agora. DATE FOUNDED: 1970. FREQUENCY: 3/yr. PRICE: $8/yr. personal. PUBLISHER: State University of New York, Potsdam, New York 13676.   EDITOR: Martin A. Bertman.   ILLUSTRATIONS. CIRCULATION: 600.   MANUSCRIPT SELECTION: Editor.   REPRINTS: author.   BOOK REVIEWS: 3 reviews, 1-2 pp., signed.   INDEXED/ABSTRACTED: PhilosI. TARGET AUDIENCE: AC.   SAMPLE COPIES: Libraries. ACCEPTANCE RATE: 17%.

Topics generally accepted in Agora cover social and humanistic theory with emphasis on politics and science.   Humanism receives a unique blend of analytic and synthetic interpretations, resulting in a scope that differs widely from the sociologic orientations of The Humanist, and Humanities and Society.   Academic contributors from scientia may sacrifice objectivity for a new outlook on evolutionary dynamics in human communication.
   Each issue of Agora is a collage of four to five short articles leading to a series of book reviews.   Readers may find Agora complementary to lighter essays on the arts, sciences, and politics of human nature that appear in Aitia and the Cornell Journal of Social Relations.

5.   Aitia. DATE FOUNDED: 1972. FREQUENCY: 3/yr. PRICE: $16/2 yrs. institutions, $14/2 yrs. personal. PUBLISHER: James P. Friel, Knapp Hall 15, State University of New York Farmingdale, Farmingdale, New York 11735.   EDITOR: James P. Friel. ILLUSTRATIONS. ADVERTISEMENTS.

CIRCULATION: 3,000. MANUSCRIPT SELECTION: Refereed, editorial board. BOOK REVIEWS: 5 reviews, 1-2 pp., signed. INDEXED/ABSTRACTED: PhilosI. TARGET AUDIENCE: AC, GP.

In its eleventh year of publication, Aitia represents the first magazine in the United States to focus on the problem of teaching humanities. Members of the Center for Philosophy, Law, Citizenship, Incorporated, a nonprofit corporation, took over Aitia in 1974, promoting the idea that philosophy is a central force in society. Articles highlight ethics, peace and paramount issues in the fight against military armament. Unlike Ethics and the British Journal of Aesthetics, this journal strives for an objective portrayal of education by presenting course curricula, poetry, and criticisms of art, theatre and film.

The type of article commonly found in Aitia is not overly technical and is relatively jargon-free. A single issue contains five to six short articles interspersed with editorial commentary. Book reviews clearly integrate philosophy with worldwide branches of modern life. It is noteworthy that Aitia is the Greek word for "goal" or "purpose," which certainly fits its overall contents.

6. Ajatus. DATE FOUNDED: 1926. FREQUENCY: a. PUBLISHER: The Philosophical Society of Finland, Department of Philosophy, University of Halsinki, Unioninkatu 40-B, 00170, Helsinki 17, Finland. EDITOR: Juha Manninen. ADVERTISEMENTS. CIRCULATION: 500. MANUSCRIPT SELECTION: Refereed, editorial board. REPRINTS: author. BOOK REVIEWS: 1-4 reviews, 2 pp., signed. SPECIAL ISSUES: Occasional. INDEXED/ABSTRACTED: PhilosI. TARGET AUDIENCE: AC. SAMPLE COPIES: Libraries.

Ajatus is regarded as a forum for Finnish thought, covering such major categories as epistemology, morality, religion, social sciences, and logic. Organized, in part, to facilitate a national platform for the Philosophical Society of Finland, Ajatus publishes articles by local scholars written mostly in Swedish or Finnish, especially from Volume 40 onwards. Dominance of cultural coverage, much like Acta Philosophical Fennica, limits the global scope of the journal and this may account for the small circulation.

The one yearly volume is a compendium of extensive articles and short book reviews, in large part focused on current Finish philosophy or indigenous publications.

7. Aletheia. DATE FOUNDED: 1977. FREQUENCY: a. PRICE: $15/yr. institutions. PUBLISHER: The International Academy of Philosophy Press, 403 South Britain Road, Irving, Texas 705060. EDITOR: Josef Seifert. ADVERTISEMENTS. MANUSCRIPT SELECTION: Refereed, editorial board. REPRINTS: authors. INDEXED/ABSTRACTED: PhilosI. TARGET AUDIENCE: AC.

Aletheia covers all major areas of philosophy essential to the scholarly appraisal of social science, art, humanities, and psychology. Formerly a phenomenological forum, Aletheia now publishes articles on ethics, metaphysics, epistemology, and logic. This expansion furthers the very definition of philosophy and scientific reasoning, from principles of ontology and language to the methodology of "objective inquiry." Concepts readily explored in the social and natural sciences (e.g., feminism, individualism) provide an objective orientation, rich in thought for graduate students. Editions of Aletheia study applied and analytic philosophy equal to articles in Contemporary Philosophy, Inquiry, and Explorations in Knowledge.

Each issue focuses on a current theme considered of merit by the editorial board. Contributions are both solicited and unsolicited and run six to ten pages long. Aletheia holds especial interest for the eclecticist who draws new insights from a collective presentation.

8.   Algemeen Nederlands Tijdschrift voor Wijsbegeerte. DATE FOUNDED: 1907.   TITLE   CHANGES: Tijdschrift   voor   Wijsbegeerte   (1907-1932), Algemeen   Nederlands   Tijdschrift   voor   Wijsbegeerte   en   Psychologie (1933-1965). FREQUENCY: q. PRICE: $20/yr. institutions, $24/yr. personal. PUBLISHER: Van Gorcum and Company, P.O. Box 43,9400, AA Assen, Netherlands.   EDITOR: Theo A.F. Kuipers.   ILLUSTRATIONS. INDEX. ADVERTISEMENTS.   CIRCULATION: 750.   MANUSCRIPT   SELECTION: Refereed, editorial board. REPRINTS: author. BOOK REVIEWS: 7 reviews, 1-2 pp., signed. INDEXED/ABSTRACTED: PhilosI. TARGET AUDIENCE: AC. SAMPLE COPIES: Libraries. ACCEPTANCE RATE: 40%.

Dutch, Flemish, and English articles by scholars cover general topics in philosophical discourse, particularly on ethics and morality.   ANTW's prestigious role in Dutch philosophy continues a long tradition of well-composed papers objectively critical of controversial themes in a direct style comparable to American Philosophical Quarterly and Metaphilosophy.

Issues of ANTW typically provide three to four original articles followed by reactions to previous articles.   This analytical exchange opens interpretations for subsequent rebuttals.   The book reviews are generally short and to an extent correspond to the list of books received.

9. American Atheist. DATE FOUNDED: 1959. FREQUENCY: m. PRICE: $25/yr. personal. PUBLISHER: American Atheist Press, Box 2117, Austin, Texas 78768.   EDITOR: Madalyn Murray O'Hair.   ILLUSTRATIONS. CIRCULATION: 5,000.   MANUSCRIPT SELECTION: Editor. REPRINTS: author.   BOOK   REVIEWS: 2-3   reviews,   500   words,   signed. INDEXED/ABSTRACTED: MPerIn. TARGET AUDIENCE: AC, GP, HS. SAMPLE COPIES: Libraries, individuals. ACCEPTANCE RATE: 20%.

AA is the official organ of the Society of Separationists, which strongly upholds the freedom of thought and dogmatic separation between State and Church.   AA encourages development and public acceptance of this philosophy through its views on art and sciences that unreservedly promote the supremacy of reason over the cosmos. In every monthly issue one finds the stern refutation of religion written primarily by featured columnists. The permeable aim of AA is a Darwinian revivalism. But this radical perspective tends to lose objectivity, lagging behind articles in, for instance, Inquiry or even American Rationalist.

Common issues of AA begin with six to seven original articles and then short commentaries by regular columnists. Two or so selections of poetry are interspersed with creative illustrations, all encased in an impressive artistic layout.

10. American Imago. DATE FOUNDED: 1939. FREQUENCY: q. PRICE: $21/yr. institutions, $16/yr. personal. PUBLISHER: Wayne State University Press, Leonard N. Simons Building, 5959 Woodward Avenue, Detroit, Michigan 48202. EDITOR: Harry Slochower. ILLUSTRATIONS. INDEX. MANUSCRIPT SELECTION: Refereed, editorial board. REPRINTS: KR. INDEXED/ABSTRACTED: PsyAb, SSCI. TARGET AUDIENCE: AC.

AI symbolizes a long tradition of psychoanalytic philosophy as originated by Sigmund Freud and Hans Sachs. The official journal of the Association for Applied Psychoanalysis, AI is devoted to criticism of culture, science, the arts and general humanities, and is perhaps the only psycho-dynamically-oriented journal featuring interdisciplinary scholars. Aitia and Humanities in Society, by comparison, accept articles along a wider continuum of disciplines but mostly by philosophers. Because theoretical doctrines in AI are limited to those psychoanalytic sympathizers, the journal functions more as a newsletter than a scholarly resource.
A typical issue contains five to seven original unsolicited articles running about ten to thirty pages long. The printed pictures of individuals on whom biographical sketches are written impart an impressive aesthetic to the artistic design.

11. American Philosophical Quarterly. DATE FOUNDED: 1964. FRE-QUENCY: q. PRICE: $30/yr. institutions, $15/yr. personal. PUBLISHER: Basil Blackwell, 108 Crowley Road, Oxford, England OX4 1JF. EDITOR: Nicholas Rescher. ADVERTISEMENTS. CIRCULATION: 1,600. MANU-SCRIPT SELECTION: Refereed, editorial board. REPRINTS: author. INDEXED/ABSTRACTED: ArtHumCitI, CurrContAH, HumI, PhilosI. TARGET AUDIENCE: AC. SAMPLE COPIES: Libraries.

Esteemed journal among philosophers, APQ welcomes articles by philosophers of any country on modern or historical subjects reflective of an analytical orientation. Over 30 acclaimed scholars on the editorial board represent a continuum of contemporary topics from ethics and morality to political science and epistemology. Articles define principal arguments in unambiguous terms that readily serve as a model structure for such journals as Nous, Dialogue, and Synthese.
A typical issue contains from nine to ten articles, with a list of books received at the back. Article length varies from ten to twenty pages and occasionally those along a theme are published in a monograph series.

12. The American Rationalist. DATE FOUNDED: 1956. FREQUENCY: bm. PRICE: $6/yr. personal. PUBLISHER: Rationalist Association, Incorporated, P.O. Box 994, St. Louis, Missouri 63188. EDITOR: Gordon Stein. ILLUSTRATION. ADVERTISEMENTS. CIRCULATION: 975. MANUSCRIPT SELECTION: Editor. MICROFORMS: UMI. REPRINTS: Editor. BOOK REVIEWS: 8 reviews, 300 words, signed. TARGET AUDIENCE: GP. SAMPLE COPIES: Libraries, individuals.

Rationalism as viewed by the AR magazine is an alternative to religious superstition. Articles focus on atheism, free-thought, history, and separation between Church and State. Criticism of theology employs the moral and ethical stratagem of Robert G. Ingersoll, America's greatest free-thinker who reinforced independence from fundamentalism. The anthology of atheism and rationalism resembles articles in Free Inquiry and are written by strongly vocal members and academic sympathizers of the Rationalistic movement.

A typical issue of AR is a potpourri of the Association's announcements, original articles, and book reviews on a wide variety of topics from creationism to religious suppression. Noteworthy are the insightful letters-to-the-editor, which reverberate animosity toward organized religion and call for a return to Darwinism.

13. The American Theosophist. DATE FOUNDED: 1915. FREQUENCY: sa. PRICE: $5.50/yr. personal. PUBLISHER: Theosophical Society, 1926 North Main, Box 270, Wheaton, Illinois 60189. EDITORS: Dora Kunz, Scott Miners. ILLUSTRATIONS. CIRCULATION: 7,000. MANUSCRIPT SELECTION: Editors. BOOK REVIEWS: 2 reviews, 1-2 pp., signed. SPECIAL ISSUES: Occasional. TARGET AUDIENCE: AC, GP. SAMPLE COPIES: Libraries. ACCEPTANCE RATE: 20%.

AT is the official journal of the Theosophical Society in America and as such reserves for each member full freedom to interpret the teachings of theosophy that embody a world-wide vision of brotherhood. This journal claims to impose no dogmas, but only points toward sources of unity such as devotion to truth, love for all living things, and commitment to altruism. To promote this egalitarian humanism, articles on ancient history, the cosmos, ethics, and religion are written by scholars. Although theosophic arguments resist dogma, the articles themselves do convey a definite and pursuasive tone similar to the Monist.

Nine articles usually appear per issue, accompanied by editorial commentary and a collection of short book reviews. Readers interested in the scientificism of "psychical phenomena" may view AT in juxtaposition to The American Atheist and Zetetic Scholar.

14. Analele Universitatii Bucuresti series Filozofia. DATE FOUNDED: 1969. TITLE CHANGES: Filozofie (1969-1973), Filozofie, Drept, Istorie (1974-1976). FREQUENCY: a. PUBLISHER: Tipografia Universitatii Bucuresti, Soseaua Panduri, Romania. EDITOR: Universitatea Bucuresti. ILLUSTRATIONS. MANUSCRIPT SELECTION: Editor. BOOK REVIEWS: 6 reviews, 1-3 pp., signed. TARGET AUDIENCE: AC, GP. SAMPLE COPIES: Libraries, individuals. ACCEPTANCE RATE: 5%.

AUBF is a major vehicle for expression in Romanian philosophy. Profiles connected with general areas of aesthetics, epistemology, ethics, morality, and history of law advance the journal's specialization in scientific objectivity. The competence of contributors comes across by the depth of discussions on multidisciplinary trends, many using quantitative data. Applied philosophy is exploratory, whereas the International Journal of Applied Philosophy and even Thinking are both more direct upon practical methods of application.

Issues of AUBF contain twenty to thirty articles apparently representative of major developments in Romanian study. Books selected for review are largely in Romanian.

15. Analysis. DATE FOUNDED: 1933. FREQUENCY: q. PRICE: $33/yr. institutions, $21/yr. personal. PUBLISHER: Basil Blackwell Publishers, 108 Crowley Road, Oxford, England OX4 1JF. EDITOR: Christopher Kirwan. INDEX. ADVERTISEMENTS. CIRCULATION: 1,700. MANUSCRIPT SELECTION: Refereed, editorial board. INDEXED/ ABSTRACTED: ArtHumCitI, PhilosI. TARGET AUDIENCE: AC. SAMPLE COPIES: Libraries, individuals. ACCEPTANCE RATE: 18%.

Analysis is one of the few forums for active debate among scholars of modern contemporary philosophy. Exchanges of the analytical tradition surface in articles on denotation (semantics), physicalism, and thorough criticism against epistemology and morality. Rejoinders raise awareness to pitfalls in logical arguments and mistranslations of another philosopher's revered works. Articles do not normally exceed 3,000 words in length or survey purely historical and exegetical topics, although varying degrees of exception appear from time to time. Authors are mostly scholars in what could easily become an egocentric portrait of British philosophy such as British Journal for the Philosophy of Science.
  Like Philosophical Quarterly and Mind, Analysis presents an anthology of twelve to thirteen articles, some book reviews and a statement of aims and purposes of the journal.

16. Annales D'Esthetique/Chronika Aesthetikes. DATE FOUNDED: 1962. FREQUENCY: a. PRICE: $7/yr. institutions, $4/yr. personal. PUBLISHER: The Hellenic Society of Aesthetics, 79 Vasilissis Sophias, Athens, 140 Greece. EDITOR: Hellenic Society of Aesthetics. ILLUSTRATIONS. INDEX. CIRCULATION: 700. MANUSCRIPT SELECTION: Refereed, editorial board. REPRINTS: author. BOOK REVIEWS: 9-12 reviews, 700 words, signed. INDEXED/ABSTRACTED: PhilosI. TARGET AUDIENCE: AC. ACCEPTANCE RATE: 10%.

ACA offers reflections of ancient and modern Greek aesthetics and general issues in the philosophy of art. It is an official outlet for the Hellenic Society of Aesthetics and publishes specialty papers which compare cultural and architectural evolutions with early Roman civilizations. While similar to Journal of the History of Ideas and Journal of the History of Philosophy, ACA departs from pure history in articles on current ecological movements and the exigency of artistic liberation.
  Thirteen original articles comprise the first portion of an annual edition. Short book reviews are followed by a bibliography of selected, annotated articles in the philosophy of aesthetics. Together with the British Journal of Aesthetics and Aitia, ACA provides useful guidance for readers studying the antecedents of art, allegory, imagination, and structural development.

17. Annales Universitatis Mariae Curie-Sklodowska. DATE FOUNDED: 1976. FREQUENCY: a. PUBLISHER: UMCS, Pl. Marii Curie-Sklodowskiej 5, 20-031, Lublin, Poland. EDITOR: Zdzislaw Cackowski. CIRCULATION: 525. MANUSCRIPT SELECTION: Editor. TARGET AUDIENCE: AC. SAMPLE COPIES: Libraries, individuals. ACCEPTANCE RATE: 90%.

AU is primarily the Polish equivalent to American Philosophical Quarterly, Dialogue, and those periodicals identified as the mainstays of aesthetics, epistemology, ethics, religion, and social sciences. AU invites cross-cultural essays which interrelate dynamics of philosophical thought with sociology. Articles that extend or evaluate theory objectively cover certain philosophers (e.g., Hume, Kant) as well as relevant historic   periods (e.g., French enlightenment, Soviet communism).   Discussions are polemical, but they encapsulate the many charted ideas in Polish philosophy.

AU contains ten to fifteen articles, no book reviews, and English translations of the summary of each foreign paper. Noteworthy is that Philosophia-Sociologia represents only one section in a series of different areas of this journal.

18.   Annual Proceedings of the Center for Philosophic Exchange.   DATE FOUNDED: 1969.   FREQUENCY: a.   PRICE: $6.50/yr. institutions. PUBLISHER: Center   for   Philosophic   Exchange,   State   University College, Brockport, New York   14420.   EDITOR: Jack Glickman. CIRCULATION: 400.   MANUSCRIPT SELECTION: Editor.   REPRINTS: Editor. TARGET AUDIENCE: AC. SAMPLE COPIES: Libraries, individuals.

APCPE publishes the papers of guest lecturers presenting at the Center for Philosophic Exchange.   This is a nonprofit organization founded on the principle that academic and public issues express basic educational values. The Center conducts conferences and seminars on a variety of philosophical topics and makes available the transcripts in television tapes or through the proceedings.   The collected papers of extensive international programs appear in annual editions.   Invited scholars   seemingly orient their material around the needs of faculty and students as might appear in The Modern Schoolman.

19.   Antioch Review. DATE FOUNDED: 1941. FREQUENCY: q. PRICE: $20/yr. institutions, $15/yr. individuals. PUBLISHER: The Antioch Review, P.O. Box 148, Yellow Springs, Ohio   45387.   EDITOR: Robert S. Fogarty. ILLUSTRATIONS.   INDEX.   ADVERTISEMENTS. CIRCULATION: 4,500. MANUSCRIPT   SELECTION: Editors.   MICROFORMS: BHW,   UMI. REPRINTS: author.   BOOK REVIEWS: 37 reviews/yr., 1-2 pp., signed. INDEXED/ABSTRACTED: AbEnSt, BRI, CurrContAH, HistAb, InAmPerV, LLBA, PhilosI, SocAb, SSCI. TARGET AUDIENCE: AC, GP. ACCEPTANCE RATE: 5%.

AR is an independent journal of critical and creative thought with articles of interest to both the liberal scholar and educated layman. It attracts international readership by reflecting the zeitgeist of arts, poetry, politics, and current affairs. Underlying this orientation is a strong interest in magic. The art of illusion speaks through cartoons, satires, and explorations of classic epistemology, the latter being most infrequent.   Reduced to a few words, AR is an experiment in playful imagination. Fiction writers compete for the $10 per page of manuscript and engender a softer approach to philosophy as appear in Aitia or Teaching Philosophy.

Typical issues are divided into four basic parts. First there are three to four articles, sometimes related thematically. Second, three to four fictional stories give flexibility to the contents. Third, a healthy assortment of over twelve poems, a page or so long, touch upon improvisation. Finally, announcements, editorials, indices, and a brief description of contributors fall under the category of "Etcetera."

20. Archiv Fuer Rechts-und Sozialphilosophie. DATE FOUNDED: 1907. FREQUENCY: q. PRICE: 108 Deutch Marks/yr. institutions. PUBLISHER: Franz Steiner Verlag, 6MBH, 62 Wiesbaden, Friedrichstr. 24, West Germany. EDITOR: Werner Maihofer. ILLUSTRATIONS. INDEX. ADVERTISEMENTS. CIRCULATION: 1,000. MANUSCRIPT SELECTION: Editor. BOOK REVIEWS: 10-15 reviews, 1-3 pp., signed. SPECIAL ISSUES: Occasional. INDEXED/ABSTRACTED: PhilosI. TARGET AUDIENCE: AC.

AFRS concentrates heavily on philosophy of law and social philosophy relative to the cultural matrix of West Germany. International articles trace the manifestation of legal and ethical policy, with direct implications for interdisciplinary studies (i.e., education, anthropology, sociology, psychology, etc.). Central to most essays is the act of political injustice and invasive mechanisms for social control. Contributions to AFRS are similar in style and content to Philosophy and Public Affairs and Philosophy and Social Action, but these latter periodicals are less ambitious as statements against the practices of government. Authors are well known scholars in areas related to social science.

21. Artificial Intelligence. DATE FOUNDED: 1970. FREQUENCY: q. PRICE: 400 Dutch Guilders/yr. personal. PUBLISHER: Elsevier- North Holland, 52 Vanderbilt Avenue, New York, New York 10017. EDITOR: Daniel G. Bobrow. ILLUSTRATIONS. INDEX. ADVERTISEMENTS. MANUSCRIPT SELECTION: Refereed, editorial board. REPRINTS: author. INDEXED/ABSTRACTED: CA, EI, MathR, SocAb. TARGET AUDIENCE: AC. SAMPLE COPIES: Libraries.

AI offers a medium of publication for papers dealing with theory and practice of computer programs and other artifacts that manifest "intelligent" behavior. Papers spread over a wide variety of topics including computer science, mathematics, linguistics, logic, psychology, and aspects of technological advancement. AI is not for cognitive and computer scientists alone, since the philosophy of language is present in nearly every objective essay on communication theory. In some respects, AI follows from traditions found in Philosophy of Science, Review of Metaphysics, and Nature and System.
   A typical issue publishes five to seven high-quality articles representative of this interdisciplinary approach. Articles, critical notes, and editorials soften the potential complications of technical reading.

22. Arzt und Christ. DATE FOUNDED: 1955. FREQUENCY: q. PRICE: 53 Deutch Marks/yr. institutions. PUBLISHER: Verlag Arzt und Christ, Verlag und Redaktion, Wahringer Strabe 2, Germany. EDITOR: Wolfgang Muller-Hartburg. INDEX. ADVERTISEMENTS. CIRCULATION: 1,600. MANUSCRIPT SELECTION: Editor. REPRINTS: author. BOOK REVIEWS: 6 reviews, 1-2 pp., signed. INDEXED/ABSTRACTED: SSCI. TARGET AUDIENCE: AC, SP. SAMPLE COPIES: Libraries, individuals.

Serials on biomedical ethics atypically cover principles of theology. AC differs in that articles view borderline problems between medicine and philosophy as indicative of unresolved religious issues. Religious doctrines are expanded within a social context relative to hospital policy and scientific decisions, which also might appear in Bioethics Quarterly, Hastings Center Report, and Human Rights Quarterly. Contributions are written largely by academicians.

Most issues contain three to nine lead articles followed by a series of book reviews. English language summaries are scarce and may prevent English-speaking subscribers from appreciating the journal's high caliber scholarship.

23. Ascent. DATE FOUNDED: 1968. FREQUENCY: 3/yr. PRICE: $12/yr. institutions, personal. PUBLISHER: Yasodhara Ashram, Box 9, Kootenay Bay, BC, Canada UOB 1X0. EDITOR: L.R. Halldorson. ILLUSTRATIONS. CIRCULATION: 1,000. MANUSCRIPT SELECTION: Editor. REPRINTS: author. BOOK REVIEWS: 3 reviews, 1-2 pp., signed. SPECIAL ISSUES: Occasional. TARGET AUDIENCE: AC, GP. SAMPLE COPIES: Librarians, individuals.

Ascent communicates the principles of Swami Radha, founder of Yasodhara Ashram, and focuses on spiritual awareness and physical development. The metaphysical and moralistic tone of articles is exploratory rather than dogmatic and provides general audiences with a calming sense of transpersonal, self-assurance comparable to that of Yoga, One Earth, and Prana Yoga Life. Some amount of literary abstraction, however, separates Ascent from cosmologic philosophies in Ultimate Meaning and Reality and the objective scholarship found in Philosophy and Phenomenological Research.

Ascent begins most issues with editorial statements about the Swami's current insights. Short articles and books chosen for review carry this transcendental theme through a number of interesting interpretations.

24. Augustinian Studies. DATE FOUNDED: 1970. FREQUENCY: a. PRICE: $15/yr. institutions. PUBLISHER: Augustinian Institute, Villanova University, Villanova, Pennsylvania 19085. EDITOR: Robert P. Russell. ILLUSTRATIONS. CIRCULATION: 1,000. MANUSCRIPT SELECTION: Editor. MICROFORMS: Publisher. REPRINTS: editor. BOOK REVIEWS: 4 reviews, 1-3 pp., signed. INDEXED/ABSTRACTED: PhilosI. TARGET AUDIENCE: AC.

AS champions the scholarly study, theology, and cultural history associated with the influence of St. Augustine (354-430). Augustine was an eyewitness and participant in philosophical movements during the pagan impact on Roman civilization. Augustine's classic work, De Civitate Dei, speaks of faith in God, eternity, and spiritual achievment, which articles in AS interpret and translate for modern application. Besides pure exegetics, articles also have an almost paleoanthropic purpose behind each analysis similar to the Journal of the History of Ideas and Proceedings of the Aristotelian Society. Critical essays are written by prestigious Augustinian scholars and institutes.

A typical issue is an encyclopedia of annual papers and concepts developed thematically around prevalent social problems. Selected book reviews also deal with Augustine and may additionally appear in a supplementary series.

25. Auslegung. DATE FOUNDED: 1973. TITLE CHANGES: Auslegung: A Graduate Journal of Philosophy (1973-1979). FREQUENCY: 3/yr. PRICE: $10/yr. institutions, $6/yr. personal ($4/yr. unemployed philosophers and students). PUBLISHER: Graduate Association of Studies in Philosophy, Philosophy Department, University of Kansas, Lawrence, Kansas 66045. EDITOR: David A. Duquette. INDEX. ADVERTISEMENTS. CIRCULATION: 200. MANUSCRIPT SELECTION: Refereed, editorial board. REPRINTS: author. BOOK REVIEWS: 3 reviews, 1-2 pp., signed. SPECIAL ISSUES: Occasional. INDEXED/ABSTRACTED: ArtHumCitI, PhilosI. TARGET AUDIENCE: AC. SAMPLE COPIES: Libraries, individuals. ACCEPTANCE RATE: 20%.

Auslegung is one of the first pioneering achievements to recognize out-standing work by graduate students and non-tenured philosophers. Papers address an interdisciplinary variety of topics on metaphysics, psychology, cybernetics, anthropology, existentialism, and phenomenology. Foremost in editorial policy is the encouragement toward "experimental" topics, that is, papers dealing more with social science than classic analytic issues. Published seminars on Marx, Hagel, Einstein and from graduate student conferences enhance the blend of innovation and intellectualism. Auslegung, like Kinesis and Gnosis, is run primarily by students under faculty supervision.
   Issues of Auslegung typically feature eight original articles, book reviews, announcements regarding undergraduate and graduate philosophical activity, and a list of books received. Graduate students in philosophy hoping to publish or read articles by their peers may find this periodical a source of motivation.

26. Australian Journal of Philosophy. DATE FOUNDED: 1923. TITLE CHANGES: Australasian Journal of Psychology and Philosophy (1923- 1946). FREQUENCY: q. PRICE: $34/yr. institutions, $17/yr. personal. PUBLISHER: Australasian Association of Philosophy, Department of Philosophy, La Trobe University , Bundoora, Vic 3083, Australia. EDITOR: Brian Ellis. ILLUSTRATIONS. INDEX. ADVERTISEMENTS. CIRCULATION: 1,200. MANUSCRIPT SELECTION: Refereed, editorial board. MICRO-FORMS: KR. REPRINTS: author. BOOK REVIEWS: 9-12 reviews, 1-3 pp., signed. SPECIAL ISSUES: Occasional. INDEXED/ABSTRACTED: ArtHumCitI, PhilosI. TARGET AUDIENCE: AC. SAMPLE COPIES: Individuals. ACCEPTANCE RATE: 20%.

AJP maintains a high regard for original articles in controversial areas of philosophy within the Anglo-American tradition. Authors are primarily members of the Australasian Association of Philosophy and either teach or conduct research in philosophy.Substantial coverage is made of aesthetics, epistemology, ethics, religion, history, and political science. Because of the overseas distribution, selected articles seemingly reflect, first, trends in American scholarship, and, second, the views of the Australasian Association. As with International Philosophical Quarterly and International Studies in Philosophy, an eclectic orientation provides a forum for objective criticism.
   Each edition of AJP contains five to six original articles, discussion and critical note sections, and several book reviews. News and notes follow with announcements about relevant journals and visiting scholars in Australia.

27.   Australian Logic Teachers Journal.   DATE FOUNDED: 1976.
FREQUENCY: 3/yr.   PRICE: $12/yr. institutions, $6/yr. personal.
PUBLISHER: Australian Logic Teachers Association, Philosophy Department,
University of Queensland, St. Lucia, Qld, Australia 4067.   EDITORS: R.A.
Girle, T.A. Halpin. ADVERTISEMENTS. CIRCULATION: 120. MANUSCRIPT
SELECTION: Refereed, editorial board.   REPRINTS: author.   BOOK
REVIEWS: 1 review, 600 words, signed.   TARGET AUDIENCE: AC.
SAMPLE COPIES: Libraries, individuals. ACCEPTANCE RATE: 50%.

ALTJ consists largely of papers, teaching notes, and course outlines relevant
to the teaching of logic (formal and informal) and elementary philosophy in
schools and universities.   Philosophy on the primary and secondary school
levels has accelerated since Lipman's "Philosophy for Children" (e.g.,
Metaphilosophy, 7, January 1976) and the story version of symbolic logic in
Harry Stottlemier's Discovery.   Articles view philosophy as propaedeutic to
computer literacy   and social adjustment skills.   Articles are written by
teachers who re-assess education in ways similar to the essays in Teaching
Philosophy and Thinking.
    Discussion papers in logic and educational areas are followed by news and
information for Australian-based subscribers.

28.   Aut Aut.   DATE FOUNDED: 1951. FREQUENCY: bm. PRICE: 25
Lira/yr. personal. PUBLISHER: La Nuova Italia Edihice, Via A. Giacomini,
8, 50132 Firenze.   EDITOR: Pier Aldo Rovatti. ILLUSTRATIONS. INDEX.
ADVERTISEMENTS.   CIRCULATION: 4,000.   MANUSCRIPT SELECTION:
Refereed, editorial board.   REPRINTS: author. SPECIAL ISSUES: 2/yr.
TARGET AUDIENCE: AC.   SAMPLE COPIES: Libraries, individuals.
ACCEPTANCE RATE: 20%.

AA is devoted to general philosophical issues in the mainstream of politics
and social science.   Predominately in Italian, articles review the current
underpinnings of liberalism within a social action framework.   Authors are
scholars, specialists, and radical revisionists who support partisan
interpretations of social justice and human rights.   Contemporary political
theory is depicted as vividly as can be found , for example, in Soviet Studies
in Philosophy.
    An issue of AA is divided into two thematic sections, each containing four
to six original articles.   On occasion, editors may publish a commentary
profile on outspoken officials or leaders in the political scene.

29. Beacon Magazine. DATE FOUNDED: 1922. FREQUENCY: bm. PRICE:
$10/yr. institutions.   PUBLISHER: Lucis Press Limited, Suite 54, 3
Whitehall Court, London SW1A 2EF, England.   EDITOR: Mary Bailey.
INDEX.   CIRCULATION: 4,000. MANUSCRIPT SELECTION: Editor. BOOK
REVIEWS: 10 reviews, 1-3 pp., signed.   SPECIAL ISSUES: Occasional.
TARGET AUDIENCE: AC, PG. SAMPLE COPIES: Libraries, individuals.

Beacon is devoted to principles of esoteric philosophy of ageless wisdom as a
contemporary way of life.   The aim is to encourage esotericists to apply
their knowledge and spiritual resources toward furthering human
consciousness.   Toward this end, articles focus on the nature of man, of God
and universe, on the plan of humanity, the hierarchy of masters, the solutions

of human problems and principles in the world. Original and reprinted articles vary in languages but all recognize the expression of religion and ideology in the form of teaching, training, and active work. This subjective synthesis of ideas, drawn from scholars and laymen, resembles the style of the American Theosophist, Idealistic Studies, and Religious Humanism.

Regular issues typically feature an editorial on Christian human relationships, then seven to nine short articles, and either book reviews or a list of books and publications. A famous quotation interspersed between articles and on the back cover enhances the unique artistic layout.

30. Behaviorism. DATE FOUNDED: 1973. FREQUENCY: sa. PRICE: $20/yr. institutions, $13/yr. personal. PUBLISHER: Department of Psychology, University of Nevado-Reno, Reno, Nevada 89557. EDITOR: Willard Day. INDEX. ADVERTISEMENTS. CIRCULATION: 1,200. MANUSCRIPT SELECTION: Refereed, editorial board. REPRINTS: author. INDEXED/ABSTRACTED: PsyAb, PhilosI. TARGET AUDIENCE: AC. SAMPLE COPIES: Libraries.

Behaviorism is a forum for critical discussion of issues pertaining to the contemporary practice of behavioral psychology. Conceptual, logical and methodological problems associated with the Skinnerian outlook on applied and experimental areas are proposed by philosophers and psychologists, both clearly represented among consulting editors. Behaviorism, like Psychological Record, serves the expanding readership of academicians and practitioners displeased by the number of unresolved theoretical issues in the current behavioral paradigm. Because philosophers are invited to deal technically with learning theory, occasional debates and ethical inquiries maintain an objective balance.

A typical issue contains six to seven original articles either along some theme (e.g., verbal behavior, freedom vs. determinism, epistemology), or on independent topics. Students and scholars desiring an interdisciplinary dialogue about the science of human behavior would find this an appropriate periodical.

31. Bibliographie de la Philosophie. DATE FOUNDED: 1937. FREQUENCY: 3/yr. PRICE: $47.50/yr. institutions. PUBLISHER: Librairie Philosophique J. Vrin, 6, Place de la Sorbonne, 75005, Paris, France. EDITOR: Institut International de Philosophie. INDEX. ADVERTISEMENTS. CIRCULATION: 1,100. MANUSCRIPT SELECTION: Editor. TARGET AUDIENCE: AC, GP.

BP is a leading authority on bibliographic reviews of current literature in philosophy of history, social sciences and most general disciplinary subjects. Analytic reviews are written by international scholars and clarify the rudimentary pitfalls and value of these contributions. Coverage resembles the prevalent themes found in Philosophical Books, and, regarding aesthetics, in Philosophy and Literature.

A single issue may survey twenty to thirty books with critical discussion and provides text in English, French, German and Italian. Publications are also selected from outside the field of philosophy.

32. Black Male/Female Relationships. DATE FOUNDED: 1979. FRE-
QUENCY: 3/yr. PRICE: $10/yr. institutions. PUBLISHER: Black Think
Tank, 1801 Bush Street, Suite 127, San Francisco, California   94109.
EDITOR: Nathan Hare. ILLUSTRATIONS. ADVERTISEMENTS. CIRCULA-
TION: 5,000. MANUSCRIPT SELECTION: Editor. MICROFORMS: UMI.
REPRINTS: author. BOOK REVIEWS: 2-3 reviews, 1-3 pp., signed.
SPECIAL ISSUES: Occasional. INDEXED/ABSTRACTED: FamAb. TARGET
AUDIENCE: AC, GP. ACCEPTANCE RATE: 40%.

BMFR explores contemporary theory and social problems related to Black
family relationships. Examined are the racial, ethnic, and religious forces
interwoven into personal life-styles, contrasted against a backdrop of
historico-African perspectives. Original articles stress the stability of
interpersonal commitments as being essential for cultural assimilation and
the recognition of Black human rights. Unlike Afro-American Journal of
Philosophy, authors of BMFR are both scholars and laymen with unilaterally
subjective orientations about political influence and nonBlack prejudices.
  A typical issue contains two to five articles, editorial commentary, and
book reviews. Occasionally series articles and original material appear in a
book supplement.

33. British Journal of Aesthetics. DATE FOUNDED: 1960. FREQUENCY:
q. PRICE: $49/yr. institutions. PUBLISHER: Oxford University Press for
British Society of Aesthetics, Walton Street, Oxford OX2 6DP, England.
EDITOR: T.J. Diffey. ILLUSTRATIONS. INDEX. ADVERTISEMENTS.
CIRCULATION: 2,000. MANUSCRIPT SELECTION: Refereed, editorial
board. MICROFORMS: KR, UMI. REPRINTS: author. BOOK REVIEWS: 10
reviews, 1-4pp., signed. INDEXED/ABSTRACTED: ArtHumCitI, ChemAb,
CurrContAH, HumI, PhilosI. SAMPLE COPIES: Libraries, individuals.

BJA has become a respectable authority for international discussion on
philosophy of art, principles of aesthetic appreciation and judgment, and
theoretical criticism from the vantage of psychology, sociology, history, and
modern philosophy.   Analogous to Journal of Aesthetics, BJA treats
aestheticism as a natural science, where intellectual debate supersedes
enduring traditions and logical assumptions of Kant, Kierkegaard, and
Wittgenstein.   BJA assumes a more academic posture than Aitia, since it
explores the deontologic implications of art criticism.
  Each issue publishes nine to ten articles, book reviews, and brief
descriptions about contributors. Editorial policy discourages essays on
individual artists, studies in literary criticism, and art history.

34. British Journal for the Philosophy of Science. DATE FOUNDED: 1950.
FREQUENCY: q. PRICE: $44/yr. institutions, $22/yr. personal. PUBLISHER:
British Society for the Philosophy of Science, Department of History and
Philosophy of Science, Chelsea College, University of London, Manresa Road,
London SW3 6LX, England. EDITOR: Donald A. Gillies. ILLUSTRATIONS.
INDEX.   ADVERTISEMENTS.   CIRCULATION: 1,500.   MANUSCRIPT
SELECTION: Refereed, editorial board. MICROFORMS: KR. BOOK
REVIEWS: 6 reviews, 1-4 pp., signed.   INDEXED/ ABSTRACTED:
ArtHumCitI, HumI, PhilosI. TARGET AUDIENCE: AC. SAMPLE COPIES:
Libraries, individuals.

BJPS is the official organ of the British Society for the Philosophy of Science, whose purpose is "to study the logic, the method and the philosophy of science as well as those of the various special sciences, including social sciences." Representative articles on ontology, experimental ethics, physics and cosmology all clearly conform to the canons of objective inquiry. BJPS publishes discussions, reviews, rebuttals, and abstracts from such journals as Dialectica, and Philosophy of Science. The coverage of exigent themes in international scientific development appears similar to Nous, Ratio, Review of Metaphysics, and Notre Dame Journal of Formal Logic.
   A typical issue features six to eight articles and lengthy book reviews. Books posted in the "recent publications" list are never guaranteed a full review nor returnable. Noteworthy is that Society membership is international and probably the reason for BJPS's prolific reputation.

35. Bulletin de Philosophie Medievale. DATE FOUNDED: 1958. TITLE CHANGES: Bulletin de la Societe Internationale pour l'Etude de la Philosophie Medievale (1958-1964). FREQUENCY: a. PRICE: $20/yr. institutions. PUBLISHER: Secretariat de la Societe Internationale pour l'Etude de la Philosophie Medievale, College Thomas More, Chemin d'Aristote, 1, B-1348, Louvain-La-Neuve, Belgium. EDITOR: Christian Wenin. INDEX. ADVERTISEMENTS. CIRCULATION: 800. REPRINTS: Editor. BOOK REVIEWS: 30-40 reviews, 1-4 pp., signed. INDEXED/ABSTRACTED: MedL, PhilosI, RBibPhil. TARGET AUDIENCE: AC. SAMPLE COPIES: Libraries. ACCEPTANCE RATE: 75%

Medieval philosophy recounted by the Latin, Greek, Arabic and Hebrew ancients is the subject of critical analysis in BPM. International contributions in French, German, English, Italian and Spanish branch into two major sections of the journal. Section I covers bibliographic lists and reviews of relevant texts from the Middle Ages, plus notices from esteemed institutions. Section II elaborates on extant works, corrections and objective scholarly findings in historiographic records, short of the "technical" enumeration that might appear in Isis and the Journal of the History of Ideas.
   A typical issue contains short book reviews, original papers, and occasional editorials. The Medieval Institute represents only a fraction of rich historical information in growing demand by students and scholars.

36. Bulletin de la Societe Francaise de Philosophie. DATE FOUNDED: 1901. FREQUENCY: q. PRICE: 55 French Francs/yr. institutions, PUBLISHER: Librairie Armand Colon, 103 B, Saint-Michel, 75240 Paris, France. EDITOR: Suzanne Delmore. INDEX. MANUSCRIPT SELECTION: Refereed, editorial board. INDEXED/ABSTRACTED: PhilosI. TARGET AUDIENCE: AC, HS.

The Society of French Philosophy is devoted to espousement of general topics reflected in the cultural concerns of Society members. Topics vary from aesthetics, epistemology, metaphysics and law to articles on logic, language and anthropology. Pubished papers are usually from Society conferences of French scholars allegiant to materialism. Papers on moral philosophy also strive for wider appeal among general French audiences. Texts and communications of the Society largely resemble the Polish version of Studia Filozoficzne.

Papers in a regular issue of BSFP may revolve around particular themes. In some cases, transcripts from a debate depart from the orthodoxy of papers on pure theoretical criticism, which is a nice embellishment for general and student readers.

37. Bulletin of the Section of Logic. DATE FOUNDED: 1972. FREQUEN-CY: q. PRICE: free. PUBLISHER: Institute of Philosophy and Sociology, PAN, Nowy Swiat 72.00-330 Warszawa, Poland. EDITOR: Polish Academy of Sciences, Institute of Philosophy and Sociology. ADVERTISEMENTS. CIRCULATION: 150. MANUSCRIPT SELECTION: Refereed, editorial board. INDEXED/ABSTRACTED: MathR, PhilosI, RZ. TARGET AU-DIENCE: AC. SAMPLE COPIES: Libraries, individuals. ACCEPTANCE RATE: 80%.

BSL focuses on analytical trends largely advanced by the Polish Academy of Sciences. Articles selected for publication deal entirely with symbolic logic applications, especially in semantics. Still a young journal, the readership alone already spans over sixteen nations from Canada to the Soviet Union. Scholarly contributors write about mathematical and metalogical principles along American-tradition themes. Technical sophistication matches the depth of analysis found in Studia Logica, Reports on Mathematical Logic and Notre Dame Journal of Formal Logic.
   A single issue covers about seven to eight original papers, news, and announcements of the contents of sibling journals. Readers intrigued by classic syllogism would welcome this addition to American journals.

38. Business and Professional Ethics Journal. FREQUENCY: q. Price: $25/yr. institutions, $12/yr. personal. PUBLISHER: Science and Technology Division, Rensselaer Polytechnic Institute, Troy, New York 12181. EDITORS: Robert J. Baum, Norman E. Bowie, Deborah G. Johnson. ILLUSTRATIONS. INDEX. ADVERTISEMENTS. MANUSCRIPT SELECTION: Refereed, editorial board. REPRINTS: author. BOOK REVIEWS: 5-6 reviews, 1-2 pp., signed. SPECIAL ISSUES: Occasional. INDEXED/ABSTRACTED: BPI, PhilosI. TARGET AUDIENCE: AC. SAMPLE COPIES: Libraries.

BPEJ is a reaction to the number of ethical problems associated with business enterprises and the professions. Papers published in BPEJ cover a broad spectrum of institutional doctrines on morality highly relevant to the rights and obligations of working individuals. Readers with a theoretical and practical interest in professional ethics can gain insight on the nature, origin and significance of essentially egalitarian aspects of health, safety, security, discrimination, privacy, and employee attitudes. Articles are written objectively by academicians and specialists in the business field. BPEJ complements the topics considered in International Journal of Applied Philosophy and Creativity and Innovation Network.
   Each issue of BPEJ features eight to ten original articles on a selected ethical issue. This is followed by book reviews, and then announcements of conferences, workshops, and other opportunities for involvement in business affairs.

39. Cahiers Albert Schweitzer. DATE FOUNDED: 1955. FREQUENCY: q. PRICE: 75 Francs/yr. institutions. PUBLISHER: 5, Rue de la Monnaie, F, 67000 Strasbourg, France. EDITOR: Madeleine Horst. ILLUSTRATIONS. INDEX. CIRCULATION: 3,000. MANUSCRIPT SELECTION: Editor. REPRINTS: editor. BOOK REVIEWS: 12 reviews, 1-2 pp., signed. TARGET AUDIENCE: AC, GP, HS. SAMPLE COPIES: Libraries.

Memorial tributes to the famous Alsatian medical missionary and theologian in Africa, Albert Schweitzer (1875-1965), carry on the tradition of moral reform. CAS is a medium for the disciples of Schweitzer's philosophy and rediscovery of his educational principles in view of modern devastations in underdeveloped countries. Schweitzer's work and critical thoughts undergo reformulation by admirers and scholars affiliated with similar occupations, but perhaps ill-versed in his teaching methods. Although articles are for general audiences, theoretical arguments may introduce ethical and moral ideas that with additional space could be clarified.

Whenever possible, articles identify a theme or comprise an anthology of papers presented at conferences. Sections on religious ethics closely approximate articles in Public Choice and Journal of Medicine and Philosophy.

40. Canadian Journal of Philosophy. DATE FOUNDED: 1971. FREQUENCY: q. PRICE: $30/yr. institutions, $20/yr. personal, $13/yr. students. PUBLISHER: University of Calgary Press, University of Calgary, Calgary, Alberta, Canada T2N 1N4. INDEX. ADVERTISEMENTS. CIRCULATION: 900. MANUSCRIPT SELECTION: Refereed, editorial board. REPRINTS: author. SPECIAL ISSUES: Occasional. INDEXED/ ABSTRACTED: ArtHumCitI, PhilosI, RBibPhil. TARGET AUDIENCE: AC. SAMPLE COPIES: Libraries.

CJP is the official arm of the Canadian Association for Publishing in Philosophy and dedicated to superior works in French and English. Recognized for its excellence in argumentation, this eclectic journal draws leading experts from fields of humanities, ethics, psychology, and epistemology to the forefront of North American intellectualism. Quality papers appeal to the objectively-minded scholar duly open to repudiations of ancient (e.g., Aristotle) and contemporary (e.g., Sellars) thinkers. CJP is complementary to such respectable serials as the Monist, the Philosophical Quarterly, and Mind.

A single issue can expect to run seven to eight original articles and a "critical note" to replace cursory reviews of important books.

41. Canadian Philosophical Review. DATE FOUNDED: 1981. FREQUENCY: bm. PRICE: $34/yr. institutions, $16/yr. personal. PUBLISHER: Academic Printing and Publishing, Box 4834, South Edmonton, Alberta, Canada T6E 5G7. EDITOR: Roger A. Shiner. INDEX. ADVERTISEMENTS. CIRCULATION: 350. REPRINTS: editor. BOOK REVIEWS: (entire journal). INDEXED/ABSTRACTED: PhilosI. TARGET AUDIENCE: AC. SAMPLE COPIES: Libraries.

CPR is a bilingual journal for publication in academic philosophy and for theoretical works in sibling fields of interest to philosophers. Originally for philosophy only, demands for rapid dissemination of publications in other fields resulted in a broader perspective, now including such areas as law, psychology, literary criticism, physics, medicine, linguistics, and classical studies. CPR is the first Canadian journal to systematically meet this need on a par with Philosophical Books, and Philosophy and Literature. Selected reviews also assemble recommendations on educational textbooks for classroom use.

Single issues contain eighteen to twenty individually signed reviews. Occasional unsolicited reviews are published under the category of educational textbooks. This comprehensive reference of essential works provides utmost assistance in serious research.

42.   Centennial Review. DATE FOUNDED: 1955. FREQUENCY: q. PRICE: $5/yr. institutions. PUBLISHER: Michigan State University, 110 Morrill Hall, East Lansing, Michigan 48824-1036. EDITOR: Linda C. Wagner. ILLUSTRATIONS. INDEX. ADVERTISEMENTS. CIRCULATION: 1,200. MANUSCRIPT SELECTION: Refereed, editorial board. MICROFORMS: UMI. REPRINTS: author. BOOK REVIEWS: 7-12 reviews, 1-3 pp., signed. TARGET AUDIENCE: AC. ACCEPTANCE RATE: 10%.

CR is a publication concerned with the interrelations among the disciplines of anthropology, art, biology, communication, economics, history, literature, music, philosophy, and political and social sciences. General epistemologic branches of interdisciplinary study are considered from scholars in the United States and abroad. Central themes orient around culturalization and twentieth century idealism, much like Daedalus. Literature interpretations and occasional poems provide interest in aestheticism equal to Philosophy and the Arts and British Journal of Aesthetics.

A typical issue contains eleven to thirteen original full length articles, poems, and short book reviews. In the frontmatter appear brief biographical sketches of each contributor, many of whom work in academia or lead prolific writing careers.

43.   Chinese Studies in Philosophy. DATE FOUNDED: 1969. TITLE CHANGES: Chinese Studies in History and Philosophy (1969). FREQUENCY: q. PRICE: $170/yr. institutions. $44/yr. personal. PUBLISHER: M.E. Sharpe, Incorporated, 80 Business Park Drive, Armonk, New York 10504. EDITOR: Chung-Ying Cheng. ILLUSTRATIONS. INDEX. ADVERTISEMENTS. INDEXED/ABSTRACTED: ArtHumCitI, CurrContAH, PhilosI. TARGET AUDIENCE: AC. SAMPLE COPIES: Libraries.

CSP contains unabridged translations of articles from Chinese sources, primarily scholarly journals and collections of articles published in book form. The aim of CSP is to present the more important Chinese studies in this field for those professionally concerned with it. Translations into English avail English-speaking readers of contemporary Oriental thinkers, the origins of their ancient heritage, and major points of convergence between American and Eastern-Asian philosophy. Metaphysical and epistemological studies tend to overshadow explorations in aesthetics or, to a lesser extent, those of political and social sciences. CSP differs from Journal of Chinese Philosophy and New Confucians by its de-emphasis upon religiosity .

A regular issue offers two to three lengthy translations embodied with exegetical analysis. Sources used in the translation appear on the editorial page, and serve as reference points. Since most journals rarely devote space to works printed in another medium, CSP may be a welcome resource to many Oriental institutes.

44. CLIO: A Journal of Literature, History and the Philosophy of History. DATE FOUNDED: 1971. TITLE CHANGES: CLIO: An Interdisciplinary Journal of Literature, History and Philosophy of History (1971-1980). FREQUENCY: q. PRICE: $26/yr. institutions, $10/yr. personal. PUBLISH-ER: CLIO, Indiana University-Purdue University, Fort Wayne, Indiana 46805. EDITORS: Robert H. Canary, Henry Kozicki, Clark Butler. ILLUSTRATIONS. INDEX. ADVERTISEMENTS. CIRCULATION: 500. MANUSCRIPT SELECTION: Refereed, editorial board. MICROFORMS: UMI. REPRINTS: author. BOOK REVIEWS: 12 reviews, 1-2 pp., signed. SPECIAL ISSUES: annual fourth number devoted to Hegel. INDEXED/ABSTRACTED: AbEnSt, AmerH, ChildDevAb, HistAb, HumI, LLBA, PhilosI, SocAb. TARGET AUDIENCE: AC. SAMPLE COPIES: Libraries, individuals. ACCEPTANCE RATE: 20%.

CLIO is a creative anthology of four broad categories. First, it publishes critiques of literature in which history or the philosophy of history functions as an ordering principle. Second, it publishes literary analyses of historical writing. Third, it presents historiography that deals with the nature of historical and literary knowledge and narrative. Fourth, it surveys the speculative philosophy of history a la Hegel from an interdisciplinary application. Lexical and biographical appraisals of historians and historical domination in the arts and sciences are also found in Apeiron and Hume Studies. Contributors are primarily scholars.
   Most issues of CLIO begin with four to six original articles and reviews of fiction and nonfiction books. Noteworthy is that the Hegel edition speaks to a number of questions focused on the late twentieth century "Hegel renaissance."

45. Cognition. DATE FOUNDED: 1972. FREQUENCY: 6/yr. PRICE: $96/yr. institutions. PUBLISHER: Elsevier Sequoia, SA., P.O. Box 851, 1001 Lausanne 1, Switzerland. EDITOR: Jacques Mehler. ILLUSTRATIONS. INDEX. ADVERTISEMENTS. MANUSCRIPT SELECTION: Refereed, editorial board. REPRINTS: author. BOOK REVIEWS: 1-3 reviews/yr., 500 words, signed. SPECIAL ISSUES: Occasional. INDEXED/ABSTRACTED: ComDevAb, CurrConSocBS, LLBA, PhilosI, PsyAb, PsyRG, SCI. TARGET AUDIENCE: AC. SAMPLE COPIES: Libraries. ACCEPTANCE RATE: 18%.

Cognition publishes theoretical and experimental papers covering all aspects of the mind. Papers in the field of psychology, linguistics, neurophysiology, ethology, philosophy and epistemology are common. The epistemological renewal of the field, also reflected in Linguistics and Philosophy, accounts for essays that evaluate meaning and reference. Cognition also acts as a forum for debates on the social and ethical questions facing scientists and philosophers. Contributors consist of philosophers and psychologists in a mutual exchange of current trends.

A typical issue contains three to four original articles, short reports, notes and discussions. Reviews of recent or reprinted books and letters to the editors are irregular and their publication depends on the relevance to Cognition.

46. Conceptus. DATE FOUNDED: 1967. FREQUENCY: 3/yr. PUBLISHER: Verlag der Wissenschaftlichen Gesellschaften Osterreichs, Lindengasse 37, Germany. EDITOR: Josef Zelger. ILLUSTRATIONS. INDEX. ADVERTISEMENTS. CIRCULATION: 2,500. MANUSCRIPT SELECTION: Refereed, editorial board. MICROFORMS: KR. Reprints: KR. BOOK REVIEWS: 5 reviews, 1-4 pp., signed. SPECIAL ISSUES: 1/yr. INDEXED/ ABSTRACTED: PhilosI. TARGET AUDIENCE: AC, GP, HS. SAMPLE COPIES: Libraries, individuals. ACCEPTANCE RATE: 50-60%.

Conceptus takes account of practically all relevant philosophy, advancing discussion between philosophical disciplines and those in the social sciences. Editorial policy favors unconventional theoretical approaches written in clear, objective styles, regardless of analytic or scientific tradition. Essays appear on aesthetics, epistemology, foundations of mathematics, philosophy of language, cognitionism, and Marxism. Conceptual applications in logic are less technical than, for instance, Journal of Philosophical Logic and Logique et Analyse.
Papers in a typical issue are largely in German and only occasionally in English. English summaries provide an intelligible translation for foreign scholars.

47. Conservative Judaism. DATE FOUNDED: 1946. FREQUENCY: q. PRICE: $67/yr. institutions, $30/yr. personal. PUBLISHER: Human Sciences Press, Incorporated, 72 Fifth Avenue, New York, New York 10011. EDITOR: Harold Kushner. ILLUSTRATIONS. INDEX. ADVERTISEMENTS. CIRCULATION: 1,500. MANUSCRIPT SELECTION: Refereed, editorial board. REPRINTS: author. SPECIAL ISSUES: Occasional. INDEXED/ABSTRACTED: CurrContAH, EM, IMed, PsyAb, SSCI. TARGET AUDIENCE: AC, SP. SAMPLE COPIES: Libraries.

This distinguished journal is devoted to the examination of three vital aspects of Judaism: Jewish texts and sources; conservative Jewish ideology; and the role of the Rabbi today. CJ extends beyond denominational lines in articles about Jews in the French Foreign Legion, in Latin America, in Sweden, and in the Havurah movement in the United States. Topics of current stimulation relate to medical ethics, Jewish women, theology and biblical studies, and the challenges of new secular religions. Scholarly papers fit into the political and social dimensions of conservative world issues much as Tradition projects the orthodox world issues.
Issues in CJ vary from six to ten articles, including a regular feature on "A Letter from Jerusalem" by Theodore Friedman. General readers outside the academic community may appreciate the contemporary focus on divorced parents, the synogogue, and Jewish learning.

48. Contemplative Review. DATE FOUNDED: 1960. FREQUENCY: q. PRICE: $8/yr. institutions. PUBLISHER: Association of Contemplative Sisters, Beckley Hill, Barre, Vermont 05641. EDITOR: Mary Roman. ADVERTISEMENTS. CIRCULATION: 5,500. MANUSCRIPT SELECTION: Editor. BOOK REVIEWS: 20 reviews, 750 words, signed. INDEXED/AB-STRACTED: CathI. TARGET AUDIENCE: AC, GP. SAMPLE COPIES: Libraries. ACCEPTANCE RATE: 50%.

CR is in response to the growing American interest in meditation and mysticisim. Articles, poetry, and book reviews explore an awareness of Christian tradition, contemplative prayer, and broaden the vision of spiritual fulfillment. In general, this journal remains a speculative inquiry into the mastery of self-truth and wisdom, unlike the emphases in Journal of Religion and Journal for the Scientific Study of Religion. Topics about death and dying, for instance, prey on beliefs in immortality, reincarnation and the romanticism of eternity. CR is analogous to the American Theosophist and Arzt und Christ in that transcendental views upstage the affirmation of legitimate religious arguments.
   In a typical issue of CR one finds twelve to thirteen short articles, book reviews, and a list of books recieved. The exhortative tone of these papers is with a conviction strongly based in human faith.

49. Contemporary Philosophy. DATE FOUNDED: 1957. TITLE CHANGES: Philosophic Research and Analysis (1957-1966). FREQUENCY: bm. PRICE: $15/yr. institutions. PUBLISHER: Institute for Advanced Philosophic Research. P.O. Box 1373, Boulder, Colorado 80306. EDITOR: Alfred E. Koenig. ILLUSTRATIONS. CIRCULATION: 1,000. MANUSCRIPT SELECTION: Refereed, editorial board. REPRINTS: author. BOOK REVIEWS: 1-20 reviews, 2pp., signed. SPECIAL ISSUES: Occasional. INDEXED/ABSTRACTED: ArtHumCitI. TARGET AUDIENCE: AC. SAMPLE COPIES: Libraries.

CP emerges as a forum for scholarly dialogue of problems in philosophy. Articles describe future-oriented and contemporary prospects of philosphy's role in sociocultural issues and regarding the fate of intellectualism. Realistic threats to the profession are contrasted with useful solutions for today's educational programs and for employment. Philosophy qua the philosopher is the outlook that resembles passages in the Proceedings and Addresses of the American Philosophical Association.
   A typical issue of four to six original papers establishes an objective basis for evaluation by students in graduate school or by unemployed philosophers.

50. Cornell Journal of Social Relations. DATE FOUNDED: 1966. FREQUENCY: sm. PRICE: $10/yr. institutions, $5/yr. personal. PUBLISHER: Department of Sociology, Uris Hall, Cornell University, Ithaca, New York 14853. EDITOR: Herman Schwartz. INDEX. ADVERTISEMENTS. CIRCULATION: 271. MANUSCRIPT SELECTION: Refereed, editorial board. MICROFORMS: UMI. REPRINTS: UMI. BOOK REVIEWS: 2 reviews, 500 words, signed. SPECIAL ISSUES: Occasional. INDEXED/ABSTRACTED: ArStAb, PsyAb, PubAdAb, SocAb, SSCI. TARGET AUD-IENCE: AC. SAMPLE COPIES: Libraries, individuals. ACCEPTANCE RATE: 10%.

CJSR falls under the guise of interdisciplinary investigation. Articles are concerned with psychology, sociology, political science, planning, organizational behavior, anthropology, human and family service studies, and nearly anything that authors convincingly demonstrate has relevance for social interactions. Special issues focus on rural policy and program utilization that are anathemic to consumerism groups. Developmental, industrial and epistemological subjects draw from a variety of original papers by graduate students. The quality and artistic structure of CJSR upgrades its presentation of professional papers to that of Public Choice and Humboldt Journal of Social Relations.
Typical issues present three to four original essays with a book review, notes and occasional deaprtmental announcements. The excitement about CJSR is the centralization of theoretical issues in such topics as "agricultural economics" and "industrial and labor relations," both important for applied philosophy.

51. Creation/Evolution. DATE FOUNDED: 1980. FREQUENCY: q. PRICE: $9/yr. institutions. PUBLISHER: American Humanist Association. 7 Harwood Drive, Amherst, New York 14226. EDITOR: Frederick Edwords. ILLUSTRATIONS. CIRCULATION: 1,800. REPRINTS: author. BOOK REVIEWS: 2-3 reviews, 500 words, signed. TARGET AUDIENCE: AC, GP. SAMPLE COPIES: Libraries, individuals. ACCEPTANCE RATE: 50%.

Ever since the Scopes Monkey Trial in 1925 aroused controversy over the separation between Church and State, a deepening interest in prayer and subjection to religion in schools has thwarted the debate between creationism and evolutionism. CE represent another partition in this intense struggle for truth. Its papers are well-researched, scientific answers to creationist arguments, including responses to legal and educational actions (e.g., Supreme Court decisions, literature censorship). Mainstream solutions also cover comparative physiology, psychology, atheism, and economic interests. Authors are distinguished paleontologists, philosophers and general skeptics allured to issues against fundamentalism. CE combats tenets of creationism as vigorously as the American Rationalist and the American Atheist defend Darwinism.
A typical issue fills the reader with inspiration. Four original articles follow with reports, news briefs, book reviews, and enthusiastic letters to the editor. For both religious and nonreligious readers, CE presents a circumscribed account of human civil rights from a historical science.

52. Creation Research Society Quarterly. DATE FOUNDED: 1963. FREQUENCY: q. PRICE: $16/yr. institutions, personal. PUBLISHER: Creation Research Society, 2717 Cranbrook Road, Ann Arbor, Michigan 48104. EDITOR: Harold Armstrong. ILLUSTRATIONS. INDEX. CIRCULATION: 2,700. MANUSCRIPT SELECTION: Refereed, editorial board. BOOK REVIEWS: 3-4 reviews, 1-2 pp., signed. INDEXED/ABSTRACTED: BioAb, CathI. TARGET AUDIENCE: AC, GP.

Scientists embrace a myriad of nonscientific behaviors from atheism to fundamentalism and this has direct bearing upon the validity of that science. Here, CRSQ advocates creationism with the same relentless objectivity that Creation/Evolution used to dispute it. Members of Creation

Research Society must subscribe to the Bible as the written word of God, claiming that all biblical assertions are historically and scientifically true. To the student of nature, this means the account of origins in Genesis is factual and that living things, including man, come from creative acts of God. Essentially, this corpus of Christian writers envision salvation as the outcome of creationistic commitments. However, the Society refuses affiliation with any religious or Church group and believes that a rapprochement between science and Christianity is hopeful. Contributors are polemicists from physics, engineering, zoology, chemistry, and most other natural sciences.

A single issue features reprisals to highly disputed events in Biblical history, such as the "Great Flood" (Noachian Deluge), plus news and notes regarding the Society's activities. Sympathetic readers of CRSQ may struggle with the ambivalence of defining "science" in transcendental terms. Though assuredly "objective," the journal's underlying principles harbor questionable scientific validity.

53. Creativity and Innovation Network. DATE FOUNDED: 1975. TITLE CHANGES: Creativity Network (1975-1983). FREQUENCY: q. PRICE: 20 Pounds/yr. institutions, 15 Pounds/yr. personal. PUBLISHER: Creativity Programme, Room 31, Manchester Business School, Booth Street West, Manchester M15 6PB, England. EDITOR: Tudor Rikards. ILLUSTRATIONS. INDEX. ADVERTISEMENTS. CIRCULATION: 1,000. REPRINTS: editor. BOOK REVIEWS: 7-20 reviews, 1-2 pp., signed. SPECIAL ISSUES: Occasional. TARGET AUDIENCE: AC. SAMPLE COPIES: Libraries, individuals. ACCEPTANCE RATE: 70%.

CIN is one of the few publications dealing with all aspects of industrial, economic, management, social , psychological, and complex philosophical aspects of man. It provides a unique medium for exchange between universities and technical colleges, research centers, and persons in supervisory positions. The latest editorial policy is to stress objective reports, surveys, and book reviews concerned with marketing, aspects of innovation (e.g., cost, ethics, organizational philosophy). A section on "Selective Reading" and "Alternative Community Cooperatives" encompass worldwide attitudes about work and public participation in consumerism. The consultive panel of distinguished editors contribute most of the papers on topics also found in Humboldt Journal of Social Relations and Business and Professional Ethics Journal.

Each issue covers the mainstays of business leadership and technology in three to four original articles. Books chosen for review directly relate to innovation in practice.

54. Critica: Revista Hispanoamericana de Filosofia. DATE FOUNDED: 1967. FREQUENCY: 3/yr. PRICE: $12/yr. institutions. PUBLISHER: J.A. Rubles, Javier Esquivel, Enrique Villanueva, Apartado Postal 70-447, Coyoacan, 04510, Mexico. EDITOR: Instituto de Investigaciones Filosoficas, Universidad Nacional Autonoma de Mexico. ADVERTISEMENTS. CIRCULATION: 1,000. REPRINTS: author. BOOK REVIEWS: 5 reviews, 1-2 pp., signed. INDEXED/ABSTRACTED: ArtHumCitI, PhilosI. TARGET AUDIENCE: AC. SAMPLE COPIES: Libraries. ACCEPTANCE RATE: 60%.

Critica publishes informative, critical papers on any topic with an analytic approach. This bilingual journal (Spanish and English) surpasses the outmoded conventions of esoteric formal and symbolic logic (e.g., Reports on Mathematical Logic) with a fresh variety of papers on epistemology, ethics, metaphysics, political law, language, and philosophy of science. In keeping with an eclectic format, Critica welcomes international contributions by scholars, although dealing with specific themes. As in Analysis and Nous, the philosophy of logic is presented without excessive jargon.

55. Critical Inquiry. DATE FOUNDED: 1974. FREQUENCY: q. PRICE: $55/yr. institutions, $27.50/yr. personal, $20/yr. students. PUBLISHER: University of Chicago Press, Journal Division, P.O. Box 37005, Chicago, Illinois 60637. EDITOR: W.J.T. Mitchell. ILLUSTRATIONS. INDEX. ADVERTISEMENTS. CIRCULATION: 5,000. MANUSCRIPT SELECTION: Refereed, editorial board. REPRINTS: author. SPECIAL ISSUES: 1/yr. INDEXED/ABSTRACTED: HumI. TARGET AUDIENCE: AC. SAMPLE COPIES: Libraries, individuals. ACCEPTANCE RATE: 50%.

CI is an interdisciplinary journal devoted to publishing the best critical thought in the arts and humanities. Combining a commitment to rigorous scholarship with a vital concern for dialogue, the journal presents articles by eminent artists on a wide variety of topics from architecture to history. Special issues, for instance, on "metaphor" or "narrative" assemble the liveliest essays on contemporary theory, written in an objective style orthogonal to Philosophy and Literature, CLIO, and Philosophy and the Arts. CI is also like Aitia in the interpretive criticisms given to film and poetry.
A typical issue contains eight original articles and an invited article by some leading figure (e.g., Joyce Carol Oates) in the section titled "Artists on Art." Aesthetic readers are sure to discover valuable insights in contemporary literature.

56. Chroniques de Philosophie. DATE FOUNDED: 1958. TITLE CHANGES: Philosophie au Milieu du Loeme Siecle (1958-1959), Philosophie Contemporaine (1968-1971), Philosophie Contemporaine, A New Survey (1971-1981). FREQUENCY: 10/yr. PRICE: 160 Florins/yr. institutions. PUBLISHER: Institut International de Philosophie, Montreal, Canada. EDITOR: R. Klibansky. INDEX. MANUSCRIPT SELECTION: Editor. REPRINTS: KR. TARGET AUDIENCE: AC, GP, HS.

CP is a chronicle devoted to intraphilosophy and its contemporary phases of intellectual growth in history and sciences. Articles in English and French sample analytical traditions in epistemology, ethics, and political philosophy. Canadian academicians write for general audiences. These essays typically assume a posture similar to that in Contemporary Philosophy and Acta Philosophica Fennica.
Most issues contain six original short papers that are appropriate for supplementary reading in graduate and undergraduate philosophy courses.

57. Cross Currents. DATE FOUNDED: 1950. FREQUENCY: q. PRICE: $12.50/yr. institutions, $10/yr. personal. PUBLISHER: Convergence Incorporated, 103 Van Houten Fields, West Nyack, New York 10994. EDITOR: Joseph Cunneen. ILLUSTRATIONS. INDEX. ADVERTISEMENTS. CIRCULATION: 5,200. MANUSCRIPT SELECTION: Refereed, editorial board. MICROFORMS: UMI. REPRINTS: KR. BOOK REVIEWS: 12 reviews, 1-2 pp., signed. SPECIAL ISSUES: Occasional. INDEXED/ ABSTRACTED: ChiPerI, HumI. TARGET AUDIENCE: AC. SAMPLE COPIES: Libraries, individuals. ACCEPTANCE RATE: 8%.

CC acts as an international forum for dialogue between religion and contemporary world. Ecumenical and interdisciplinary from the start, it rejects the liberal illusion that religion belongs to the "moral majority" or old-time fundamentalism. Instead, CC challenges anti-intellectualism and the monopolization of ersatz religions. Readers looking for instant salvation or revolutionary slogans as in the Beacon, Contemplative Review, and Dawn are surprised by the sturdy ediface of politics, scholarly judgment, and substantive Christendom. Such world renown contributors as Ivan Illich, Thomas Merton and Karl Rahner give impetus to pragmatic debates on race, theology, freedom, metaphysics, spirituality, and existentialism.

A typical issue features six to seven original articles, book reviews, and occasionally a biographical sketch on some leading or deceased innovator. While not primarily a "philosophical journal," articles may be found published on Jaspers, Husserl, Kierkegaard, Merleau-Ponty and others. In fact, the specimen copy alone (Spring, 1982) contained a superlative annual survey of philosophical literature by Professor James Collins.

58. Crucible and Scientific Atheist. DATE FOUNDED: 1964. FREQUENCY: m. PRICE: $5/yr. institutions. PUBLISHER: De Young Press, Box 14, Route 2, Perkins Hull, Iowa 51239. EDITOR: Mary De Young. ILLUSTRATIONS. ADVERTISEMENTS. CIRCULATION: 250. MANUSCRIPT SELECTION: Editor. MICROFORMS: UMI. REPRINTS: author. BOOK REVIEWS: 1 review, 750 words, signed. SPECIAL ISSUES: Occasional. TARGET AUDIENCE: AC. SAMPLE COPIES: Libraries, individuals. ACCEPTANCE RATE: 5%.

CSA is primarily the internal organ of the Minnesota Institute of Philosophy and is committed to critical expression of human rights, civil rights, social justice and philosphical underpinnings thereto. Biological sciences related to anthropology, metaphysics, and religion have been in recent issues. The atheistic ideology bequeathed to CSA is more exploratory than methodological, similar to American Atheist. CSA rejects articles that ostensibly condemn pornography, sports and racism. Contributors are members of the Institute and seek an objective profile of current issues.

Each issue features materialistic views in three to five articles. Reviewers for books are selected based on their expertise in atheism or membership in the society.

59. Das Argument: Zeitschrift fur Philosophie und Sozialwissenschatten.
DATE FOUNDED: 1959. FREQUENCY: 6/yr. PRICE: 63.80 Deutsche
Mark/yr. institutions, 50 Deutche Mark/yr. students. PUBLISHER:
Argument-Verlag, 6MGH, Altensteinstrabe 48a, D-1000, Berlin, West
Germany. EDITORS: Frigga Haug, Wolfgang Fritz Haug. ILLUSTRATIONS.
INDEX. ADVERTISEMENTS. MANUSCRIPT SELECTION: Refereed, editorial
board. REPRINTS: author. BOOK REVIEWS: 35-40 reviews, 1-2 pp.,
signed. SPECIAL ISSUES: 1 supplement/yr. TARGET AUDIENCE: AC.
SAMPLE COPIES: Libraries, individuals. ACCEPTANCE RATE: 5%.

DA is the voice of German thought. Published articles tap the flow of
intellectual criticism on literature, art, culture, sociology, education,
psychology, history, policy movements, and German economics. Political
examinations introduce a unique hybrid of idealism and socialism in
understanding the motivation of government, underground groups, and
subversive practices. Scholarly inquiries assume an objective outlook on
equality, since the authors are largely academicians. In short, this portrait
of German culture reads with the same political skepticism as Aut Aut and
Seikyo Times.
     A typical issue covers editorials, approximately nine to ten original
dialogues on philosophical ideology, and book reviews. English summaries
translate the critical themes inherent in the articles.

60. Dawn Magazine. DATE FOUNDED: 1981. FREQUENCY: q. PRICE:
$8/yr. institutions, personal. PUBLISHER: Himalayan International Institute
of Yoga Science and Philosophy, RD1, Box 88, Honesdale, Pennsylvania
18431. EDITOR: Lawrence Clark. ILLUSTRATIONS. ADVERTISEMENTS.
CIRCULATION: 3,000. MANUSCRIPT SELECTION: Editor. REPRINTS:
editor. TARGET AUDIENCE: GP. SAMPLE COPIES: Libraries, individuals.

DM is a modern statement of the ancient yoga tradition and philosophy
handed down by the sages of the Himalaya Mountains. Through the teachings
of Sri Swami Rama, this contemporary expression of ancient truth helps
readers search for the inner light of wisdom. Specifically, articles explore
yoga, meditation, philosophy, psychology, and the principles of holistic living.
Indian philosophy is converted into the "cosmopolitan" ways of American
subscribers. Himalayian spirituality tries to answer intriguing psychological
questions also solved in Ascent, Prana Yoga Life, or through the
transpersonal emotionalism of Iconoclast. Spiritual panaceas for life's
complex problems may oversimplify the commitments of DM, despite its
wide appeal. In fact, these original ideas risk becoming egocentric and may
confuse optimistic readers.
     A single issue has an impressive aritistic layout. Published are five to six
featured papers and three to four regular installments on holistic medicine,
yoga, phenomenology, and "Nature's Pharmaçy." The idolism surrounding
Swami Rama, for some, may arouse interest in concepts of altruism.

61. Death and Dying A to Z. DATE FOUNDED: 1981. FREQUENCY: q.
PRICE: $69/yr. institutions. Publisher: Croner Publications, Incorporated,
211-05 Jamaica Avenue, Queens Village, New York 11428. EDITOR: Kurt J.
Guggenheimer. SPECIAL ISSUES: q. TARGET AUDIENCE: AC, GP, HS.

In our youth oriented society, old age, sickness and death have been taboo. DD circumvents this tradition in a series of quarterly supplements that cover every single aspect of death and dying in a truly encyclopedic approach to cultural problems in the modern world. Six sections produced by a board of esteemed scholars meet this need. Section I deals with new approaches in law, geriatrics, and social work devoted to bereavement. Section II gives a directory of United States and Canadian hospices, organizations for organ donations, and also services for grief counseling. Section III contains a thorough bibliography covering books, pamphlets, articles, and audio-visual material. Section IV looks at death and religion, death and philosophy, and legal implications regarding protection of an estate. Section V provides an indispensable glossary and latest statistics of interest to those in thanatology. And Section VI lists historical milestones in all fields covered by the periodical, as well as outlooks for the foreign scene.

As a reference alone, DD updates the field of death and dying unmatched by either spiritual and mystic magazines or such educational tools as Omega.

62. Degres. DATE FOUNDED: 1973. FREQUENCY: q. PRICE: 1300 Belgium Francs/yr. institutions. PUBLISHER: Degres-Sqare Sainctelette, 8-1000 Brussels, Belgium. EDITOR: Andre Helbo. ILLUSTRATIONS. ADVERTISEMENTS. CIRCULATION: 10,000. MANUSCRIPT SELECTION: Refereed, editorial board. REPRINTS: editor. BOOK REVIEWS: 20 reviews, 1-3 pp., signed. SPECIAL ISSUES: Occasional. TARGET AUDIENCE: AC, GP, HS.

Degres offers an unusual combination of fine arts, social sciences, and general semiotics. Narratives on international development in aesthetic criticism rest on the mantel of epistemological philosophies and works of twentieth century Belgium thinkers. A center for independent exchange, Degres communicates the renaissance of early contemporary ideas as shifting from abstractionism to surrealism. Authors are scholars and laymen who deeply believe in the preservation of old tradition as viewed in Annals d'Esthetique.

Original articles have recently shifted attention to topics in semiotics. Short articles are followed by book reviews and occasional notes.

63. Dharma. DATE FOUNDED: 1949. FREQUENCY: q. PRICE: $6/yr. institutions. PUBLISHER: Pure Life Society, 6th Mile, Puchong Road, Petaling, Kuala Lumpur. EDITOR: Sister A. Mangalam. INDEX. CIRCULATION: 3,000. MANUSCRIPT SELECTION: Editor. BOOK REVIEWS: 1 review. SPECIAL ISSUES: Occasional. INDEXED/ABSTRACT-ED: NewTAb. TARGET AUDIENCE: AC, GP. SAMPLE COPIES: Libraries, individuals.

"Dharma" means conformity to one's deity and laws of cosmic nature. Consequently, Dharma promotes the study of comparative theology and philosophy in its widest form. Devoted to universal religion, righteousness and culture, articles stimulate spiritual truth as the ideal discernment of self-fulfillment. Articles are written by revered Swamis, yoga specialists, and members of the Pure Life Society. Metaphysical and cosmic papers on peace and harmony consider human freedom the enlightenment of misguided ways. While sounding dogmatic, this same fervorance appears in Cross Currents, Dawn and Beacon.

A normal issue typically contains a medley of anecdotes and original guidance for spiritual edification. Editorials follow with eight to nine short articles, and then regular features on "Salient Thought" and newsletter announcements.

64. Diafora. DATE FOUNDED: 1970. FREQUENCY: q. PRICE: 6,000 Lire/yr. institutions. PUBLISHER: Grafiche Elmas-09100 Cagliari, v. le Elmas, Italy. EDITOR: Egidio Muraglia. INDEX. CIRCULATION: 1,500. MANUSCRIPT SELECTION: Editor. BOOK REVIEWS: 5-10 reviews, 750 words, signed. SPECIAL ISSUES: Occasional. TARGET AUDIENCE: AC. SAMPLE COPIES: Libraries, individuals.

Diafora is a multilingual forum for the review and critical discussion of various philosophical sciences. Increasing debate between monism and antimonism, between mathematics and mathematicism, and between political philosophy and politicizing give rise to sound arguments. Different from Philosophy of Science and British Journal for Philosophy of Science, Diafora may accept articles providing that authors agree to have it followed by refutations. Concise, objective rebuttals complement the original presentations of general and social dialogue, written by scholars.
A typical issue contains six to seven articles followed by book reviews and editorial refutations. Papers at times suffer from pedantry, which obscures important flaws in argument. For instance, one editorial rejoinder, apparently angry about certain prejudices, calls the authors "donkeys" and "subjecting [themselves] to the worst. . .highbrow bondage."

65. Dialectica. DATE FOUNDED: 1947. FREQUENCY: q. PRICE: 55 Swiss Francs/yr. institutions. PUBLISHER: Dialectica, c/o Association F. Gonseth, Case Postale 1081, 2501, Bienne, Switzerland. EDITOR: Henri Lauener. ILLUSTRATIONS. INDEX. ADVERTISEMENTS. REPRINTS: editor. BOOK REVIEWS: 9-10 reviews, 600 words, signed. SPECIAL ISSUES: Occasional. INDEXED/ABSTRACTED: ArtHumCitI, PhilosI. TARGET AUDIENCE: AC.

Dialectica is an international review of philosophy of knowledge ideally suited for the serious investigator of epistemological research. Mostly in English, articles survey the continuum of social action theory related to philosophical method,logic, and rationality. Authors, largely scholars, address the republic of science in ongoing modes of analyticity. Fundamental questions touch upon mainstream issues such as feminist philosophy (e.g., Hypatia), ethicality (e.g., Ethics and Animals) and Hegelian axioms for marriage and social dialectic (e.g., Owl of Minerva). Special issues assemble proceedings of colloquia sponsored by the Swiss Academy of Sciences and Humanities.
A typical issue contains four to five original features and book reviews, plus a list of books received. Dialectica provides a novel interdisciplinary approach to problems of knowing without much jargon.

66. Dialogos. DATE FOUNDED: 1964. FREQUENCY: sa. PRICE: $10/yr. institutions, $7/yr. personal. PUBLISHER: Departamento de Filosofia, Universidad de Puerto Rico, P.O. Box 21572 Rio Piedras, Puerto Rico 00931. EDITOR: Roberto Torretti. ILLUSTRATIONS. INDEX. ADVERTISEMENTS.

CIRCULATION: 800. MANUSCRIPT SELECTION: Refereed, editorial board. REPRINTS: author. BOOK REVIEWS: 6-8 reviews, 1-2 pp., signed. INDEXED/ABSTRACTED: PhilosI. TARGET AUDIENCE: AC. SAMPLE COPIES: Libraries, individuals. ACCEPTANCE RATE: 50%.

Dialogos publishes articles in English and Spanish on current themes relevant for practical philosophical application. Metaphysics and morality dominate the historical bias in theoretical criticism. Papers carefully examine Hume, Sartre, Freud, and dichotomies such as freedom vs. determinism. Interposed between this science and metaphilosophy (e.g., hermeneutism) are representative ethical arguments about crime, psychopathy, and civil disobedience. Similar articles appear in Philosophy and Mental Health and the Journal of Philosophy. Scholarly treatments of obligationism, games, and social choice also resemble the discussions in Nous and Ratio.
  A single issue contains original articles and a healthy assortment of book reviews. Selection of books is perhaps more tedious than usual, since the editor prefers reviews be finished before a specific publication deadline.

67. Dialogue. DATE FOUNDED: 1956. FREQUENCY: 3/yr. PRICE: $5/yr. institutions. PUBLISHER: Phi Sigma Tau, Department of Philosophy, Marquette University, Milwaukee, Wisconsin 53233. EDITOR: Thomas Prendergast. ILLUSTRATIONS. INDEX. ADVERTISEMENTS. CIRCULATION: 1,500. MANUSCRIPT SELECTION: Refereed, editorial board. REPRINTS: ISI. BOOK REVIEWS: 1-2 reviews, 750 words, signed. INDEXED/ABSTRACTED: ArtHumCitI, CurrContAH, PhilosI. TARGET AUDIENCE: AC. SAMPLE COPIES: Libraries, individuals.

Active chapters of Phi Sigma Tau, the national honor society for philosophy, responsibly recruit graduate and undergraduate students every year for intellectual advancement of the discipline. Original articles of these members (or nonmembers) appear in Dialogue. Articles are accepted in the entire field of philosophy whether or not the author comes from an institution endorsed by the Society. However, work is rejected from authors whose degree program is finished or are teaching. Contributors write on ancient history, experimental philosophy, and general trends. As observed in Auslegung and Cornell Journal of Social Relations, the student contribution marks a critical turning point in polemical traditions, perhaps with unwelcome reception.
  A typical issue of Dialogue features five to six student articles and book reviews. A list of books received and description of contributing authors follows with a regular column on "Careers in Philosophy." Along with Jobs for Philosophers, this career section highlights the placement opportunities in demand.

68. Dialogue: Canadian Philosophical Review. DATE FOUNDED: 1962. FREQUENCY: q. PRICE: $40/yr. institutions, $30/yr. personal, $10/yr. students. PUBLISHER: Wilfred Laurier University Press, Wilfred Laurier University, Waterloo, Ontario, Canada N2L 3C5. EDITORS: Francois Duschesneau, Michael McDonald. INDEX. ADVERTISEMENTS. CIRCU-LATION: 1,300. MANUSCRIPT SELECTION: Refereed, editorial board. REPRINTS: author. BOOK REVIEWS: 15 reviews, 1-2 pp., signed. INDEXED/ABSTRACTED: ArtHumCitI, PhilosI. TARGET AUDIENCE: AC. ACCEPTANCE RATE: 5-10%.

DCPR is the official publication for the Canadian philosophial Association covering mainstream topics in general philosophy. Bilingual articles in French and English broadly explore the conceptual tours de force of assumptions in psychologism, epistemology, ethics and philosophy of sciences. Historical philosophy and original theories on intentionality and rationality draw from the ethos of such contemporary movements as cognitive psychology, artificial intelligence and sociobiology. As with Philosophiques, editors of DCPR subscribe to an objective overview of recent scholarly thought and typically accept contributions by American academicians.

A typical issue of DCPR contains nine to ten original essays followed by a series of two to three critical reviews on controversial themes or books. The Book Review section and list of books received reflect an interdisciplinary orientation toward domestic and foreign publications. Since DCPR extends beyond Canadian philosophy, readers may find its contents complementary to American Philosophical Quarterly and Journal of Philosophy.

69. Dianoia, Anvario de Filosofia. DATE FOUNDED: 1955. FREQUENCY: q. PRICE: 4 Pesos/yr. institutions. PUBLISHER: Enrique Villanueva, Apartado Postal 70-447, Coyoacan, 04510-Mexico, D.F. EDITOR: Instituto de Investigaciones Filosoficas, Universidad Nacional Autonoma de Mexico. CIRCULATION: 1,200.   MANUSCRIPT SELECTION: Refereed, editorial board. REPRINTS: author. BOOK REVIEWS: 8 reviews, 1-2 pp., signed. INDEXED/ABSTRACTED: BibFE, RBibPhil. TARGET AUDIENCE: AC. SAMPLE COPIES: Libraries. ACCEPTANCE RATE: 60%.

DAF accepts quality essays, discussions, exegetical papers, and investigative reports regardless of the philosophical school or point of view. The standard authoritative issues underlying rationalism and empiricism lend contrast to major enigmas in modern philosophy. Like Critica, bilingual articles in Spanish and English are objectively probing for practical implications in areas of aesthetics, epistemology, metaphysics, history and social sciences. Moreover, the fresh examination of skeptical themes in political philosophy reflect the revival in dialectic traditions. Authors are international scholars whose papers are less technical than those found in Annales Universitatis Mariae Curie-Sklodowska.

70. Dignity. DATE FOUNDED: 1969. FREQUENCY: m. PRICE: $10/yr. institutions. PUBLISHER: Dignity Incorporated, 1500 Massachusetts Avenue, North West (#11), Washington, D.C. 20005. EDITOR: Michael Bushek. ILLUSTRATIONS.   CIRCULATION: 4,200.   REPRINTS: editor. BOOK REVIEWS: 1 review, 700 words, signed. TARGET AUDIENCE: AC, GP, HS. SAMPLE COPIES: Libraries, individuals.

Dignity provides rapid publication of news, events, and controversial issues affecting the religious community on certain topics. Politically supportive of gay liberation, Dignity combines a pastoral perspective with the views of interdenominational   ethics.   This   active   ministry   features   short communications from liturgy groups nationwide who adopt the "Dignity" philosophy. Articles are written by enthusiasts in the regional offices. The Christian orientation invites dialogue and reflection on meaningful changes within the social context. However, these morally strong protestations can resemble the subjective styles of Beacon, Cross Currents ,and the Movement.

A typical issue is in newsletter format and contains five to seven half-page articles, followed by newsbriefs. The newsbriefs review organizational and membership activities or preponderant legislative action nationwide.

71. Diogenes. DATE FOUNDED: 1952. FREQUENCY: q. PRICE: $20/yr. institutions. PUBLISHER: Casalini Libri, 50014 Fiesole (Firenze), Italy. EDITOR: Jean d'Ormesson. ILLUSTRATIONS. INDEX. ADVERTISEMENTS. CIRCULATION: 3,000. MANUSCRIPT SELECTION: Refereed, editorial board. MICROFORMS: UMI. SPECIAL ISSUES: Occasional. INDEXED/ABSTRACTED: ArtHumCitI, BoA, HistAb, HumI, PhilosI. TARGET AUDIENCE: AC, GP. SAMPLE COPIES: Libraries, individuals.

Diogenes is an international review of human sciences. It publishes parallel editions in English, French, and Spanish. Articles concern the broad scientific fields, cultivating a synthesis more than analysis of semantics, demography, epistemology, political economy, psychiatry, and history of commerce. Original essays provide a justly demanding account of accurate and objective information concerning recent advances in society. Topical selections offer ideas for other disciplines in a refreshing style similar to that of Antioch Review and Human Studies. Contributors are scholars and professionals from different groups of general culture. Diogenes also contains literary works on themes about Africa, aesthetic problems, Marxism, language, and the concept of history in the Orient.

A normal issue contains six to seven unsolicited articles. Articles are followed by brief notes about contributors. Since Diogenes represents worldwide scientific organizations, the link it establishes between specialists and scholars is unique to most periodicals.

72. Dionysius. DATE FOUNDED: 1977. FREQUENCY: a. PRICE: $10/yr. institutions. PUBLISHER: Dionysius, Department of Classics, Dalhousie University, Halifax, Nova Scotia, B3H 3J5, Canada. EDITORS: A.H. Armstrong, R.D. Crouse, J.A. Doull. ILLUSTRATIONS. CIRCULATION: 350. MANUSCRIPT SELECTION: Refereed, editorial board. REPRINTS: author. INDEXED/ABSTRACTED: AP, PhilosI, RedG, SciHu. TARGET AUDIENCE: AC. SAMPLE COPIES: Libraries.

The interest of Dionysius is to make available a more accurate knowledge of ancient philosophy (Greek and Latin) and its relation to both Christian belief and the secular forces opposed to Christian belief in ancient and modern times. Distinctively a Canadian journal, articles do not rely on assumptions of European or American cultures. Rather, philosophical essays by scholars concern classical and later literature, the arts, and a clarification of Christian, Jewish, and Islamic religions. This emphasis on antiquity and criticism may lay beyond the scope of such journals as Journal of the History of Ideas, History and Theory and Bulletin de Philosophie Medievale. Contributions in the Christian heritage resemble articles in CLIO but only regarding interpretations of neo-Platonic studies.

An issue features eight to ten original essays on the interaction of ancient thinking.

73. Diotima. DATE FOUNDED: 1973. FREQUENCY: a. PRICE: $20/yr. institutions. PUBLISHER: Hellenic Society for Philosophical Studies, 40, Hypsilantou Street, Athens 140, Greece. EDITOR: E. Moutsopoulos. INDEX. ADVERTISEMENTS. MANUSCRIPT SELECTION: Editor. MICROFORMS: Publisher. REPRINTS: author. BOOK REVIEWS: 20 reviews, 1-2 pp., signed. SPECIAL ISSUES: Occasional. INDEXED/ ABSTRACTED: PhilosI. TARGET AUDIENCE: AC. SAMPLE COPIES: Libraries, individuals.

Diotima is the official publication of the Hellenic Society for Philosophical Studies. Among the topics given historical treatment include epistemology, ethics, metaphysics, cosmology, aesthetics, and the philosophical roles of Greek culture. Rational belief systems in the value and existence of logic, skepticism, and sociological ideology are presented against an objective backdrop of interdisciplinary science. Contributors are mostly academicians invited from the Society. Discussions on historical Greece vary in technicality in relation to the synthetical sophistication of Augustinian Studies and Dionysius.
Annual issues compile proceedings and from three to fifteen selected articles, followed by book reviews. The criticism acts as an essential lesson for introductory students of Hellenic philosophy.

74. Divus Thomas. DATE FOUNDED: 1979. FREQUENCY: q. PRICE: $14/yr. institutions. PUBLISHER: Collegio Alberoni, Via Emilia Parmense 77, 29100 Piacenz, Italia. EDITOR: Giuseppe Perini. INDEX. CIRCULA-TION: 600. MANUSCRIPT SELECTION: Refereed, editorial board. REPRINTS: author. BOOK REVIEWS: 30 reviews, 1-3 pp., signed. TARGET AUDIENCE: AC. SAMPLE COPIES: Libraries, individuals. ACCEPTANCE RATE: 70%.

DT draws on the relevant works of advancing theories in Thomism. Philosophy and theology extend Spanish scholasticism according to the writings of St. Thomas Aquinas. Original articles apply Thomistic principles to modern social and political problems, providing a compelling argument for mind-body inquiries. Critical essays also encompass the continental traditions in philosophy underlying Thomistic thinkers. Theoretical positions are by no means parochial, since they assimilate with intellectual changes typically found in Thomist.
A typical issue provides three to six unsolicited articles and several reviews of current books. Largely an international medium, DT suffers from limited exposure and the dying interest in Thomistic philosophy.

75. Dreamworks. DATE FOUNDED: 1980. FREQUENCY: q. PRICE: $46/yr. institutions, $19/yr. personal. PUBLISHER: Human Sciences Press, Incorporated, 72 Fifth Avenue, New York, New York 10011. EDITORS: Kenneth Atchity, Marsha Kinder. ILLUSTRATIONS. INDEX. ADVERTISEMENTS. CIRCULATION: 2,000. MANUSCRIPT SELECTION: Refereed, editorial board. REPRINTS: author. INDEXED/ABSTRACTED: CurrConSocBS, EM, IMed, PsyAb, SSCI. TARGET AUDIENCE: AC. SAMPLE COPIES: Libraries.

Dreamworks is the only periodical devoted to the interdisciplinary study of the relationship between dream and art. Essays bring together the latest thinking on dream process from aesthetics, anthropology, neurophysiology, philosophy and psychology. Dreamworks also gathers reports and adaptations from artists in the popular media. Explored is a vital part of human consciousness that focuses on creative and symbolic experiences. Original articles by scholars and scientists analyze these phenomena objectively. Dreamworks is a meeting place for artists and scientists much as American Imago centralizes disciplines in psychoanalysis.

Each issue of Dreamworks features three to six articles. Enlightening assays of nightmares and psychology make the journal an important acquisition for university libraries.

76. Educational Philosophy and Theory. DATE FOUNDED: 1969. FRE-QUENCY: sa. PRICE: $8/yr. institutions. PUBLISHER: University of New South Wales, School of Education, P.O. Box 1, Kensington, NSW, Australia 2033. EDITORS: L.M. Brown, J.H. Gribble. CIRCULATION: 600. MANUSCRIPT SELECTION: Refereed, editorial board. MICROFORMS: UMI. REPRINTS: author. BOOK REVIEWS: PhilosI. TARGET AUDIENCE: AC. SAMPLE COPIES: Libraries.

EPT is one of the few international journals for philosophy of education. Contributors include leading scholars in America, England, and Australasia. In general, editors view philosophy of education as a branch of philosophy analogous to philosophy of science, of law, and of the social sciences. Articles draw on a variety of disciplines in order to explain ideas for theory and practice. This international forum complements the pragmatism found in articles of Australasian Logic Teachers Journal and Educational Theory. Essays further promote particular ideologies concerned with a more analytical and objective approach.

A typical issue of EPT features four to six original articles and general notes about professional trends. Editorial invitations for book reviews are rare.

77. Educational Studies. DATE FOUNDED: 1970. FREQUENCY: q. PRICE: $21/yr. institutions. PUBLISHER: Robert R. Sherman, Managing Editor, Norman Hall, University of Florida, Gainesville, Florida 32605. EDITOR: Wayne J. Urban. INDEX. ADVERTISEMENTS. CIRCULATION: 1,500. MANUSCRIPT SELECTION: Editor. MICROFORMS: UMI. BOOK REVIEWS: 30 reviews, 1-3 pp., signed. INDEXED/ABSTRACTED: ArtHumCitI, PsyAb, PhilosI, SSCI. TARGET AUDIENCE: AC. SAMPLE COPIES: Libraries, individuals. ACCEPTANCE RATE: All solicited reviews are accepted.

ES is exclusively devoted to book reviews. Review essays cast much philosophical light on the perplexing problems of practical concern to scholars and educators. Coverage spans the interdisciplinary foundations of education, from history to philosophy, and through social policy issues. Contributors are well-known philosophers of education writing in the Anglo-American tradition of conceptual analysis. Their thought-provoking appraisals wrestle with the labyrinth of judgments and current aims of child and adult education. Books on morality, community, and idealist systems are often featured which add merit to the timely nature of the selections. Like Philosophical Books, ES advances various works to the forefront of college research.

78. Educational Theory. DATE FOUNDED: 1951. FREQUENCY: q. PRICE: $12/yr. institutions. PUBLISHER: University of Illinois, 1310 South Sixth Street, Champaign, Illinois 61820. EDITOR: Ralph C. Page. ILLUSTRATIONS. INDEX. ADVERTISEMENTS. CIRCULATION: 2,500. MANUSCRIPT SELECTION: Refereed, editorial board. MICROFORMS: UMI. REPRINTS: UMI. BOOK REVIEWS: 2 reviews, 2-3 pp., signed. INDEXED/ABSTRACTED: PhilosI. TARGET AUDIENCE: AC. ACCEPTANCE RATE: 10%.

ET consists of position papers by the rank of social scientists who explore central problems in the basic concepts, principles, categories, and questions of education. Perspectives reflect philosophical, historical and sociological foundations as consistently rich, wide-ranging, and incisive as the articles in Educational Philosophy and Theory. Education and the development of reason, knowledge and curricula are among the frequent issues included during recent years of ET's publication.

A typical issue contains four to five articles followed by essay reviews of current books. ET is highly recommended for undergraduates and graduates who seek to become familiar with contemporary academia.

79. Energy and Character: Journal of Biosynthesis. DATE FOUNDED: 1970. FREQUENCY: sa. PRICE: $20/yr. institutions. PUBLISHER: Abbotsbury Publications, Rodden, Dorset, England. ILLUSTRATIONS. INDEX. ADVERTISEMENTS. MANUSCRIPT SELECTION: Editor. MICROFORMS: Publisher. SPECIAL ISSUES: Occasional. TARGET AUDIENCE: AC, GP.

ECJB has published a wealth of articles in thirty-eight issues on a wide range of themes relevant to the theory and practice of therapy and of personal change. Contributions are from all over the world and directly reflect an awareness that "bio-energetic" concepts have existed in many cultures. The central concept in biosynthesis is that there are three energetic currents of life-stream flowing in the body out of which the distinctive organ-systems are formed. These streams express themselves as (a) a flow of perceptions, (b) a flow of emotional life, and (c) a flow of muscle movement. The roots of ECJB are found in works by Wilhelm Reich (1897-1957). As such, ECJB articulates the Reichian therapies of the "Centre for Biosynthesis" by integrating psychology and biology. Articles on this process share the basic principle of essays in Journal of Somatic Experience.

A typical issue contains four to five feature articles focused on self-regulation, then followed by announcements of the Center. Research completed and planned in this highly esoteric discipline has received worldwide attention.

80. Environmental Ethics. DATE FOUNDED: 1979. FREQUENCY: q. PRICE: $24/yr. institutions, $18/yr. personal. PUBLISHER: University of Georgia and Environmental Philosophy, Incorporated, Department of Philosophy and Religion, UGA, Athens, Georgia 30602. EDITOR: Eugene C. Hargrove. ILLUSTRATIONS. INDEX. ADVERTISEMENTS. CIRCULATION: 1,200. MANUSCRIPT SELECTION: Editor. MICROFORMS: UMI. BOOK REVIEWS: 3 reviews, 1-2 pp., signed. INDEXED/ABSTRACTED: ArtHumCitI,

CurrContSocBS, EcolAb, EnInAb, PhilosI, PolAb, RBibPhil, RZ, SafSciAb, SSI, SocAb, URS. TARGET AUDIENCE: AC,GP. SAMPLE COPIES: Libraries. ACCEPTANCE RATE: 10%.

EE is an interdisciplinary journal dedicted to the philosophical aspects of environmental problems including ethics, values clarification, and national affairs. It serves as a forum for diverse interest and attitudes that bring together newly emerging questions in business, biology, public policy, health, and environmental standards. More than an "ecophilosophy," EE is "environmental philosophy" dealing with history and contemporary aesthetics. Contributors are mainly scholars whose skepticism of current ecology throws an objective light on the far-reaching consequences of technology and natural environment. The profile of criticism is directed toward applied topics similar to Inquiry and Ethics and Animals.

A typical issue provides views and notes from the editor, followed by two to five feature and discussion papers and book reviews. While not every professional shares concern for environmental ethics, EE does attest to movements in philosophy toward practical matters of social theory.

81. Epistemologia. DATE FOUNDED: 1978. FREQUENCY: sa. PRICE: $20.50/yr. institutions. PUBLISHER: Editrice Tilgher-Genova, via Assarotti 52, 16122 Genova, Italy. ILLUSTRATIONS. INDEX. ADVERTISEMENTS. MANUSCRIPT SELECTION: Refereed , editorial board. REPRINTS: author. BOOK REVIEWS: 7 reviews, 1-2 pp., signed. SPECIAL ISSUES: 1/yr. INDEXED/ABSTRACTED: PhilosI. TARGET AUDIENCE: AC. SAMPLE COPIES: Libraries, individuals. ACCEPTANCE RATE: 40%.

Epistemologia symbolizes the influence of modern philosophy upon contemporary thinkers in semantics, logic and science. The journal covers a wide spectrum of original polemical writings on developments in history associated with meaning and values of social life. The best and most important feature is its extended analysis of twentieth century arguments about human action; essays examine interrelations between rationality, belief and the liberation of social institutions. Articles are written by an interdisciplinary network of scholars. Topics in epistemology survey unresolved issues typically of interest in American Philosophical Quarterly and Canadian Philosophical Review.

An issue contains five to seven original contributions and a series of book reviews. The clear and comprehensive treatment of human knowledge makes Epistemologia a nice supplement to introductory texts.

82. Erfahrungswissenschaftliche Blatter. DATE FOUNDED: 1954. TITLE CHANGES: Psychophysikalischezeitschrift (1955-1963). FREQUENCY: 7/yr. PRICE: 8 Deutsche Marks/yr. institutions. PUBLISHER: Wolfgang Ehrenberg, Vorsitzender der PPG, D-8000 Munchen 19, Klarastr, 22, West Germany. CIRCULATION: 500. MANUSCRIPT SELECTION: Editor. REPRINTS: editor. BOOK REVIEWS: 2-3 reviews, 1-3 pp., signed. SPECIAL ISSUES: Occasional. TARGET AUDIENCE: AC, GP. SAMPLE COPIES: Libraries, individuals.

EWB devotes itself to an exploration of social and theoretical topics, usually connected with parapsychology and metaphysics. Abstracts of featured articles are in English and occasionally there are English papers. Articles are generally polemical and follow neo-transcendental approaches toward scientific theory. Self-development is a secondary interest related to the existence of psychical and psychosomatic phenomena. It is difficult to tell whether this cross-section of science and supernaturalism takes seriously the implications of philosophy for advanced study in human technology and social sciences. Unlike Light and Energy and Character, EWB refrains from imposing dogmatism and contains relatively objective perspectives.

The contents are unique in several respects. An issue features five to six original essays followed by a section on correspondences. Invited and unsolicited criticism of previous articles are summarized briefly. Book reviews and a list of bibliographic sources in other journals further provide the reader with a current context.

83. Erkenntnis. DATE FOUNDED: 1930. TITLE CHANGES: Journal of Unified Science (1930-1946). FREQUENCY: 3/yr. PRICE: $137/yr. institutions, $44/yr. personal. PUBLISHER: D.Reidel Publishing Company, P.O.Box 17, 1300 AA Dorecht, Holland. EDITORS: Carl G. Hempel, Wolfgang Stegmuller, Wilhelm K. Essler. ILLUSTRATIONS. INDEX. ADVERTISEMENTS. MANUSCRIPT SELECTION: Refereed, editorial board. REPRINTS: author. BOOK REVIEWS: 1-3 reviews, 2 pp., signed. SPECIAL ISSUES: Occasional. INDEXED/ABSTRACTED: InPhil, PhilosI, RG, SocAb. TARGET AUDIENCE: AC. SAMPLE COPIES: Libraries.

Erkenntnis is a philosophical journal for foundational studies and scientific methodology covering analytic, normative, social and historical disciplines. One of its primary objectives is the provision of a suitable platform for the discussion of controversial issues in logic and natural sciences. Language, mathematics, and physics are topics that represent expanding trends in interdisciplinary study. Original essays by known scholars furnish reliable and timely reviews in topics of interest to Studia Logica, Journal of Philosophy and Critica.

A typical issue contains roughly eight articles and a collection of book reviews. The technical sophistication of articles presupposes at least a general, if not advanced, knowledge of symbolic logic and philosophic methodology.

84. ETC: A Review of General Semantics. FREQUENCY: q. PRICE: $20/yr. institutions. PUBLISHER: International Society for General Semantics, Box 2469, San Francisco, California 94126. EDITOR: Neil Postman. ILLUSTRATIONS. INDEX. ADVERTISEMENTS. CIRCULATION: 2,808. MANUSCRIPT SELECTION: Refereed, editorial board. MICRO-FORMS: UMI. REPRINTS: author. BOOK REVIEWS: 3-4 reviews, 500 words, signed. SPECIAL ISSUES: Occasional. INDEXED/ABSTRACTED: ChemAb, HumI, PsyAb, SSI. TARGET AUDIENCE: AC. SAMPLE COPIES: Libraries.

ETC is the official organ of the International Society for General Semantics. Original articles offer a thematically unified treatment of many central questions within contemporary philosophy of language. The varieties of referential construction, truth-theory, causal modalities, and specific applications of semantics receive an objective critique. ETC studies language variations as part of the larger workings of social practice and hence may include authors from different disciplines. Aiming to bridge the academic-social gap, ETC sits in a class of journals with Semiotics, Analysis, and especially Critical Inquiry, which mutually seek a wider perspective of topics.

A typical issue of ETC is broken into four basic parts: Articles, media, books, and end papers. All of these sections, except "Articles," are critical commentaries regarding previous articles, mainstream issues, and current publications.

85. Ethical Record. DATE FOUNDED: 1890. TITLE CHANGES: The Monthly Record (1890-1965). FREQUENCY: m. PRICE: 5 Shillings/yr. institutions. PUBLISHER: South Place Ethical Society, Conway Hall, 25 Red Lion Square, London WC1R 4RL, England. EDITOR: Peter Hunot. CIRCULATION: 1,000. MANUSCRIPT SELECTION: Editor. MICROFORMS: UMI. REPRINTS: UMI. BOOK REVIEWS: 1-2 reviews, 1-2 pp., signed. TARGET AUDIENCE: AC, GP. SAMPLE COPIES: Libraries, individuals.

ER publishes primarily the lectures that are delivered to the South Place Ethical Society. Topical themes cover natural and social sciences, humanities, history, and current politics. Critical talks examine the fundamental values and principles of conduct in professional roles, issues concerning discrimination, and of the moral framework in institutions. Invited lecturers are renown scholars on ethical subjects. The result is a coherent collection of objective appraisals in the strictest tradition of philosophical criticism.

A single issue contains a varying number of entire and abridged transcripts of Society lectures. Occasional book reviews give a lucid and informative survey of outstanding contributions in related fields.

86. Ethics. DATE FOUNDED: 1890. TITLE CHANGES: International Journal of Ethics (1890-1938). FREQUENCY: q. PRICE: $38/yr. institutions, $24/yr. personal. PUBLISHER: University of Chicago Press, Journals Division, P.O. Box 37005, Chicago, Illinois 60637. EDITOR: Russell Hardin. ILLUSTRATIONS. INDEX. ADVERTISEMENTS. CIRCULATION: 3,300. MANUSCRIPT SELECTION: Refereed, editorial board. MICROFORMS: UMI. REPRINTS: author. BOOK REVIEWS: 75 reviews, 1-2 pp., signed. SPECIAL ISSUES: Occasional. INDEXED/ABSTRACTED: ABC, ArtHumCitI, ChemAb, PhilosI, SocAb, SSCI, SSI. TARGET AUDIENCE: AC. SAMPLE COPIES: Libraries, individuals. ACCEPTANCE RATE: 5%.

Now in its 91st year, Ethics is one of the leading philosophical journals in America. It has become a centrally important medium of exchange between moral philosophers and those scholars with moral concerns in social science, politics, and law. Ethics is not the organ of any group and is not committed to any policy or program. Rather, articles draw out ideas and principles from an interdisciplinary approach. The editorial board and authors include distinguished names in psychiatry, theology, and social action theory. Topics in priority entail jurisprudence, and values of civilized society. Other journals on these subjects include Philosophical Studies and Inquiry.

Each issue of Ethics contains three to five major articles as well as discussion of current theory. Reviews of important books often appear, and special symposia have assessed the exigencies of "rights" and "moral development."

87. <u>Ethics and Animals</u>. DATE FOUNDED: 1980. FREQUENCY: q. PRICE: $7/yr. institutions, $5/yr. personal. PUBLISHER: Society for the Study of Ethics and Animals, c/o Department of Philosophy, Virginia Polytechnic Institute and State University, Blacksburg, Virginia 24061. EDITOR: Harlan B. Miller. ILLUSTRATIONS. INDEX. ADVERTISEMENTS. CIRCULATION: 225. MANUSCRIPT SELECTION: Editor. REPRINTS: author. BOOK REVIEWS: 5 reviews, 1-2 pp., signed. TARGET AUDIENCE: AC, GP, SP. SAMPLE COPIES: Libraries, individuals. ACCEPTANCE RATE: 60%.

<u>EA</u> is provided for the exchange of information between individuals interested in ethical questions concerning humane treatment of non-human animals. Members of the Society for the Study of Ethics established this medium in response to growing concern for animal liberation. Major articles stress the ascription of independent moral values to species, and the imminent dangers in science and technology toward animal abuse. Since authors are primarily philosophers, a recent editorial appealing to nonphilosophers re-stated the principal goals of the journal as being relevant for biologists, veterinarians, historians, legal scholars, sociologists, political scientists, and students of religion. The welfare of animals crosses over into biomedical camps of inquiry found in the <u>Hastings Center Report</u>, <u>Philosophy and Public Affairs</u> and <u>Journal of Medicine and Philosophy</u>.
  Each issue of <u>EA</u> features two to three major articles and a series of critical reviews on both books and previously published articles. A directory of organizations and periodicals affiliated with the aims of animal rights provide current perspective on different sides of the argument.

88. <u>European Journal of Humanistic Psychology</u>. DATE FOUNDED: 1973. TITLE CHANGES: <u>Self and Society</u> (1973-1979). FREQUENCY: bm. PRICE: 28 Shillings/yr. institutions. PUBLISHER: Milroy Productions, Limited, 62 Southwark Bridge Road, London SE1 0AS, England. EDITOR: Vivian Milroy. ILLUSTRATIONS. INDEX. ADVERTISEMENTS. CIRCULATION: 2,850. MANUSCRIPT SELECTION: Refereed, editorial board. REPRINTS: editor. BOOK REVIEWS: 4 reviews, 750 words, signed. SPECIAL ISSUES: 3/yr. TARGET AUDIENCE: AC, GP. SAMPLE COPIES: Libraries, individuals. ACCEPTANCE RATE: 35%.

<u>EJHP</u> is the official organ of the Association for Humanistic Psychology in Great Britian. Humanistic psychology looks up to people rather than looking down on them. Authors share their attempts to experience ecstasy, creativity, and transpersonal states as well as everyday functioning. These approaches emphasize a motivation arising from "wanting more of life," and toward a set of values which the founding father, Abraham Maslow, calls the "Being-values." In recent years, <u>EJHP</u> published a considerable number of special issues (e.g., on "experiencing") that explored this theme of human potential. Because authors are both philosophers and psychologists, contributions are integrative and better establish a common aim as viewed in <u>Journal of Transpersonal Psychology</u>.
  A typical issue covers eight to nine short articles and an assortment of poems, notes and announcements. Book reviews and occasional annotated bibliographies are useful to students in phenomenology who seek solid, pragmatic direction.

89. Explorations in Knowledge. DATE FOUNDED: 1983. FREQUENCY: a.
PRICE: 20 Shillings/yr. institutions, 16 Shillings/yr. personal. PUBLISHER:
Avebury Publishing Company, Limited, Olympic House, 63 Woodside Road,
Amersham, Bucks, HP6 6AA, England. EDITORS: David Lamb, Gonzalo
Muneyar. ADVERTISEMENTS. CIRCULATION: 500. MANUSCRIPT
SELECTION: Refereed, editorial board. BOOK REVIEWS: 10 reviews, 1-2
pp., signed. SPECIAL ISSUES: Occasional. TARGET AUDIENCE: AC.
SAMPLE COPIES: Libraries.

The inception of EK is the result of epistemological and ethical problems
arising in all branches of science. Articles set out to re-examine the
relationship between science and philosophy, encouraging critical discussion
of natural laws. Radically new forms of knowledge reflect scientific
methodology and trends in philosophy. One form in particular views the
limits of endurance in human experience. Authors are primarily scholars who
extend the classic theorists in many ways similar to   efforts in
Epistemologia and Dialectica.
   Each issue of EK presents four to five unsolicited articles and book
reviews. Considering the attraction for non-doctrinaire information, EK may
afford introductory students a realistic look at internal conflicts in the
theory of knowledge.

90. Explorations in Medicine. DATE FOUNDED: 1984. FREQUENCY: a.
PRICE: 20 Shillings/yr. institutions, 16 Shillings/yr. personal. PUBLISHER:
Avebury Publishing Company, Limited, Olympic House, 63 Woodside Road,
Amersham, Bucks, HP6 6AA, England. EDITORS: David Lamb, Teifion
Davies. ILLUSTRATIONS. ADVERTISEMENTS. CIRCULATION: 500.
MANUSCRIPT SELECTION: Refereed, editorial board. REPRINTS: author.
BOOK REVIEWS: 10 reviews, 1-3 pp., signed. SPECIAL ISSUES: Occasional.
TARGET AUDIENCE: AC, SP. SAMPLE COPIES: Libraries.

EM examines important issues in medicine requiring a philosophical critique
of both technical and theoretical underpinnings. To fulfill this need, EM
utilizes philosophical analysis in an endeavor to review clinical and ethical
issues. Theories of knowledge lend insight into the beliefs and
socio-economic conventions of modern life. The scope of topics on abortion,
euthanasia, patient compliance and principles of equality are discussed
beyond the limits of moral philosophy. In essence, scholars try to show how
these controversies have their roots in more basic dilemmas dealing with
applied philosophy. These objective positions provide intelligible answers to
the problems raised in Ethics and Journal of Medical Ethics.
   Each issue of EM publishes five to seven original essays and the book
reviews include resources of beneficial interest to physicians and applied
philosophers alike.

91. Filosofia. DATE FOUNDED: 1950. FREQUENCY: q. PRICE: 25
Lira/yr. institutions. PUBLISHER: Augusto Guzzo, Piazza Statuto 26,
I-10144 Torino, Italy. EDITOR: Augusto Guzzo. INDEX. MANUSCRIPT
SELECTION: Editor. REPRINTS: publisher. BOOK REVIEWS: 7 reviews,
1-2 pp., signed. INDEXED/ABSTRACTED: ArtHumCitI, PhilosI. TARGET
AUDIENCE: AC. SAMPLE COPIES: Libraries. ACCEPTANCE RATE: 70%.

Filosofia is the systematic study of philosophically-based reasons and causes of human behavior. It covers the entire corpus of philosophy topics from classicism to contemporary problems with science and physicalism. Ethics, law, moral responsibility, and even well-developed essays on aesthetics sample the vast directions in Italian thought. Contributors are primarily academicians who carefully unravel and fit back together the pieces of many arguments in the process of redefinition and change. Timely criticisms comport to the overall styles of Chroniques des Philosophie and Dialogue.

A typical issue contains a varying number (six to eight) of articles followed by book reviews in English and Italian. Philosophers of social theory are perhaps the best candidates to appreciate this journal.

92. Foresight. DATE FOUNDED: 1970. FREQUENCY: q. PRICE: $4/yr. institutions.   PUBLISHER: Foresight, 29 Beaufort Avenue, Hodge Hill, Birmingham B34 6AD, England. EDITORS: John and Judy Barklam. ADVERTISEMENTS.   CIRCULATION: 800.   MANUSCRIPT SELECTION: Editors. REPRINTS: editors. BOOK REVIEWS: 6 reviews, 1-2 pp. TARGET AUDIENCE: GP. ACCEPTANCE RATE: 80%.

Foresight researches and publishes subjects on psychic phenomena, UFO's, significant world events, conspiracies, and revolutionary   discoveries not normally found in regular media sources. Great emphasis is placed on paranormal, including spiritual awareness and evolutionism. Contributors range in specialization from the laymen to expert scientists. Authors present their   findings   with   supposed   detachment   and   precision.   Although quantification is not required, this material clearly lends itself to sensationalism, reinforced by a liberal editorial policy.   Articles on mysticism resemble the foci of Psychic Observer and Prediction.

The contents of Foresight magazine is a portfolio of anecdotal stories, featured articles, regular columns, and occasional reviews of books in general studies of supernaturalism. One advantage of Foresight is that it piques the curiosity of young readers interested in espionage and planetary motion (astronomy).

93. Fortean Times. DATE FOUNDED: 1973. FREQUENCY: q. PRICE: $12/yr. institutions. PUBLISHER: BM-Fortean Times, London WC1N 3XX, England.   EDITOR: Robert J.M. Rickard.   ILLUSTRATIONS. INDEX. ADVERTISEMENTS.   CIRCULATION: 1,500.   MANUSCRIPT SELECTION: Editor. REPRINTS: editor. BOOK REVIEWS: 15 reviews, 1-3 pp., signed. SPECIAL ISSUES: Occasional.   TARGET AUDIENCE: AC, GP, SP. SAMPLE COPIES: Libraries, individuals. ACCEPTANCE RATE: 80%.

The main interests of FT center on strange or anomalous phenomena relating to (a) altered and higher states of consciousness, (b) eyewitness, (c) mass hysteria, (d) psychosocial aspects of abductions, out-of-body and death experiences, and (e) history and methodology of scientific revolutions (Kuhnian paradigm). Unorthodox phenomena and reports of their devastation are interpreted through Jungian archetypes. Authors trained in this area or into   psychical research are both scholars and laymen.   The presentation of material is slightly more objective than Foresight, but below criteria in academic periodicals.

A single issue features three to four original short articles by "authorities" in the psychic field. Following this are books reviews, special announcements and local events. A relatively strong clue that psychical research is popular in the United Kingdom is the increasing number of subscriptions to FT over the past year.

94. Franciscan Studies. DATE FOUNDED: 1941. FREQUENCY: a. PRICE: $14/yr. institutions. PUBLISHER: The Franciscan Institute, St. Bonaventure University, St. Bonaventure, New York 14778. EDITOR: Conrad Harkins. INDEX. ADVERTISEMENTS. CIRCULATION: 750. MANUSCRIPT SELECTION: Refereed, editorial board. REPRINTS: editor. INDEXED/ABSTRACTED: CathI, PhilosI. TARGET AUDIENCE: AC. SAMPLE COPIES: Libraries, individuals. ACCEPTANCE RATE: 50%.

FS publishes articles and texts concerned with Franciscan contributions to theology, philosophy, science, and to the historical evolution of the Franciscan movement around the medieval period. Articles are in English, Italian, French, German, and Latin. The order that St. Francis of Assisi (1181-1226) had founded numbered at his death at some 5,000 members and had spread to Hungary, Germany, England, France, and Spain. Today the literature on Francis is partly history, partly legend. Since these legends are among the masterpieces of medieval literature, great interest is shown in FS to separate fact from fiction and myth. Franciscans consist of scholars and disciples who interpret historical events in ways similar to that found in Augustinian Studies and Bulletin de Philosophie Medievale.
   Each issue of FS provides thirteen to fifteen stimulating articles ranging from historical to contemporary criticism. This journal would make an excellent addition to a medieval studies library.

95. Free Inquiry. DATE FOUNDED: 1980. FREQUENCY: q. PRICE: $14/yr. institutions. PUBLISHER: 1203 Kensington Avenue, Buffalo, New York 14215. EDITOR: Paul Kurtz. ILLUSTRATIONS. ADVERTISEMENTS. CIRCULATION: 10,000. MANUSCRIPT SELECTION: Editor. MICROFORMS: UMI. REPRINTS: publisher. BOOK REVIEWS: 3 reviews, 1-2 pp., signed. SPECIAL ISSUES: 2-3/yr. INDEXED/ABSTRACTED: PhilosI. TARGET AUDIENCE: AC. SAMPLE COPIES: Libraries.

FI is a magazine dedicated to rational inquiry, critical of dogmatic religions and ideologies. It is interested in constructive dialogue without fear of social pressure or censure. Original articles follow the general orientation of secular humanism that (1) the best available method of truth is scientific method, (2) right behavior is what contributes to natural and physical life, and (3) political systems should be based on democratic principles. Authors are primarily religious leaders, scholars and scientists all actively supportive of ethical alternatives to orthodox religion. The challenge of controversy in such articles as "Was Jesus a Magician?" communicate this new perspective on a level equal to articles in American Rationalism, Creation/Evolution, and Crucible and Scientific Atheist.

The approach in each issue is unique in shaking the foundations of religion. A typical issue begins with letters to the editor, a special feature article on scientific or ethical suppression, and followed by six to eight short articles. Viewpoints, poetry, books, and a classified section completely fill the magazine with an ambience of religion-state separationism.

96. Free Mind. DATE FOUNDED: 1944. FREQUENCY: bm. PRICE: $30/yr. personal (includes membership to American Humanist Association). PUBLISHER: American Humanist Association, 7 Harwood Drive, Amherst, New York 14226. EDITOR: Bette Chamber.ILLUSTRATIONS. ADVERTISEMENTS. CIRCULATION: 4,500. MANUSCRIPT SELECTION: Editor. REPRINTS: editor. SPECIAL ISSUES: Occasional. TARGET AUDIENCE: AC, GP. SAMPLE COPIES: Libraries, individuals.

FM is the optimistic voice of the American Humanist Association. Published are articles relating to the institution of humanistic philosophy and activities of chapters or associated groups who continue to keep a watchful eye on freedom of choice.   Brief essays, usually solicited, express the negative impact of science on society and promote civil liberties in the twentieth century.   Contributors are members of the Association.   In many ways, FM stretches the nature of arguments reported in Free Inquiry.

Differences in style and format qualify FM more as a newsletter than standard periodical.   Each issue contains a lead article plus letters to the editor, news of members' activities, and overseas contributions to humanism. Ads for reprints and for special "humanistic" calendars further this manifesto of theory.   In fact, FM is a good device for political conversion, despite its discussion of seemingly complex issues.

97.   Freedom.   DATE FOUNDED: 1968.   FREQUENCY: bm.   PRICE: $12/yr.   institutions.   PUBLISHER: Church of Scientology, 4833 Fountain Avenue, Los Angeles, California 90029. EDITOR: Thomas G. Little. ILLUSTRATIONS. INDEX. ADVERTISEMENTS. CIRCULATION: 25,000. MANUSCRIPT SELECTION: Editor. REPRINTS: editor. BOOK REVIEWS: 1 review, 1-2 pp., signed. SPECIAL ISSUES: 8/yr. TARGET AUDIENCE: AC, GP. SAMPLE COPIES: Libraries, individuals.

Freedom is a syndicated magazine devoted to the exposure of corruption in governmental, psychiatric, and capitalistic establishments.   Carefully researched news covers vital issues regarding the denial of human rights and philosophy of the Church of Scientology.   Contributors range from news correspondents to guest professionals, in both cases using investigative methods to qualify statements about the invasion of privacy. By the large circulation alone, Freedom attracts a cross-section of secular and religious readers.   At times, this so-called investigative journalism may overstate moral accusations or the facts surrounding some controversy.   Clearly, however, it does seek the same humanistic goals as Free Inquiry and the Humanist.

A typical issue features six to eight original and regular brief articles on controversial themes in the nation.   This newspaper-styled periodical best appeals to educated readers.

98. Gnosis: A Journal of Philosophic Interest. DATE FOUNDED: 1973. FREQUENCY: sa. PRICE: free. PUBLISHER: Philosophy Department, Concordia University, 1455 Demaisonneuve, West Montreal, Quebec H3G 1M8. EDITORS: Graduate and undergraduate students. ILLUSTRATIONS. CIRCULATION: 600. MANUSCRIPT SELECTION: Editors. REPRINTS: author. INDEXED/ABSTRACTED: PhilosI. TARGET AUDIENCE: AC. SAMPLE COPIES: Libraries, individuals. ACCEPTANCE RATE: 30%.

Gnosis is a philosophy journal devoted largely to the publication of student papers for exposure, evaluation and criticism among the philosophical community. Graduate and undergraduate students co-edit and review articles on the humanities, historical issues, ethics, and public policy. Papers in the past have been by Concordia students but students elsewhere are welcome to submit essays covering a wide range of schools or traditions in philosophy. Because of this general scope, Gnosis reaches more interdisciplinary readers than might other graduate-student journals such as Auslegung and Dialogue.
   Each issue of Gnosis fulfills the prophecy of its subtitle, "a journal of philosophic interest." Four to five original articles or extracts from students' theses and dissertations are followed by insightful notes and discussions for student research. Gnosis defines its commitment as improving graduate studies.

99. Gralswelt: Zeitschrift fur Wahren Aufbau durch neues Wissen (Magazine for True Upbuiling through New Knowledge). DATE FOUNDED: 1947. TITLE CHANGES: Gralsblatter (1947-1950). FREQUENCY: bm. PRICE: 25.80 Deutsche Marks/yr. institutions. PUBLISHER: Verlag der Stiftung Gralsbotschaft, Zenzhalde 15, D-7000, Germany. EDITOR: Edith Janson-Runge. INDEX. CIRCULATION: 2,300. MANUSCRIPT SELECTION: Editor. INDEXED/ABSTRACTED: SLPrW. TARGET AUDIENCE: GP. SAMPLE COPIES: Libraries, individuals.

Gralswelt publishes articles based on the spiritual knowledge contained in the work "In the Light of Truth" (by Verlag Alexander Berhardt). Essays on morality, religion, and self-fulfillment help the reader to find a solution to his personal problems or philosophical questions about laws of nature and creation. Contributors are both laymen and scholars. Probing inquiries discuss everyday issues within the realm of Bernhardt's "Grail Message of Abd-ru-Shin." This mixture of cosmology and psychologism resembles the topics in European Journal of Humanistic Psychology and Dharma.
   A typical issue of Gralswelt features a combination of original papers and regular columnists. Notes, announcements, and editorials appraise the current status of religion with an authoritarian voice, somewhat like Rand's editorializing in the Objectivist Forum.

100. Grazer Philosophisce Studien. DATE FOUNDED: 1975. FREQUENCY: sa. PRICE: $16/yr. institutions. PUBLISHER: Editions Rodopi B.V., Keizersgracht 302-304, NL-1016 Amsterdam. EDITOR: Rudolf Haller. ADVERTISEMENTS. CIRCULATION: 500. MANUSCRIPT SELECTION: Refereed, editorial board. BOOK REVIEWS: 10 reviews, 1-2 pp., signed. SPECIAL ISSUES: 1/yr. INDEXED/ABSTRACTED: PhilosI. TARGET AUDIENCE: AC. ACCEPTANCE RATE: 60%.

GPS is an open forum for philosophical debate on contemporary subjects ranging from aesthetics and epistemology to analytic logic. Bilingual articles bridge the international gap between Anglo-American and European schools of thought and allow for critical examination of reasonable and intriguing aspects of metatheory. Authors are mainly scholars. GPS draws on the foundational works of epistemological and applied philosophers in each objective account of current ideas. Like Synthese and Erkenntnis, criticism usually centers on the unresolved problems in semantics and human action.

Issues of GPS feature five to six original essays and major articles followed by book reviews. Reviews are regarding the exceptional achievements of a given book.

101. Heytings Center Report. DATE FOUNDED: 1971. FREQUENCY: bm. PRICE: $35/yr. institutions, $26/yr. personal, $22/yr. student. PUBLISHER: The Hastings Center, 360 Broadway, Hastings-on-Hudson, New York 10706. EDITOR: Carol Levine. INDEX. CIRCULATION: 9,500. MANUSCRIPT SELECTION: Refereed, editorial board. MICROFORMS: UMI. REPRINTS: author. BOOK REVIEWS: 2-3 reviews, 1-2 pp., signed. SPECIAL ISSUES: Occasional. INDEXED/ABSTRACTED: CurrContSocBS, IMed, PhilosI, SSCI. TARGET AUDIENCE: AC, GP, SP.   SAMPLE COPIES: Libraries. ACCEPTANCE RATE: 10%.

HCR is the premier journal of biomedical ethics. Its reputation alone is that of central organ for discussion of ethical problems associated with medicine, professionalism, and applied disciplines. HCR represents the devotion of the Hastings Center to explore and disseminate objective facts in behavioral sciences. Among its high caliber essays include topics on organ transplants, human experimentation, prenatal diagnosis of genetic disease, and life-extending technology. Solicited and unsolicited articles draw from a team of medical experts and scholars. Practical statements about health policy and human rights extend the opinions usually found in Explorations in Medicine, Cahiers Albert Schweitzer, and the Journal of Medicine and Philosophy.

Contained in HCR are five or more major articles followed by featured reviews on case studies. The news, notes, and calendar of events that follow provide current information on continuing education for students. There is no doubt that HCR is the ideal serial for medical and university libraries.

102. Heythrop Journal. DATE FOUNDED: 1960. FREQUENCY: q. PRICE: $20/yr. institutions. PUBLISHER: Heythrop College (University of London) 11-13 Cavendish Square, London WIM OAN, England. ILLUSTRATIONS. INDEX.   ADVERTISEMENTS.   CIRCULATION: 800.   MANUSCRIPT SELECTION: Refereed, editorial board. REPRINTS: author. BOOK REVIEWS: 60 reviews, 1-3 pp., signed. INDEXED/ABSTRACTED: ArtHumCitI, CurrContAH, CathI, PhilosI, NewTAb. TARGET AUDIENCE: AC. ACCEPTANCE RATE: 25%.

HJ contains a systematic and critical account of disciplines within the religious enterprise. Examined are translations, the emergence of theological movements, and social teachings of Christianity advanced from classic periods.   Topics of major focus include individual freedom, women's ordination, liturgy, and inherent contradiction of scientific philosophy. Articles are written primarily by scholars. Links between historical and modern contemporary ideas reflect intellectual originality. In short, this religious literature strives to achieve skeptic perspectives. Such perspectives can be found in Philosophy of Religion and Journal for the Scientific Study of Religion.

A typical issue contains four to five articles and the remainder is book reviews and notes. Since half the journal is bibliographic, students and scholars may enjoy the combined benefits of advanced criticism in theology and an anthology of recent works.

103. History and Theory: Studies in the Philosophy of History. DATE FOUNDED: 1960. FREQUENCY: q. PRICE: $25/yr. institutions, $15/yr. personal. PUBLISHER: Wesleyan University, Wesleyan Station, MIddletown, Connecticut 06457. EDITOR: George H. Nedel. ILLUSTRATIONS. INDEX. ADVERTISEMENTS. CIRCULATION: 2,200. MANUSCRIPT SELECTION: Refereed, editorial board. MICROFORMS: UMI. REPRINTS: editor. BOOK REVIEWS: 4 reviews, 10-12 pp., signed. SPECIAL ISSUES: Every fourth issue (called a Beiheft). INDEXED/ ABSTRACTED: CurrContAH, HistAb, HumI, PhilosI, SocAb. TARGET AUDIENCE: AC. ACCEPTANCE RATE: 15%.

HT champions the philosophic coverage of history in a variety of expressions. Published are essays, monographs, reviews, notes and also bibliography principally covering theories of history, historical figures, methods of historiography, and the relationship of problems in theory to economic, psychological, and other social sciences. Articles confine the analysis to facts, objectivity, and social and cultural implications of value to historical scholarship. Contributors are distinguished academicians and frequently pioneers of such intellectual schools as "psychohistory" and "instrumentalism." Essays present a vision of history in a lucid and accessible form that captures the nuances of sociohistorical revolutions. Of no less interest are the compelling text translations and criticisms against century thinkers in areas also probed by Conceptus, Dionysius, and CLIO. Specialty journals such as Augustinian Studies and Franciscan Studies equally match the intensity of special issues in HT.

A single issue features four to five major articles and a series of book reviews followed by short book summaries. Historians and philosophers alike can appreciate logical theory derived from methods and principles of schools in history.

104. History of Universities. DATE FOUNDED: 1981. FREQUENCY: a. PRICE: 20 Pounds/yr. institutions, 16 Pounds/yr. personal. PUBLISHER: Averbury Publishing Company, Limited, Olympic House, 63 Woodside Road, Amersham, Bucks HP6 6AA. EDITOR: Charles Schmitt. ILLUSTRATIONS. ADVERTISEMENTS. CIRCULATION: 500. MANUSCRIPT SELECTION: Refereed, editorial board. BOOK REVIEWS: 10-15 reviews, 2-5 pp., signed. INDEXED/ABSTRACTED: HistAb. TARGET AUDIENCE: AC.

HU departs from the usual panorama of classic studies and historiography. Rather, it publishes papers primarily concerned with the history of development, structure and teaching of institutions of advanced education. Subjects cover the history of European and American universities before the outbreak of the second world war , including the comparative histories of current institutions. All contributions are expected to reflect an awareness of the cultural context and contain documentation from primary sources. Substantial studies of the modern period may follow a theme such as "specialized academies" (e.g., College royal, Ecole Polytechnique of Paris) or support the impact of documents upon pedagogy. Articles are written primarily by historians and scholars at British universities, although submissions are encouraged internationally. Papers on higher education and learning set HU apart from Educational Theory or Teaching Philosophy by the fact that no single periodical devotes entire space to university histories.

Each issue provides a compendium of introductory and complex analyses. Contained are ten to twelve original studies as well as a section of book reviews, research notes, and reports. The main language of the articles is English, but contributions also have been in French, German, Italian and Spanish.

105. Hsinjuchia: New Confucians. DATE FOUNDED: 1967. FREQUENCY: q. PRICE: $5/yr. institutions. PUBLISHER: Chen Chien-Fu, P.O. Box 22239 Taipei, Taiwan, Republic of China. EDITOR: Chen Chien-Fu. ILLUSTRATIONS. INDEX. CIRCULATION: 1,000. MANUSCRIPT SELECTION: Editor. BOOK REVIEWS: 3 reviews, 1-2 pp., signed. TARGET AUDIENCE: GP. SAMPLE COPIES: Libraries, individuals. ACCEPTANCE RATE: 50%.

Hsinjuchia represents a flowing dialogue of China's new values. It has its origin in China's traditional Buddhist beliefs, merging the best of Buddhism and Christianity. Founder Chen Chien-Fu views Confucianism as the truths from personal moral culture to ruling the State and pacifying the world. Old Confucianism lost interest when Chinese culture entered into modern times, coming in contact with Western influence. Hsinjuchia introduces a New Confucianism that does not speak of divinity and human desires. Articles directly speak to the energy of life, the awakening of spirit and good behavior, and establish a code of morality full of world affairs. A crystallization of New China, Hsinjuchia has been called the "philosophy of the new world." Contributing authors are philosophers, theologians, and laymen. This journal opens its channels of social commentary beyond the focus of Journal of Chinese Philosophy.

A typical issue features three to four articles in English and Chinese. New Confucianism Magazine Company encourages distribution to European and American universities in the hopes of establishing international recognition.

106. Human. DATE FOUNDED: 1973. TITLE CHANGES: Uncertified Human (1973-1981). FREQUENCY: m. PRICE: $10/yr. institutions. PUBLISHER: 1295 Gerrard Street East, Toronto, Canada M4L 148. EDITOR: Jessica Pegis. ILLUSTRATIONS. ADVERTISEMENTS. CIRCULATION: 10,000. MANUSCRIPT SELECTION: Editor. REPRINTS: publisher. BOOK REVIEWS: 1-3 reviews, 2 pp., signed. TARGET AUDIENCE: AC, GP, HS, SP. SAMPLE COPIES: Libraries, individuals. ACCEPTANCE RATE: 15%.

Human is a magazine of life issues from conception through natural death. Strong coverage is given to uses and abuses of medical technology. Articles with general appeal on abortion, surgery and the bereavement process report on the dangers surrounding a given problem. Innovative reports always present the facts objectively. The biomedical information is written by freelance and staff authors. Like Freedom, Human employs investigative journalism to dispel the myths of the medical establishment. In this sense, Human is a popularized version of Hastings Center Report.

Each issue of Human divulges the latest warnings and violations against clinical safety. Four to five brief articles follow with book reviews and a section for each regular department. Human is by no means bereft of religious orientation. Implicitly, perhaps, the messages of Christianity underlie each article.

107. Human Rights Quarterly. DATE FOUNDED: 1979. TITLE CHANGES: Universal Human Rights (1979-1981). FREQUENCY: q. PRICE: $40/yr. institutions, $18/yr. personal. PUBLISHER: John Hopkins University Press, Baltimore, Maryland 21218. EDITOR: Bert B. Lockwood. ILLUSTRATIONS. INDEX. ADVERTISEMENTS. CIRCULATION: 1,000. MANUSCRIPT SELECTION: Refereed, editorial board. MICROFORMS: UMI. REPRINTS: author. BOOK REVIEWS: 5 reviews, 2-5 pp., signed. SPECIAL ISSUES: Occasional. INDEXED/ABSTRACTED: CurrContAH, PhilosI. TARGET AUDIENCE: AC. SAMPLE COPIES: Libraries, individuals. ACCEPTANCE RATE: 15%.

HRQ offers a forum for international dialogue among the disciplines of law, philosophy and social sciences concerning research on public policy and universal human rights. While free from any single ideology, the scope of articles centers largely on the constitutionality of justice, equality, and egalitarian philosophy. Examined are realistic as well as contradictory transformations of human rights for moral problems (freedom, abuses of speech, etc.). "Foreign policy attitudes of American human rights" represents another major focus, presented in contrast to the unique status of decisions in the United Nations. Essays thus attempt an objective outlook on current politics. This approach bears some similarity to viewpoints in Aut Aut and Acta Philosophical Fennica.

A typical issue contains four to six major articles and book reviews. At the back is a description of contributors.

108. Human Studies. DATE FOUNDED: 1978. FREQUENCY: q. PRICE: $47/yr. institutions, $21/yr. personal. PUBLISHER: Ablex Publishing Corporation, Norwood, New Jersey 07648. EDITOR: George Psathas. INDEX. ADVERTISEMENTS. CIRCULATION: 300. MANUSCRIPT SELECTION: Refereed, editorial board. REPRINTS: author. BOOK REVIEWS: 2 reviews, 2-6 pp., signed. SPECIAL ISSUES: 1/every 2 yrs. TARGET AUDIENCE: AC. SAMPLE COPIES: Libraries. ACCEPTANCE RATE: 50%.

HS is a journal primarily dedicated to advancing discussion between philosophy and the social sciences, in particular, between phenomenological and existential thinking. It is a problem-oriented journal in that ideas draw on theory and practice to solve everyday human problems. Articles provide a clear statement of the nature and strategy underlying science, objectivism, and methodology. Authors are primarily scholars and specialists in psychology and natural sciences. This interdisciplinary communication enhances the reader's ability to place HS in current context along with Degres and British Journal for the Philosophy of Science.

A typical issue contains five feature articles followed by an occasional, lengthy book review. The impressive quality of HS is in its concern for social and technical principles interposed between actual facts and hypothetical constructs. Students in social science disciplines can benefit from this approach.

109. Humanist. DATE FOUNDED: 1941. TITLE CHANGES: New Humanist (1941). FREQUENCY: bm. PRICE: $15/yr. institutions. PUBLISHER: American Humanist Association, 7 Harwood Drive, Amherst, New York 14226. EDITOR: Lloyd L. Morain. ILLUSTRATIONS. ADVERTISEMENTS. CIRCULATION: 14,000. MANUSCRIPT SELECTION: Editor. REPRINTS: publisher. BOOK REVIEWS: 5 reviews, 750 words, signed.   SPECIAL ISSUES: Occasional. INDEXED/ABSTRACTED: CurrContAH, HumI, PhilosI, RG, SSCI. TARGET AUDIENCE: AC, GP. SAMPLE COPIES: Libraries. ACCEPTANCE RATE: 2%.

Humanist is probably the most widely circulated and well known of the humanist or "free thought" journals published in the United States. It offers a high quality of objective reading matter for the educated person on anthropology, education, ethics, and philosophy of religion. Constructively discussed are social issues and personal concerns in the light of humanistic studies and developments in society. In pursuit of free and open dialogue, authors are mainly scholars and staff writers whose opinions are similar to those found in Free Inquiry and Free Mind. Interesting and lively debates cover world religions, creationism, and cultural consciousness. Parallels to such serials as Crucible and Scientific Atheist and Creation/Evolution are striking.
A typical issue contains ten to twelve original articles and regular departments. One department called the "Philosopher's column" comments on prevalent themes (e.g., nuclear war, pursuit of knowledge, etc.).

110. Humanities in Society. DATE FOUNDED: 1978. FREQUENCY: q. PRICE: $26/yr. institutions, $20/yr. personal. PUBLISHER: Center for the Humanities, 326 Taper Hall of Humanities, University of Southern California, Los Angeles, California 90089-0350. EDITORS: Mark E. Kahn, Katherine S. Kovacs. ILLUSTRATIONS.   ADVERTISEMENTS. CIRCULATION: 500. MANUSCRIPT SELECTION: Refereed, editorial board. REPRINTS: author. SPECIAL ISSUES: Occasional. INDEXED/ ABSTRACTED: MHRA, PhilosI, SocAb, SSCI. TARGET AUDIENCE: AC, GP. SAMPLE COPIES: Libraries, individuals.

HS is an interdisciplinary journal concerned with the role of ideas in modern society. The aim is to situate intellectual endeavors in a social context and to explore the power relations that govern society. Starting from the premise that no inquiry is value-free, HS investigates the currents of thought in the academic community regarding politics, militarism, psychoanalysis, religion, pornography, and east/west emigrationism. Humanistically treated topics challenge the domination of hegemonic groups and propose alternative perspectives on the past, present and future. HS publishes articles, essays, translations, and special dialogues by prominent scholars. The intersection of society, idealism, and university resembles the themes in History of Universities and Human Rights Quarterly.

A typical issue contains five to seven original discourses in critical theory and a pervasive social science.   The authority HS commands in the humanities area owes much to its commitment to global issues.

111.   Humboldt Journal of Social Relations.   DATE FOUNDED: 1972. FREQUENCY: sm.   PRICE: $15/yr., institutions, $11/yr. personal. PUBLISHER: 55 Library, Humboldt State University, Arcata, California 95521.   EDITOR: James Carroll.   ILLUSTRATIONS.   ADVERTISEMENTS. CIRCULATION: 700.   MANUSCRIPT SELECTION: Refereed, editorial board.   REPRINTS: author.   BOOK REVIEWS: 10 reviews, 1-3 pp., signed. SPECIAL ISSUES: 1/yr. INDEXED/ABSTRACTED: AbSocW, PsyAb, SocAb. TARGET   AUDIENCE: AC.   SAMPLE   COPIES: Libraries, individuals. ACCEPTANCE RATE: 20%.

HJSR is an interdisciplinary approach to the social sciences and publishes original research in areas of sociology, anthropology, social welfare, geography, history, philosophy and psychology.   Potential contributors span a large class of specialists and students active in practical studies. Central questions concern scientific history, ethnicity, and cross-cultural developments.   The distinct character of HJSR is its broader-based evaluation of human and environmental factors, which contrasts with Cornell Journal of Social Relations and Agora.   However, there is a dialectic position of HJSR which is very polemical and somewhat difficult for uninformed readers.
   A regular issue of HJSR publishes fifteen to twenty major articles and a section on book reviews.   There is a list of books received and biographic statements of the contributors.

112.   Husserl Studies.   DATE FOUNDED: 1983.   FREQUENCY: 3/yr. PRICE: $50/yr. institutions, $30/yr. personal. PUBLISHER: Martinus Nijoff Publishers, B.V. P.O. Box 566 2501 CN, The Hague, Netherlands. EDITORS: J.N.   Mohanty,   Karl   Schuhmann.   ADVERTISEMENTS.   MANUSCRIPT SELECTION: Refereed, editorial board.   REPRINTS: author. BOOK REVIEWS: 3 reviews, 1-2 pp., signed.   SPECIAL ISSUES: Occasional. TARGET AUDIENCE: AC. SAMPLE COPIES: Libraries, individuals.

HS is a new international journal publishing German and English articles that emphasize the relevance of Husserl's phenomenology in contemporary as well as wider philosophical circles.   It encourages interpretive and comparative works solidly based on adequate textual research into Husserl's writings. Contributions, both historical and systematic, may be exegetical or derive from the biographic background of Husserl.   In effect, HS fulfills the need for an ontological reappraisal of transcendental logic in writings of early twentieth century phenomenologists.   Advanced criticism raises the caliber of interest in this period far more than does Philosophy and Phenomenological Research and Mind.   In fact, essays on causes and meanings of self reflect modern shifts in paradigm. This makes the interpretation more controversial and therefore enjoyable.
   Each issue of HS publishes four to six major articles and book reviews. There is also a section devoted to news from various phenomenological centers and societies, such as the Husserl Archives at Louvain.   This intellectual survey of Husserl provides a nice introduction to the topic for students.

113.   Hypatia.   DATE FOUNDED: 1982. FREQUENCY: sm.   PRICE:
$95/yr. institutions, $75/yr. personal, $24/yr. members of American
Philosophical Association.   PUBLISHER: Pergamon Press, Maxwell House,
Fairview Park, Elmsford, New York 10523.   EDITOR: Azizah al-Hibri.
ADVERTISEMENTS. MANUSCRIPT SELECTION: Refereed, editorial board.
BOOK REVIEWS: 1-2 reviews, 2-3 pp., signed.   SPECIAL ISSUES:
Occasional. TARGET AUDIENCE: AC. ACCEPTANCE RATE: 16%.

Hypatia is a special   journal emerging as the voice of feminist philosophy.
It is the first journal in North America devoted entirely to the articulation
and development of progress within the women's movement on such issues as
ethics, aesthetics, political theory, sociobiology, and sexuality. A feminist
analysis of anger, racism, spirituality, and social science addresses the
oppression women have been under since antiquity.   Originally part of the
Women's Studies International Forum, Hypatia became an independent forum
for stimualting dialogue among women philosophers and male sympathizers.
Enunciation of this seemingly "activist" philosophy does not spare objectivity
in its arguments.
    Issues of Hypatia publish six to ten articles of current interest to
feminism, followed by a small number of book reviews.   Special issues add
elements of distinction to the needs of   feminist expression that   may
challenge traditions,   but will clearly inspire future heterodoxical changes
for women readers.

114.   Iconoclast. DATE FOUNDED: 1979. FREQUENCY: m.   PRICE:
Donations.   PUBLISHER: Foundation of Human Understanding, P.O. Box
8780 Venice Boulevard, Los Angeles, California   90034.   EDITOR: Roy
Masters.   MANUSCRIPT SELECTION: Editor.   REPRINTS: publisher.
SPECIAL ISSUES: Occasional.   TARGET AUDIENCE: GP.   SAMPLE
COPIES: Libraries, individuals.

Iconoclast comes from the Greek word "icon" meaning "image." "Iconoclast"
means (1) one who destroys religious images or opposes their veneration, and
(2) one who attacks established beliefs or institutions.   Each issue of
Iconoclast certainly follows this mission. Evangelical articles focus on the role
that illusions, false religious images, misplaced beliefs, and disintegrating
institutions play in people's personal and interpersonal problems.   Readers
learn to dissolve away these illusions and misbeliefs through the practice of
meditation. Usually these   suggestions   are written by the editor, Roy
Masters, himself. On the surface, Iconoclast strikes a harmonic chord with
the valid aims of Creation/Evolution and especially Zetetic Scholar. But this
first impression ignores the cynical and driving force behind Iconoclast:
Evangelism.   What makes these evangelical statements so revealing?
Questions like this raise serious doubts about the legitimacy of scholarship in
Roy Master's crusade for transpersonal fulfillment.   Since many essays are
pontificatory, not explanatory, the empty promises simply do an injustice to
biblical and psychological interpretations. Another unfortunate aspect is that
articles will "borrow" established principles and ideas but claim originality
for them.
    A typical issue expands upon a prior theme or features new articles   by
contributing editors, and occasionally by guest writers.   There are different
departments on medicine, coping, and news and information on the
Foundation. The stress and suffering this author went through in reviewing
Iconoclast should hopefully serve as a lesson for skeptical librarians.

115.   Idealistic Studies.   DATE FOUNDED: 1970.   FREQUENCY: 3/yr. PRICE: $10/yr. institutions.   PUBLISHER: Clark University Press, c/o Philosophy Department, Clark University, 950 Main Street, Worcester, Massachusetts 01610.   EDITOR: Walter E. Wright.   INDEX.   ADVERTISE-MENTS.   CIRCULATION: 500.   MANUSCRIPT SELECTION: Editor. REPRINTS: author.   BOOK REVIEWS: Annual survey of literature, 15-20 pp., signed.   SPECIAL ISSUES: Occasional.   INDEXED/ABSTRACTED: ArtHumCitI, PhilosI.   TARGET AUDIENCE: AC.   SAMPLE COPIES: Libraries, individuals.   ACCEPTANCE RATE: 30%.

IS publishes historical and contemporary statements of idealistic arguments. Critical examinations go beyond assumptions underlying the nature of science itself, and probe into areas of logic, history, and psychology. The revival of neoidealistic intellectual movements accounts for the expansion of IS toward issues in general.   Metascience articles are   written objectively by scholars from several different branches of philosophic thought.   Proponents and opponents of idealism regularly generate theories similar in   definition   to those found in Philosophy and Social Criticism, Journal of Philosophy, and Monist.
   A typical issue contains about five original essays, a survey of recent literature, and announcements about sibling organizations and journals. The constructive criticisms in ontology, Hegelian phenomenology, and scientific progress are particularly relevant to introductory philosophy students.

116.   Independent Journal of Philosophy.   DATE FOUNDED: 1977. FREQUENCY: a.   PRICE: $18/yr. institutions, $12/yr. personal, $8.50/yr. students.   PUBLISHER: 30, Rue St-Louis-en-L'Isle, F-75004 Paris, France. EDITOR: George E. Tucker.   ADVERTISEMENTS.   CIRCULATION: 750. MANUSCRIPT SELECTION: Refereed, editorial board.   BOOK REVIEWS: 25 reviews, 2-3 pp., signed.   SPECIAL ISSUES: Half of each issue. INDEXED/ABSTRACTED: PhilosI, RBibPhil.   TARGET AUDIENCE: AC. ACEPTANCE RATE: 5%.

IJP provides an international forum for the exploration of alternatives to the positivist-analytical, Marxist, and narrowly academic trends   characterized by much of present-day philosophy. Although not aligned with any particular school or movement, IJP takes its general stance from Platonic-Aristotelian concepts of "reason," "wisdom," and "intuitive form."   Articles written by scholars oppose the nihilism latent in poor historical research, as well as in relativism and irrationalism.   Toward this aim, the papers form a rich constellation of phenomenological   and existential dialogues broadly based on special themes--literature and art, aphorisms, and idealistic topics.   IJP publishes works in English and French and is considered comparable to British Journal of Aesthetics, American Philosophical Quarterly, and Explorations in Knowledge.
   Each issue includes six to nine original articles, replies, book reviews, translations, and general editorial announcements.   Being one of the few French journals to publish English articles, IJP provides unique   opportunities for American contributors.

117.   Indian Philosophical Quarterly.   DATE FOUNDED: 1973.   TITLE
CHANGES: Philosophical Quarterly (1973).   FREQUENCY: q.   PRICE:
$16/yr. institutions, $8/yr. personal.   PUBLISHER: Department of Phi-
losophy, University of Poona, Pune-411 007, India. EDITORS: S.S. Barlingay,
Raejndra   Prasad.   ILLUSTRATIONS.   INDEX.   ADVERTISEMENTS.
CIRCULATION: 700.   MANUSCRIPT SELECTION: Refereed, editorial
board.   BOOK REVIEWS: 1-2 reviews, 1-3 pp., signed.   SPECIAL ISSUES:
Each issue contains a student supplement. INDEXED/ABSTRACTED: PhilosI.
TARGET AUDIENCE: AC. SAMPLE COPIES: Libraries.

IPQ is a revival of one of the oldest Indian philosophy journals. The clarity
and power of essays seek to unite Anglo-Saxon and Indian interactionism,
where philosophy includes the ideas implicit in great works of art and
literature.   Contributors are primarily Indian polemicists able to transform
equivocal problems into a thought-provoking and often exciting matter for
the neophyte reader.   As a model of philosophical analysis, IPQ rivals the
high research caliber   of   American Philosophical Quarterly and   the
internationalism of such serials as Acta Philosophica Fennica, Philosophy and
Philosophy and Rhetoric.
   Each issue normally contains four to six major articles including book
reviews and special notices relevant to the journal's subsequent issues.

118. Inquiry. DATE FOUNDED: 1958. FREQUENCY: q. PRICE: $32/yr.
institutions, $19/yr. personal.   PUBLISHER: Universitetsforlaget, P.O. Box
2959, Toyen Oslo 6, Norway. EDITOR: Alastair Hannay. ILLUSTRATIONS.
INDEX.   ADVERTISEMENTS.   CIRCULATION: 1,500.   MANUSCRIPT
SELECTION: Editor.   MICROFORMS: UMI.   REPRINTS: author. BOOK
REVIEWS: 2 reviews, 5-10 pp., signed.   SPECIAL ISSUES: 1/yr.
INDEXED/ABSTRACTED: ArtHumCitI, PhilosI.   TARGET AUDIENCE: AC.
SAMPLE COPIES: Libraries. ACCEPTANCE RATE: 5%.

Inquiry is the outgrowth of philosophical criticism against the absolutist
theories of knowledge in social sciences.   Values in social technology,
medicine, applied sciences, and naturalism receive an extended treatment by
internationally known scholars.   Discussion looms largely over contemporary
and historical sources, but almost invariably moves at a rapid pace through
arguments . The analysis contained in major articles clearly avoids pedantry
and displays a variety of themes commonly found in Philosophy in Context,
Philosophy and Public Affairs and Philosophy and Rhetoric.
   Issues of Inquiry feature three to four original essays and critical reviews
or rebuttals of previously published articles. The review discussion takes the
place of shorter book reviews by being especially comprehensive.

119.   Interbehaviorist.   DATE FOUNDED: 1970.   TITLE CHANGES:
Interbehavioral   Psychology   Newsletter   (1970-1974),   Interbehaviorist
Quarterly (1975-1978). FREQUENCY: q.   PRICE: $4/yr. institutions,
personal.   PUBLISHER: Department of Human Development and Family
Life, University of Kansas, Lawrence, Kansas 66045. EDITOR: Edward K.
Morris.   ADVERTISEMENTS.   CIRCULATION: 100.   MANUSCRIPT
SELECTION: Refereed, editorial board.   REPRINTS: editor.   BOOK
REVIEWS: 2-3 reviews, 300 words, signed.   TARGET AUDIENCE: AC.
SAMPLE COPIES: Libraries, individuals. ACCEPTANCE RATE: 80%.

Interbehaviorist is a publication in the behavioral and philosophical sciences. As its title indicates, Interbehaviorist takes its orientation from the interbehavioral psychology of J.R. Kantor (1888-1984). Hence, authors are primarily scholars committed to a contextualist or field-integrated theory. Essays and announcements serve a professional function that falls between archival publication and informal letters and colloquia. As such, Interbehaviorist supplements such mainstream journals as Behaviorism, Psychological Record and History and Theory. The journal strongly encourages reader submission of materials reflective of interbehavioral activities. Besides being a festschrift for Kantor, articles lend critical insight into the inadequacies of radical behaviorism.

Interbehaviorist publishes brief articles presented for peer comment and perusal, book reviews, commentaries, and other publications of interest. General observations usually reflect current practices in basic and applied research, theory and history of behavioral psychology. With philosophers turning toward applied studies, topics in Interbehaviorist may furnish practical ideas for the future.

120. Interchange. DATE FOUNDED: 1966. FREQUENCY: sa. PRICE: $10/yr. institutions. PUBLISHER: AFES Graduate Fellowship Australia, 120 Chalmers Street,, Surry Hills 2010, Australia. EDITOR: Peter Inman. CIRCULATION: 1,100. MANUSCRIPT: Refereed, editorial board. REPRINTS: publisher. BOOK REVIEWS: 1-3 reviews, 1-3 pp., signed. INDEXED/ABSTRACTED: PhilosI, PsyAb. TARGET AUDIENCE: AC. SAMPLE COPIES: Libraries, individuals.

Interchange is published as a means of putting thought and work done in evangelical circles into circulation, promoting discussion on the teachings of the Bible. Scriptual interpretation in most cases gets lost in the shuffle of polemical rhetoric. Interchange, however, prevents this obscurity by identifying the causes of moral confusion and current gravity of interest toward spiritual growth. Theologians and philosophers alike undertake a thorough account of historical as well as contemporary issues facing the practice of religion. Articulated in the aims and goals are interests similar to Heythrop Journal.

A typical issue provides four to five contributions on the doctrines of scripture and occasionally a few book reviews. Interchange closely identifies with the re-emergence of religious studies as centrally bound to curricula at schools of divinity.

121. International Forum for Logotherapy. DATE FOUNDED: 1978. FREQUENCY: sa. PRICE: $16/yr. institutions. PUBLISHER: 1 Lawson Road, Berkeley, California 94707. EDITOR: Joseph Fabry. ADVERTISEMENTS. CIRCULATION: 1,000. MANUSCRIPT SELECTION: Editor. BOOK REVIEWS: 2 reviews, 2 pp., signed. TARGET AUDIENCE: AC, GP, SP. ACCEPTANCE RATE: 80%.

IFL presents the meaning-oriented philosophy and therapy as developed by Viktor Frankl and expanded by disciples of Logotherapy. Contributors span the human and social sciences, medicine, social work, nursing, education and drug abuse fields. Such noted authors as Elisabeth Kubler- Ross and Robert Leslie publish experimental reports, theoretical papers, personal essays, research studies, and bibliographies. Like the Interbehaviorist, the specialization of topic (Logotherapy) affords a closer look at one school of thought. Articles are written primarily by clinicians and philosophers.

Each issue contains three to four lead articles on Logotherapeutic topics, and then reports on case studies relative to principles and methods. Noteworthy is that Logotherapy builds its foundation on the very same or similar psychological constructs essential in humanistic approaches.

122. International Humanist. DATE FOUNDED: 1952. TITLE CHANGES: International Humanism (1952-1981). FREQUENCY: q. PRICE: $8/yr. institutions. PUBLISHER: International Humanist and Ethical Union, Oudkerkhof 11, 3512, GH Utrecht, Netherlands. EDITOR: G.S. Soeters. CIRCULATION: 1,200. MANUSCRIPT SELECTION: Refereed, editorial board. BOOK REVIEWS: Occasional. SPECIAL ISSUES: 1/yr. TARGET AUDIENCE: AC. SAMPLE COPIES: Libraries, individuals.

IH serves as a medium for worldwide attention to the oppression of human rights and generalizations about racial, sexual, or religious stereotypes. Practical humanism takes on a nondenominational belief system prominent among disputants of Christian values. These highly readable articles by members of the International Humanist and Ethical Union provide inspiration for the acceptance of freedom and equality. Ideas resemble the portfolio of themes in Dignity, Ethics, Free Mind, and Humanities in Society. Educating the public to the realism of universal human problems represents one more step in the advances of "community philosophy."

Each issue provides a colloquium on political and ethical subjects. Regular issues contain about six short articles with news and information about the Union's activities.

123. International Journal of Applied Philosophy. DATE FOUNDED: 1982. TITLE CHANGES: Applied Philosophy (1982-1983). FREQUENCY: sa. PRICE: $7/yr. institutions, $5/yr. personal. PUBLISHER: Indian River Community College, 3209 Virginia Avenue, Fort Pierce, Florida 33454-9003. EDITOR: Elliot Cohen. ADVERTISEMENTS. CIRCULATION: 700. MANUSCRIPT SELECTION: Refereed, editorial board. REPRINTS: author. BOOK REVIEWS: 1 review, 1-3 pp., signed. SPECIAL ISSUES: Occasional. INDEXED/ABSTRACTED: PhilosI. TARGET AUDIENCE: AC. SAMPLE COPIES: Libraries, individuals. ACCEPTANCE RATE: 5%.

IJAP is dedicated to the thesis that philosophy can and should be brought to bear upon the clarification and solution of practical issues of life. Critical papers clearly exhibit the impact of philosophy upon substantial problems in education, business, law, health care, ecology, government, the economy, fine arts, and crafts. Principles in applied philosophy draw upon classic works of social scientists in examining the future of philosophers. Well-intentioned surveys create an objective range of fresh and stimulating ideas. Authors are philosophers and specialists in other disciplines. Reviews and major essays, among other things, stress the proportion of universal needs to applied methods, as made clear in Ethics and Animals, Ethics, Business Professional Ethics, and Philosophy and Public Affairs.

Each issue is handsomely printed and bound with five major articles, short reports, and brief discussion on themes or previous articles. IJAP commences a deserving trend in philosophy toward clearer articulation of the pragmatics in the field.

124. International Journal for Biosocial Research. DATE FOUNDED: 1979. FREQUENCY: q. PRICE: $24/yr. institutions, $18/yr. personal. PUBLISHER: Biosocial Publications, 505 Broadway, P.O. Box 1174, Tacoma, Washington 98401. EDITOR: Alexander G. Schauss. ILLUSTRATIONS. INDEX. CIRCULATION: 3,000. MANUSCRIPT SELECTION: Refereed, editorial board. REPRINTS: author. BOOK REVIEWS: 2 reviews, 1-2 pp., signed. SPECIAL ISSUES: Occasional. INDEXED/ABSTRACTED: ChemAb, LLBA, PSA, PsyAb, SocAb. TARGET AUDIENCE: AC, SP. ACCEPTANCE RATE: 64%.

IJBR concentrates on interdisciplinary research and findings related to environmental, biochemical, genetic, and nutritional factors that affect human behavior. Accepted papers usually cover the impact of socioeconomic, cultural, and political factors upon individual and community. Essays on the behavioral, health, and social sciences balance the conflicting values in ecological psychology and philosophy of science, including ethical subjects as abortion and right to physical fitness. Like Exploration in Medicine, studies in IJBR entertain the premise that medicinal interventions are a consumer matter. Recent work by philosophers and scholars supply the missing link, then, between pure theory and hard sciences.
A typical issue contains research reviews, update reports on continuing investigations, four to five original studies, and then a "Dialogue" section, wherein guest authors react to significant problems in social fields.

125. International Journal for the Philosophy of Religion. DATE FOUNDED: 1970. FREQUENCY: q. PRICE: $46/yr. institutions, $22/yr. personal. PUBLISHER: Martinus Nijhoff Publishers, P.O. Box 566, 2501 CN, Hague, Netherlands. EDITOR: Bowman L. Clarke. INDEX. ADVERTISEMENTS. MANUSCRIPT SELECTION: Refereed, editorial board. REPRINTS: author. BOOK REVIEWS: 1-2 pp., signed. INDEXED/ABSTRACTED: HumI, PhilosI. TARGET AUDIENCE: AC. SAMPLE COPIES: Libraries, individuals. ACCEPTANCE RATE: 20%.

IJPR provides a medium for the exposition, development, and criticism of important philosophical insights and theories relevant to religion in any of its varied forms. Articles, symposia, discussions and reviews are intended to serve the interests of a wide range of thoughtful readers, especially teachers and students of philosophy and theology. Uncommitted to a single institution or sectarian school, IJPR publishes constructive essays by leading theoreticians. Discussion related to the objective study of religion supplements the ideas found in Ajatus. Shifts in emphasis toward a more scientific paradigm even resemble Journal for the Scientific Study of Religion.
Copies of IJPR normally contain five leading articles followed by a section of brief book reviews. There is an exponential progression of scientific thought which is of interest to skeptics.

126.   International Philosophical Quarterly.   DATE FOUNDED: 1961.
FREQUENCY: q.   PRICE: $18/yr. institutions, $13/yr. personal.   PUBLISH-
ER: Fordham University, Bronx, New York 10458.   EDITOR: W. Morris
Clarke.   INDEX.   ADVERTISEMENTS.   CIRCULATION: 1,800.   MANU-
SCRIPT SELECTION: Refereed, editorial board.   MICROFORMS: UMI.
REPRINTS: author.   BOOK   REVIEWS: 6 reviews, 1-2 pp., signed.
INDEXED/ABSTRACTED: ArtHumCitI, CathI, HumI, PhilosI, SocAb, SSI.
TARGET AUDIENCE: AC.   SAMPLE COPIES: Libraries.   ACCEPTANCE
RATE: 10%.

IPQ is a highly respectable forum in English for the interchange of basic
philosophical ideas between America   and Europe and between East and
West.   Its   primary   orientation   is   to   encourage   vital   contemporary
expression--creative, critical and historical--in the intercultural tradition of
theistic, spiritualistic, and personalist humanism.   The current trends in
modernity,   rationalism,   and   empiricism   close   connections   between   the
historical world view and the views of universal interest to today's scholars.
The analytical structure of essays strives for objectivity but is weighted by
partiality   toward   a   more   metaphysical   sense   of   human life and ethics.
Contributors, mostly theorists, are prominent international leaders in general
philosophy.   Attention to political and moral problems coincides with writings
in Das Argument, Philosophy East and West, and Canadian Philosophical
Review.
   A typical issue features five or so main articles and a special article in
two sections called "Contemporary Currents" and "Feature Book Review."
Following this are briefer book reviews.

127.   International Social Science Review.   DATE FOUNDED: 1925. TITLE
CHANGES: Social Science (1925-1982).   FREQUENCY: q.   PRICE: $10/yr.
institutions.   PUBLISHER: Toledo University, Toledo, Ohio 43606. EDITOR:
Panos D. Bardis.   ILLUSTRATIONS.   INDEX.   CIRCULATION: 13,000.
MANUSCRIPT SELECTION: Refereed, editorial board.   BOOK REVIEWS: 20
reviews, 2-3 pp., signed.   INDEXED/ABSTRACTED: HistAb, IntPolSc, SocAb,
VerZ.   TARGET   AUDIENCE: AC.   SAMPLE   COPIES: Libraries.
ACCEPTANCE RATE: 25%.

ISSR is committed to the investigative study of sociohistorical and intercultural   factors   associated   with   political,   moral and ethical enterprises.
Contributions are interesting, stimulating and philosophically sophisticated,
serving a worthwhile function for readers interested in a coherent theory of
knowledge.   Social psychologists, philosophers, and anthropologists, among
others,   come   to   grips   with   the   notion   of   transcultural method and ideas
underlying several intellectual establishments.   These well- executed essays
go beyond the panoramic introduction to social philosophy and in an orderly
manner present challenges to twentieth century minds, much like Annals
Universitatis, Human Studies, and Chroniques De Philosophie.
   Regular issues contain an average of six original articles followed by book
reviews.   ISSR is beneficial in developing a general conception of social
policy and behavioral science in a clear and straightforward way.

128. International Studies in Philosophy. DATE FOUNDED: 1969. FREQUENCY: 3/yr. PRICE: $30/yr. institutions, $20/yr. personal. PUBLISHER: Scholars Press, 101 Salem Street, P.O. Box 2268,Chico, California 95927. EDITORS: Leon J. Goldstein, Norbert Hinske, Vittorio Mathieu, Stephen D. Pos. ADVERTISEMENTS. CIRCULATION: 325. MANUSCRIPT SELECTION: Refereed, editorial board. REPRINTS: author. BOOK REVIEWS: 2 reviews, 1-6 pp., signed. SPECIAL ISSUES: Occasional. INDEXED/ABSTRACTED: ArtHumCitI, PhilosI. TARGET AUDIENCE: AC.

ISP advances the originality and critical examination of topics in the general territory of philosophy. Articles attempt to bring together various reflections on principles and theories emergent in cross-cultural studies in epistemology, metaphysics, phenomenology, religion, history, and social sciences. Authors are mainly scholars in diverse branches of philosophy, sensitive to the need for a systematic presentation of ideas. Intriguing analogies and explorations into problems of interdeterminancy, quantum jumps, and the purposiveness of individual responsibility set ISP clearly apart from Independent Journal of Philosophy and Diagones.
   A typical issue of ISP is divided into three or four major articles, notes and communications, book reviews, and editorial announcements. Articles in Italian are encouraged.

129. Isis. DATE FOUNDED: 1913. FREQUENCY: q. PRICE: $55/yr. institutions, $29/yr. personal. PUBLISHER: History of Science Society, University of Pennsylvania, 214 South 34th Street, D6, E.F. Smith Hall, Philadelphia, Pennsylvania 19104. EDITOR: Arnold Thackray. ILLUSTRA-TIONS. INDEX. ADVERTISEMENTS. CIRCULATION: 3,500. MANU-SCRIPT SELECTION: Refereed, editorial board. MICROFORMS: UMI. REPRINTS: author. BOOK REVIEWS: 60 reviews, 1-2 pp., signed. SPECIAL ISSUES: 1/yr. INDEXED/ABSTRACTED: ArtHumCitI, BoA, BulSig, ChemAb, CurrContSocBS, EI, HistAb, HumI, IMed, MathR. SAMPLE COPIES: Libraries, individuals. ACCEPTANCE RATE: 50%.

Isis is an international review devoted to the history of science and its cultural influences. This journal is a definite pioneer among serials centered on scholarly research, translation, and essays exploring medical and social aspects of technology and idealism. Revolutionary trends in the scientific evolution of Anglo-American and European countries are recalled in illuminating papers that trace the roots, ascendance, and central figures of philosophical importance. The translations, judiciously abridged, capture all the drama and conviction of the original document, plus explanations which shed light on economics, sociology, psychology and anthropology. History of science and philosophy is written by experts in historiography. Their distinctively clear prose and acumen for issues still prevalent today add character to the events of prior generations. The aims of Isis are similar to Journal of the History of Medicine and Allied Sciences, History and Theory, and Psychological Record.
   Each issue contains articles, critiques, documents and translation, notes and correspondence, news of the profession, essay reviews, and a book review section classified explicitly into different branches of science. This review section alone thoroughly augments the innovative personality of Isis for any student or teacher inclined toward the sciences.

130. <u>Iyyun</u>. DATE FOUNDED: 1945. FREQUENCY: q. PRICE: $10/yr. institutions, $8/yr. personal. PUBLISHER: S.H. Bergman Center for Philosophical Studies, Hebrew University of Jerusalem, Jerusalem 91 905, Israel. EDITOR: David Heyd. INDEX. ADVERTISEMENTS. CIRCULATION: 800. MANUSCRIPT SELECTION: Refereed, editorial board. REPRINTS: author. BOOK REVIEWS: 2 reviews, 1-2 pp., signed. SPECIAL ISSUES: Occasional. INDEXED/ABSTRACTED: PhilosI. TARGET AUDIENCE: AC. SAMPLE COPIES: Libraries, individuals. ACCEPTANCE RATE: 50%.

<u>Iyyun</u> publishes articles in Hebrew and English on general areas in philosophy. Articles articulate the exigencies of human condition in contemporary culture and the relevance of analysis to classic principles in epistemology, logic, ethics, metaphysics, politics, semantics, and philosophy of social sciences. Israeli scholars blend the history of philosophical systems with the main currents of Eastern and Western writings. The creativity and logical rigor with which these authors exchange ideas heighten the objectivity and interdisciplinary nature of <u>Iyyun</u>. Critical essays bear striking resemblance to those found in <u>Filosofia</u>, <u>Grazer Philosophische</u>, and <u>International Philosophical Quarterly</u>.
  Issues of <u>Iyyun</u> contain an average of five articles and brief book reviews. Noteworthy is the representation of Judaic culture interwoven into essays on cultural heritage, morality and public policy.

131. <u>Journal of Aesthetic Education</u>. DATE FOUNDED: 1966. FREQUENCY: q. PRICE: $25/yr. institutions, $15/yr. personal. PUBLISHER: University of Illinois Press, Subscription Department, 54 East Gregory, Box 5081, Station A, Champaign, Illinois 61820. EDITOR: Ralph A. Smith. ILLUSTRATIONS. INDEX. ADVERTISEMENTS. CIRCULATION: 1,000. MANUSCRIPT SELECTION: Refereed, editorial board. MICROFORMS: Publisher. REPRINTS: author. BOOK REVIEWS: 6-7 reviews, 1-3 pp., signed. SPECIAL ISSUES: Occasional. INDEXED/ABSTRACTED: AbEnSt, CurrContAH, EdI, MusicArtG, PhilosI, PsyAb, SocEdAb. TARGET AUDIENCE: AC. SAMPLE COPIES: Libraries. ACCEPTANCE RATE: 24%.

<u>JAE</u> is an educational response to perennial challenges to improve the quality and style of civilization. The major purpose of <u>JAE</u> is to clarify the issues of aesthetic education understood in its most extensive meanings. This includes formal instruction in the arts and humanities, as well as aesthetic problems created by twentieth century existence. Articles also explore aesthetic interest in public policy, cultural administration, cultural services, and the new communication media. Authors are mainly in humanistic disciplines. This open forum of discussion further encourages an objective profile of ideology and, related to modern needs, an evaluation of occupational opportunities for training. The result is a new vision of artistic nature, much improved over articles which are entirely theoretical (e.g., <u>British Journal of Aesthetics</u>, <u>Critical Inquiry</u>). Emphasis on educational curricula embraces the same goals found in <u>Australian Logic Teachers Journal</u>.
  <u>JAE</u> publishes nine to eleven original and stimulating studies on the status of aesthetic schooling. Book reviews and a list of books received provide additional resources for the enlightened reader.

132. Journal of Aesthetics and Art Criticism. DATE FOUNDED: 1941.
FREQUENCY: q. PRICE: $20/yr. institutions. PUBLISHER: Temple
University, Philadelphia, Pennsylvania 19122. EDITOR: John Fisher.
ILLUSTRATIONS. INDEX. ADVERTISEMENTS. CIRCULATION: 3,000.
MANUSCRIPT SELECTION: Refereed, editorial board. BOOK REVIEWS: 10
reviews, 1-3 pp., signed. SPECIAL ISSUES: Occasional. INDEXED/
ABSTRACTED: ArtHumCitI, HumI. TARGET AUDIENCE: AC. ACCEPT-
ANCE RATE: 10%.

JAAC provides critical expositions highly regarded as the yardstick of
progress in contemporary aesthetics. Speculative essays on the current
intellectual revolutions in art criticism synthesize the abundance of theories
and arguments related to expression, symbolism, and intentionality. The
historical nature of art is another prominent theme. In pursuing this inquiry,
JAAC publishes a variety of objectively-based surveys by the ablest
spokesmen in the discipline. Such articles characterize aesthetics as a
rational and conscious activity grounded in scientific evidence. JAAC rivals
the prestige of British Journal of Aesthetics, but steps beyond the
interdisciplinary achievements of, for example, Aitia.
   Issues of JAAC contain six to eight original articles and a section on
comprehensive book reviews. One basic advantage is that JAAC narrows the
cultural factors to a specific few in its analysis of art.

133. Journal of Bioethics. DATE FOUNDED: 1978. TITLE CHANGES:
Bioethics Quarterly (1978-1983). FREQUENCY: sa. PRICE: $40/yr.
institutions, $18/yr. personal. PUBLISHER: Human Sciences Press,
Incorporated, 72 Fifth Avenue, New York, New York 10011. EDITOR: Jane
A. Boyajian Raible. INDEX. ADVERTISEMENTS. CIRCULATION: 1,000.
MANUSCRIPT SELECTION: Refereed, editorial board. MICROFORM: UMI.
REPRINTS: author. BOOK REVIEWS: 4 reviews, 1-3 pp., signed. SPECIAL
ISSUES: Occasional. INDEXED/ABSTRACTED: IMed, PsyAb. TARGET
AUDIENCE: AC, SP. SAMPLE COPIES: Libraries, individuals.

JB devotes itself to original articles on the dramatic changes in biomedical
technology, legislative and judicial decisions, and health care policies. Such
innovations profoundly affect the quality and ideology of health care systems
and raise essential ethical, legal, and medical questions. JB thus emerges to
assess these complex problems and openly discuss biomedical advances and
concurrent social concerns. This exchange of timely ideas is also a
pronunciation of the morality manifested in the design, implementation and
evaluation of health practices. Articles are written objectively by
physicians, philosophers, and health specialists. Experts focus on the same
paradoxes examined in Hastings Center Report and International Journal of
Biosocial Research.
   A typical issue of JB overviews concepts and developments in medicine and
human rights in five to six major articles and book reviews. Prevalent
themes in ethical theory, abortion, brain injury, and artificial insemination
make for stimulating reading .

134. Journal of the British Society for Phenomenology. DATE FOUNDED:
1970. FREQUENCY: 3/yr. PRICE: $33/yr. institutions. PUBLISHER:
Haigh and Hochland Limited, Precinct Centre, Oxford Road, Manchester M13
9QA England. EDITOR: Wolfe Mays. INDEX. ADVERTISEMENTS.

CIRCULATION: 450. MANUSCRIPT SELECTION: Refereed, editorial board. REPRINTS: author. BOOK REVIEWS: 6-9 reviews, 1-3 pp. SPECIAL ISSUES: Occasional. INDEXED/ABSTRACTED: ArtHumCitI, PhilosI. TARGET AUDIENCE: AC. SAMPLE COPIES: Libraries, individuals. ACCEPTANCE RATE: 50%.

JBSP publishes papers on phenomenology and existential philosophy as well as contributions from other branches of philosophy. Space is devoted to research in progress, interdisciplinary discussion, and works from the humanities and human sciences. Perspectives on traditional and modern philosophy consider how scientific realism embodies imagination, perception, and introspection. Contributors are usually academicians and specialists on particular writers in the field (Sartre, Heidegger, Husserl, Merleau-Ponty, Neitzsche). Analytically minded philosophers may also appreciate the systematic coverage of linguistic and ontological subjects. These are closely tantamount to criticisms in Husserl Studies and Review of Metaphysics.

Each issue of JBSP features four to six major articles, a discussion article and selected book reviews. Editorials and notes by the British Society for Phenomenology serve as tribunals to advance the research potential among local and international scholars.

135. Journal of Business Ethics. DATE FOUNDED: 1982. FREQUENCY: q. PRICE: $55/yr. institutions, $20/yr. personal. PUBLISHER: D. Reidel Publishing Company, P.O. Box 322, 3300 AH Dordrecht, Netherlands. EDITOR: Alex C. Michalos. ILLUSTRATIONS. INDEX. ADVERTISEMENTS. MANUSCRIPT SELECTION: Refereed, editorial board. REPRINTS: author. SPECIAL ISSUES: Occasional. INDEXED/ABSTRACTED: BPI, PhilosI, SSCI. TARGET AUDIENCE: AC, SP. SAMPLE COPIES: Libraries, individuals.

JBE has surpassed all pre-publication expectations. It publishes original articles from a wide variety of methodological and disciplinary perspectives concerning the ethical issues in business. The term "business" is understood widely to include all systems involved in the exchange of goods and services. "Ethics," in this case, refers to all human action aimed at securing a good life. The synthesis that results deals with intriguing professional matters about confidentiality, accountability, employee rights and the interchange of science, logic, and social sciences within formal institutions. Conspicuously similar to Business and Professional Ethics Journal, JBE nonetheless is unique in its critical reappraisals of unethical action. Contributors in the business field pay strict attention to the objectivity of their arguments.

Articles in JBE tend to revolve around a dominant theme. Four to five major articles are accompanied by a list of books received. This journal clearly advances the imperative for applied studies in philosophy.

136. Journal of Chinese Philosophy. DATE FOUNDED: 1973. FREQUENCY: q. PRICE: $73/yr. institutions, $28/yr. personal. PUBLISHER: Dialogue Publishing Company, P.O. Box 11071, Honolulu, Hawaii 96828. EDITOR: Chung-Ying Cheng. INDEX. MANUSCRIPT SELECTION: Editor. REPRINTS: author. BOOK REVIEWS: 2-4 reviews, 1-2 pp., signed. SPECIAL ISSUES: Occasional. INDEXED/ABSTRACTED: CurrContAH, PhilosI. TARGET AUDIENCE: AC. SAMPLE COPIES: Libraries.

JCP is devoted to the study of Chinese philosophy and Chinese thought in all their phases of articulation and development. The high standard of contributions generates great interest in subjects ranging from general culture to specific tribal rituals and civilization. Scope of coverage also includes legends and currents of Confucianism, Chinese sociocultural and intellectual establishments, the roots of Zen Buddhism, and effects of the Taoistic school upon scientific values. Chinese scholars provide a forum for objective review and analysis, with clarity and relevance to modern imperatives. JCP does more than simply translate texts as appear in Chinese Studies in Philosophy. Similar to New Confucians, essays attain an original quality of religious fervor mixed with heritage and allegory.

JCP publishes four to five central papers and a section on book reviews. Noteworthy is that, in combining history with current theory, concepts of nature and feeling emerge which resemble those of Anglo-Saxon tradition.

137. Journal of Critical Analysis. DATE FOUNDED: 1968. FREQUENCY: q. PRICE: $12/yr. institutions, $10/yr. personal. PUBLISHER: The National Council for Critical Analysis, P.O. Box 137 Port Jefferson, New York 11777. EDITOR: Pasqual S. Schievella. INDEX. ADVERTISEMENTS. CIRCULATION: 500. MANUSCRIPT SELECTION: Refereed, editorial board. INDEXED/ABSTRACTED: PhilosI, SocAb. TARGET AUDIENCE: AC. SAMPLE COPIES: Libraries, individuals. ACCEPTANCE RATE: 25%.

JCA publishes articles in all areas of philosophy. Particular stress is placed on analytical and naturalistic, as opposed to historical approaches, regardless of institutional affiliation. Scholarly contributions are extremely provocative and polemic, offering a fascinating glimpse into political, epistemologic, and linguistic problems of contemporary society. Critical examinations show how philosophy qua philosophy solves basic problems, and defends a humanistic view of nature. Objectively interpreted, the arguments tackle difficult questions typically raised in Grazer Philosophische, Contemporary Philosophy, Canadian Journal of Philosophy, and Diogenes.

A typical issue of JCA contains four to seven original papers and a comprehensive book review. Authors are required to pay $75 per page for accepted articles and book reviews.

138. Journal of Helen Vale Foundation. DATE FOUNDED: 1977. FREQUENCY: q. PRICE: $12/yr. institutions. PUBLISHER: Helen Vale Foundation, P.O. Box 359, Warwick 4370 Queensland, Australia. EDITOR: Shri Vijayaden Yogendra. ADVERTISEMENTS. CIRCULATION: 2,000. MANUSCRIPT SELECTION: Editor. REPRINTS: author. SPECIAL ISSUES: Occasional. INDEXED/ABSTRACTED: PhilosI. TARGET AUDIENCE: AC, GP, SP. SAMPLE COPIES: Libraries, individuals. ACCEPTANCE RATE: 70%.

JHVF is a forum for the discussion of principles for developing "total man." Official publication of the Helen Vale Foundation, its aim is to provide guidelines for living from the philosophical, cultural, humanistic and spiritual tradition of the world, as well as from ideals and research in the organization. Articles, commentaries, and reviews interrelate common values of education, psychosomatics, counseling, and comparative religion. Pastorally-oriented papers clarify the basic assertion of "truth" regarding industrial, technological, and scientific fields. The lively metaphorical writing conveys a conventional wisdom shaped by the medical health care system. This almost literary view of humanity sacrifices the objectivity one might find in Hastings Center Report, Journal of Bioethics, and Explorations in Medicine.

Each issue features ten to eleven original articles, editorials, announcements, and poems on front and back covers.

139.   Journal of Hellenic Studies. DATE FOUNDED: 1880. FREQUENCY: a. PRICE: $36/yr. institutions, $30/yr. members. PUBLISHER: Society for the Promotion of Hellenic Studies, 31-34 Gordon Square, London WC1H 0PP, England.   EDITOR: C.R.   B.   Pelling.   ILLUSTRATIONS.   INDEX. ADVERTISEMENTS.   CIRCULATION: 3,000.   MANUSCRIPT SELECTION: Refereed, editorial board.   BOOK REVIEWS: 100 reviews, 1-4 pp., signed. SPECIAL   ISSUES: Annual   supplement   (Archaeological   Reports). INDEXED/ABSTRACTED: HumI, PhilosI. TARGET AUDIENCE: AC.

JHS is among the leading international journals in the field of Greek studies. Critical essays cover art, archaeology, history, language, and philosophy of Greek-speaking lands from archaic to Byzantine periods. Esteemed scholars consider such aspects of Hellenic thought as teleology, logic, knowledge, substance, causes, the theories of motion and theology, psychology, and the philosophy of life.   Sociohistorical accounts pay close attention to the artifacts   and   objective   records   of   crucial   intellectual   movements. Interpreting the evidence with care, JHS presents many fragments of culture so deftly and convincingly that the journal rivals the caliber of Chroniques de Philosophie, History and Theory, and Dionysius.

Issues of JHS are fairly large and contain ten to twelve major articles followed by a considerable number of book reviews.   Students and teachers aspiring to learn Greek philosophy may find JHS a thorough and readable survey.

140.   Journal of the History of the Behavioral Sciences. DATE FOUNDED: 1965.   FREQUENCY: q.   PRICE: $65/yr. institutions, $25/yr. members of Cheiron and other national professional organizations. PUBLISHER: Clinical Psychology Publishing Company, 4 Covant Square, Brandon, Vermont 05733. EDITOR: Barbara Ross.   ILLUSTRATIONS.   INDEX. CIRCULATION: 1,500. MANUSCRIPT   SELECTION: Refereed,   editorial board.   REPRINTS: publisher.   BOOK REVIEWS: 10 reviews, 1-4 pp., signed.   SPECIAL ISSUES: Occasional.   INDEXED/ABSTRACTED: AbAn, AmerH, CurrContSocBS, HistAb, IMed, PsyAb, SocAb.   TARGET AUDIENCE: AC.   ACCEPTANCE RATE: 18%.

JHBS is a multidisciplinary journal devoted to the history of anthropology, sociology, political science, philosophy, psychology, linguistics, and medicine in relation to advances in behavioral human studies.   Critical discussion stresses the theoretical origins, prominance, and evolutionary influence of basic and applied research upon different scientific domains.   Contributors are mainly psychologists, philosophers and historiographers. The sociohistorical structure   underlying   the   arguments   contains   a   definite, objective character.   JHBS takes issue on theoretical paradigms, whereas Journal of the History of Medicine and Isis focus instead on behavioral technology.

JHBS publishes five to seven main articles in each issue. Book reviews and announcements of the Cheiron Society or related scholarship and education give the journal a well-rounded profile of modern history.

141. Journal of the History of Ideas. DATE FOUNDED: 1940. FRE-
QUENCY: q. PRICE: $25/yr. institutions, $15/yr. personal. PUBLISHER:
Port City Press, Incorporated, 1323 Greenwood Road, Baltimore, Maryland
21208. EDITOR: Philip P. Wiener. ILLUSTRATIONS. INDEX. ADVER-
TISEMENTS. CIRCULATION: 3,800. MANUSCRIPT SELECTION: Refereed,
editorial board. MICROFORMS: UMI. REPRINTS: author. BOOK REVIEWS:
1 review, 1-10 pp., signed. INDEXED/ABSTRACTED: ArtHumCitI, PhilosI,
SSCI. TARGET AUDIENCE: AC. SAMPLE COPIES: Libraries. ACCEP-
TANCE RATE: 10%.

JHI publishes critical papers that fall within the purview of the interdisciplinary cultural history of pivotal ideas in philosophy, literature and art, sciences,
and religion. Original essays examine the evolution of several fields of
history, from ancient to contemporary modern times. Further, JHI tries to
promote greater collaboration among scholars in all the provinces of
historical study. Toward this end, contributors are usually scholars
interested in the subsciences of systematics, biology, and transitional periods
of culture sustained in the twentieth century. Retrospective surveys touch
upon seminal issues in ways similar to History and Theory. JHI differs from
Diotima and CLIO by the presupposition that history functions as a link
between intercultural analyses.
    A typical issue of JHI contains six to seven major articles, including
obituaries, brief dialogues on previously published articles, and a comprehensive review article. The list of books received also provides brief
annotations of each book.

142. Journal of the History of Medicine and Allied Sciences. DATE
FOUNDED: 1945. FREQUENCY: q. PRICE: $45/yr. institutions, $30/yr.
personal, $15/yr. student . PUBLISHER: Journal of the History of Medicine
and Allied Sciences, Incorporated, Medical History, Uniformed Services
University of the Health Sciences, 4301 Jones Bridge Road, Bethesda,
Maryland 20814. EDITOR: Robert J.T. Joy. ILLUSTRATIONS. INDEX.
ADVERTISEMENTS. MANUSCRIPT SELECTION: Refereed, editorial board.
REPRINTS: GryEdl. BOOK REVIEWS: 25 reviews, 1-2 pp., signed. SPECIAL
ISSUES: Occasional. INDEXED/ABSTRACTED: IMed. TARGET AUDIENCE:
AC, SP. SAMPLE COPIES: Libraries.

JHMAS is a unique forum for expression of all aspects of the history of
medicine and of the various sciences related to it.   Articles give account
of political, social, economical, and medical forces contributing to the
emergence of treatment in health service fields. Histories of opthalmology,
ornithology, psychiatry, psychology, and of the transformation of American
and European medicines provide the focus for much of JHMAS' essays. Topics
closely resemble the contents of Isis and Journal of the History of the
Behavioral Sciences. One important difference is the advances JHMAS
provides on primarily clinical subjects.
    A typical issue contains five main articles followed by a section on book
reviews, books received, and notes on the contributors.

143.   Journal of the History of Philosophy.   DATE FOUNDED: 1963.
FREQUENCY: q.   PRICE: $40/yr. institutions, $20/yr. personal, $15/yr.
student.   PUBLISHER: Journal of the History of Philosophy, Incorporated,
Department of Philosophy, Washington University, St. Louis, Missouri 63130.
EDITORS: Richard Popkin, Richard Watson.   ILLUSTRATIONS. INDEX.
ADVERTISEMENTS.   MANUSCRIPT SELECTION: Refereed, editorial board.
MICROFORMS: UMI.   REPRINTS: author.   BOOK REVIEWS: 15-20 reviews,
1-2 pp., signed.   SPECIAL ISSUES: Occasional.   INDEXED/ ABSTRACTED:
ArtHumCitI, PhilosI.   TARGET   AUDIENCE: AC.   SAMPLE   COPIES:
Libraries.

JHP is an international journal publishing articles, notes, discussion and
reviews about the history of Western philosophy, broadly concerned. Articles
appear in English, French, and German over a wide spectrum of ideologies,
religions, and sociologies, which relate to culturalization. From Cartesian to
Heideggarian theories, JHP seeks answers to the central questions of man in
society.   This understanding emerges through in-depth interpretation of
antecedents to modern philosophy. Authors are primarily philosophers. JHP
shares the unifying approaches of History and Theory, Dianoia and specialty
journals in Greek and Medieval periods.
   Each issue contains six to seven articles and several short book reviews.
Published in three languages, JHP opens its doors to a wider circulation
among the history fields.

144.   Journal of Indian Philosophy.   DATE FOUNDED: 1978. FREQUENCY:
q.   PRICE: $72/yr. institutions, $22/yr. personal. PUBLISHER: D. Reidel
Publishing Company, Box 17, 3300 AA Dordrecht, Netherlands. EDITOR: J.
Moussaieff   Masson.   ILLUSTRATIONS.   INDEX.   ADVERTISEMENTS.
MANUSCRIPT SELECTION: Refereed, editorial board.   REPRINTS: author.
BOOK REVIEWS: 7 reviews, 1-3 pp., signed.   SPECIAL ISSUES: Occasional.
INDEXED/ABSTRACTED: ArtHumCitI, CurrContAH, PhilosI.   TARGET
AUDIENCE: AC.   SAMPLE COPIES: Libraries.

Indian philosophy has attracted a small audience in the West for many years.
Only recently have Western philosophers explored the anatomy of customs,
religions, and politics unique to the East.   JIP encourages this inclination
toward Eastern study.   Contributors to the journal are bound by the limits of
rational   inquiry   and   thus   avoid   abstractions   about   sociology   and
parapsychology.   Authors are primarily polemicists who, in general, aim for
rigorous precision in their assertions.   Space is devoted to works of past and
contemporary analytic philosophers, whereas such journals as Dharma and
Dawn address considerations of historical Indian religion.
   Each issue of JIP contains five to seven main articles followed by a section
of book reviews.   Because the editorial policy insists on "rationalistic
discussion," practical aspects of Indian philosophy are succinct for the
introductory student.

145.   Journal of Medical Ethics.   DATE FOUNDED: 1975.   FREQUENCY: q.
PRICE: $56/yr. institutions. PUBLISHER: Society for the Study of Medical
Ethics, Tavistock House North, Tavistock Square, London WC1H 9LG.
EDITOR: Raanan Gillon.   ILLUSTRATIONS. INDEX. ADVERTISEMENTS.
CIRCULATION: 1,000.   MANUSCRIPT SELECTION: Refereed, editorial board.
REPRINTS: author.   BOOK   REVIEWS: 4-6   reviews,   2-3   pp.,   signed.
INDEXED/ABSTRACTED: IMed, PhilosI, SSCI. TARGET   AUDIENCE: AC,

GP, SP. SAMPLE COPIES: Libraries.

JME explores the social and moral order and limits of law within the larger domain of biomedical ethics. Critical essays interpret medicine as a specific development arising among existent forces and institutions which result in an inequality of treatment. Written by high-ranking officials and scholars, articles argue for both objectivity and the significance of clinical methods impacting on client rights. Essays are perceptive, substantive, and grounded on the best evidence available. Systematic and detailed expositions of contraception, artificial insemination, sterilization, euthanasia, and the Protestant understanding of Christian ethics make JME an excellent companion to Hastings Center Report and Journal of Medicine and Philosophy.

A typical issue features five to eight original articles, book reviews, and news and information by the Society of the Study of Medical Ethics. In so many words, JME may be considered a tribunal of pure reason which judges the putative problems in medicine from a cultural perspective.

146.   Journal of Medicine and Philosophy.   DATE FOUNDED: 1976. FREQUENCY: q.   PRICE: $36/yr. institutions, $20/yr. personal. PUBLISH-ER: D. Reidel Publishing Company, Box 17, 3300 AA Dordrecht, Netherlands. EDITOR: H. Tristram Engelhardt. ILLUSTRATIONS. INDEX. ADVERTISEMENTS: MANUSCRIPT SELECTION: Refereed, editorial board. REPRINTS: author. BOOK REVIEWS: 6 reviews, 1-2 pp., signed. SPECIAL ISSUES: Occasional.   INDEXED/ABSTRACTED: IMed, PhilosI, SSCI. TARGET AUDIENCE: AC, SP. SAMPLE COPIES: Libraries.

JMP explores the shared themes and concerns of philosophy and the medical sciences.   It provides a forum for philosophers, medical practitioners, educationists, and humanists to examine the controversies stimulated by all disciplines.   New developments in medical technology frequently crate humanistic dilemmas founded on moral and ethical issues.   Contributors nationwide focus on these dilemmas.   Examples include trends in holistic medicine, hospital morality, the reification of medical treatment, nature of self, and debate on abortion.   The dialogues take head-on approaches to philosophy, probing deeply into the same biomedical problems sampled in Explorations in Medicine and Journal of Bioethics.

Issues of JMP feature four to six   full-length full-length   articles, reviews, and commentaries on previously published articles.   As innovations in medicine continue nonhumanistic goals, journals like JMP will remind society of the specific repercussions that result.

147. Journal of Mind and Behavior. DATE FOUNDED: 1980. FREQUENCY: q.   PRICE: $40/yr. institutions, $25/yr. personal. PUBLISHER: Institute of Mind and Behavior, P.O. Box 522, Village Station, New York City, New York 10014.   EDITOR: Raymond C. Russ.   ILLUSTRATIONS. INDEX. ADVERTISEMENTS.   CIRCULATION: 1,000.   MANUSCRIPT SELECTION: Refereed, editorial board. REPRINTS: author. BOOK REVIEWS: 5 reviews, 2-3 pp., signed.   SPECIAL ISSUES: Occasional. INDEXED/ABSTRACTED: PsyAb, SocAb, SSCI.   TARGET AUDIENCE: AC.   SAMPLE COPIES: Libraries, individuals. ACCEPTANCE RATE: 20%.

JMB is dedicated to the interdisciplinary approach within psychology and related fields that mind and behavior interact and causally relate to each other in multidirectional ways. Articles generally consider experimentation and scientific methods, the relationship between operationism and theory construction, the mind-body problem, and medical, philosophical, and historical implications on the course an nature of science. Meaningful statements about human behavior rest with no one scientific commitment or school, but rather on the basic paradigm of empirical study. Emphasis is upon experimental control and measures outside the laboratory, which resembles the current topics in Psychological Record and Behaviorism.

A typical issue provides seven original articles, followed by book reviews and notices of relevant conferences, symposia and letters to the editor. The editorship strongly upholds a working reciprocity between theory and method, since most periodicals stress either one.

148.   Journal of Phenomenological Psychology. DATE FOUNDED: 1970. FREQUENCY: sa. PRICE: $13.50/yr. institutions. PUBLISHER: Humanities Press, Incorporated, Atlantic Highlands, New Jersey 07716. EDITOR: Amedeo Giorgi. ADVERTISEMENTS. CIRCULATION: 1,500. MANUSCRIPT SELECTION: Refereed, editorial board.   REPRINTS: author. BOOK REVIEWS: 5 reviews, 1-5 pp., signed.   SPECIAL ISSUES: Occasional. INDEXED/ABSTRACTED: CurrContAH, PsyAb.   TARGET AUDIENCE: AC, SP. SAMPLE COPIES: Libraries, individuals.

JPP aims to approach psychology in such a way that the entire range of experience and behavior of man as a human person is studied. The challenge facing authors is to invent methods that unveil significant aspects of man's relatedness to himself, others, and the world. The term "phenomenological" means the movement as a whole, thus encompassing articles that are theoretical, empirical, polemic, applied, clinical, and which explore experiential phenomena. Contributors are philosophers, psychologists and from the humanities. Exploring such areas as personal growth, interpersonal encounters and social consciousness, JPP provides a unique and stimulating balance between practical and idealistic topics. Journals achieving this same goal include Monist, Journal of Humanistic Psychology and even Review of Metaphysics.

Each issue offers the historical and contemporary views of introspectionism in five articles, book reviews, and announcements of relevant events.

149.   Journal of Philosophical Logic. DATE FOUNDED: 1972. FREQUENCY: q. PRICE: $70/yr. institutions, $20/yr. personal. PUBLISHER: D. Reidel Publishing Company, Box 17, 3300 AA Dordrecht, Netherlands. EDITOR: Richmond H. Thomason. ILLUSTRATIONS. INDEX. ADVERTISEMENTS.   MANUSCRIPT SELECTION: Refereed, editorial board. REPRINTS: author. SPECIAL ISSUES: Occasional. INDEXED/ABSTRACTED: ArtHumCitI, CurrContAH, InPhil, LLBA, MathR, PhilosI, RZ, SocAb. TARGET AUDIENCE: AC. SAMPLE COPIES: Libraries.

JPL is the most prestigious journal specializing in philosophical logic. It utilizes formal methods of dealing with topics in logic theory. Topics include inductive logic, conditionals, and the machinery of syllogism relative to essentialism, meanings, and truth. Discussions also relate to the logical structure of language (conventionalism) and formalization of scientific theories. Treatments of this kind tend to emphasize foundational (historical) principles derived from the laws of mathematics. Contributors are primarily analytical philosophers also publishing, for example, in Critica, Erkenntnis, Ratio and Reports on Mathematical Logic. Articles in JPL may vary in degree of technicality, although serving at the same time as direction for philosophical thought.

Each issue contains detailed evaluations of logical theory in six to seven articles. JPL has no special policies to style, other than that manuscripts be typed clearly and legibly.

150.   Journal of Philosophy.   DATE FOUNDED: 1904.   FREQUENCY: m. PRICE: $20/yr. institutions, $15/yr. personal, $12/yr. student. PUBLISHER: Managing editor, 720 Philosophy Hall, Columbia, New York, New York 10027.   EDITORS: John Randall, Herbert W. Schneider, Bernard Berofsky, Arthur Danto, Sidney Morgenbesser, Charles Parsons, James J. Walsh. ILLUSTRATIONS.   INDEX.   ADVERTISEMENTS.   CIRCULATION: 4,500. MANUSCRIPT SELECTION: Refereed, editorial board.   REPRINTS: author. BOOK   REVIEWS: 2-3 reviews, 1-2 pp., signed.   SPECIAL ISSUES: Occasional.   INDEXED/ABSTRACTED: ArtHumCitI, CurrContAH, HumI, PhilosI. TARGET AUDIENCE: AC. SAMPLE COPIES: Libraries.

JP has been a pioneering vehicle for philosophical exchange for over nearly 80 years.   Its ancestry alone enshrines the study of knowledge around a unique framework unmatched by contemporary serials as   Canadian Journal of Philosophy and Filosofia.   Critical essays are written by prominent scholars and venture into speculative as well as pragmatic questions of scientific and rationalistic theories.   More technical areas such as, for example, inductive   logic   and   value   conflict,   require   relatively   little mathematical background for readers.   The debates on morality, scientism, and epistemology grapple with perennial problems not only about man, but also about complex relations between his social and cultural systems. Special attention is given to an extended analysis of topics covered in Ethics, Monist and Mind.

A typical issue features two to four original articles, commentary and criticism, book reviews, and occasionally news and notes.   The list of new books received affords further interest in the examination of current trends in philosophy.   JP is by far a required journal for every aspiring student and professional in the field.

151.   Journal of Prison and Jail Health.   DATE FOUNDED: 1981.   FRE-QUENCY: sa.   PRICE: $40/yr. institutions, $19/yr. personal. PUBLISHER: Human Sciences Press, Incorporated, 72 Fifth Avenue, New York, New York 10011. EDITOR: Nancy N. Dubler. CIRCULATION: 2,000. MANUSCRIPT SELECTION: Refereed, editorial board.   ILLUSTRATIONS.   INDEX. ADVERTISEMENTS. REPRINTS: author. BOOK REVIEWS: 2-3 reviews, 1-2 pp., signed.   SPECIAL ISSUES: Occasional.   INDEXED/ ABSTRACTED: CurrConSocBS, IMed, PsyAb, SSCI. TARGET AUDIENCE: AC, SP. SAMPLE COPIES: Libraries.

JPJH is a timely response to the interdisciplinary interest and activity in prison health.   Reform efforts among health professionals, activism among inmates, and landmark legal decisions all contribute to this imperative. JPJH marks the first publication entirely devoted to discussion of medical, ethical, and maintenance care within the criminal justice system. Authors are primarily lawyers and philosophers working inside correctional systems. In addition, there are comments by ex-offenders concerning the degradation of prison treatment. Articles present opposing points of view on the cost-benefit ratio of mental health, morality, and legal services. These themes reverberate the debates found in Freedom, Inquiry, and Ethics.

Each issue surveys developments in the reform movement in five to seven articles and book reviews. Addressed to a diverse audience, JPJH can clarify the many misconceptions of prison life.

152. Journal of Psychohistory. DATE FOUNDED: 1973. TITLE CHANGES: History of Childhood Quarterly (1973-1980). FREQUENCY: q. PRICE: $38/yr. institutions,$24/yr. personal. PUBLISHER: Institute for Psychohistory, 2315 Broadway, New York, New York 10024. EDITOR: Dave Beisel. ILLUSTRATIONS. INDEX. ADVERTISEMENTS. CIRCULATION: 1,800. MANUSCRIPT SELECTION: Refereed, editorial board. MICROFORMS: UMI. REPRINTS: author. BOOK REVIEWS: 10-12 reviews, 2-4 pp. INDEXED/ABSTRACTED: AmerH, ChildDevAb, HistAb, SocAb. TARGET AUDIENCE: AC. SAMPLE COPIES: Libraries, individuals.

JP is the official publication for the school of historiography known as "psychohistory." Psychohistory by this definition defends the Freudian theory of personality as the modus operandi for investigation of historical and psychological events. Social historians who use this method argue that decisions and actions reflect rational and irrational belief systems, complicated by impulse control. JP adopts this psychological theory over the theores of scientific history (e.g., instrumentalism) and intellectual history, but remains partial to contributions by philosophy and anthropology. Use of psychoanalysis to explore history narrows the authors to trained specialists. This aside, the biographical essays may stretch the life events of heroes, kings and politicians beyond an objective profile. JP nonetheless covers history as intensely as History and Theory, Journal of the History of Ideas, and Journal of the History of Philosophy.

Every issue provides a balance of psychodynamism and history in five to eight lead articles. News and announcements follow the book reviews. Interested readers may find JP supplemental to American Imago.

153. Journal of Psychology and Judaism. DATE FOUNDED: 1976. FREQUENCY: sa. PRICE: $40/yr. institutions, $19/yr. personal. PUBLISHER: Human Sciences Press, Incorporated, 72 Fifth Avenue, New York, New York 10011. EDITOR: Reuven P. Bulka. CIRCULATION: 2,500. MANUSCRIPT SELECTION: Refereed, editorial board. ILLUSTRATIONS. INDEX. ADVERTISEMENTS. REPRINTS: author. BOOK REVIEWS: 2-4 reviews, 1-3 pp., signed. SPECIAL ISSUES: Occasional. INDEXED/ ABSTRACTED: CurrContAH, PsyAb, SSCI. TARGET AUDIENCE: AC, SP. SAMPLE COPIES: Libraries.

JPJ is a provocative journal exploring the relationship between modern psychology and Judaism on a clinical as well as philosophical level. Contained are case histories of identity problems, essays on ancestral and cultural influence, and reports of successful treatment of Jewish patients. Probing questions into the disassimilation of Judaic traditions typically cover topics about the Holocaust, ESP and prophecy, and the break-down of Jewish families. Contributors include rabbis, philosophers, and psychologists. Their psychoanalytic views on anti-semitism further establish JPJ as a paragon for Jewish studies. As in American Imago, critical analyses of human values promote the collaboration between clergy and secular psychotherapists.

A typical issue contains six to seven major articles, followed by book reviews. In short, JPJ combines contemporary modes of religious thought with particulars of the Jewish scene.

154. Journal of Religion and Health. DATE FOUNDED: 1961. FREQUENCY: q. PRICE: $68/yr. institutions, $29/yr. personal. PUBLISHER: Human Services Press, Incorporated, 72 Fifth Avenue, New York, New York 10011. EDITOR: Harry Meserve. ILLUSTRATIONS. INDEX. ADVERTISEMENTS. CIRCULATION: 1,500. MANUSCRIPT SELECTION: Refereed, editorial board. REPRINTS: author. BOOK REVIEWS: 1-3 reviews, 2 pp., SPECIAL ISSUES: Occasional. INDEXED/ABSTRACTED: CathI, RelAb. TARGET AUDIENCE: AC, SP. SAMPLE COPIES: Libraries.

JRH critically surveys the most recent modes of religious thought, with particular emphasis on medical and psychological research. Following an eclectic approach, JRH provides scholarly dialogue for theoretical and practical issues in secular psychotherapy, death and dying, counseling for aging, and mature religious behavior. Authors are mainly polemicists commenting on the most current trends in ethics and related health professions. Articles in JRH are presented objectively as found in Free Inquiry, and Psychology and Judaism.

A typical issue features about five original articles, book reviews, and relevant editorials about journal policy.

155. Journal of Religious Ethics. DATE FOUNDED: 1973. FREQUENCY: sa. PRICE: $15/yr. institutions, $12/yr. personal. PUBLISHER: University of Notre Dame Press, Notre Dame, Indiana 46556. EDITOR: James T. Johnson. INDEX. ADVERTISEMENTS. CIRCULATION: 1,000. MANUSCRIPT SELECTION: Refereed, editorial board. MICROFORMS: UMI. REPRINTS: publisher. BOOK REVIEWS: 4 reviews, 1-2 pp., signed. SPECIAL ISSUES: Occasional. INDEXED/ABSTRACTED: CathI, RelAb. TARGET AUDIENCE: AC. SAMPLE COPIES: Libraries, individuals.

JRE is a refreshingly original exploration into the moral and applied world of ecumenical problems. Articles draw upon a wide range of historical and contemporary resources in religion, philosophy, law, and ethics to form a vital link between biblical concepts, science, and social ideology. Morality is an essential underpinning enriched by orthodox humanistic scholars. This recital of thought and spiritual exhortation provides comparisons on matters of mysticism and liturgy covered in Ascent, Cross Curents and Heythrop Journal.

JRE publishes nine original articles an issue, although this varies with special issues.   A single issue is divided into two parts: A theme, and eclectic topics.

156.   Journal of Religious Thought. DATE FOUNDED: 1944. FREQUENCY: sa.   PRICE: $10/yr. institutions, $8/yr. personal.   PUBLISHER: Howard University Divinity School and Howard University Press, 1240 Daudolph Street, NE, Washington, D.C.   20017.   EDITOR: Cain H. Felder.   ILLUS-TRATIONS.   INDEX.   ADVERTISEMENTS.   CIRCULATION: 1,200. MANUSCRIPT SELECTION: Refereed, editorial board.   MICROFORMS: UMI. REPRINTS: UMI.   BOOK REVIEWS: 5-6 reviews, 1-3 pp., signed. SPECIAL ISSUES: Occasional. INDEXED/ABSTRACTED: ArtHumCitI, CathI, LLBA, PhilosI, SSCI.   TARGET AUDIENCE: AC.   SAMPLE COPIES: Libraries, individuals. ACCEPTANCE RATE: 60%.

JRT provides a forum for discussion on Afro-American, Caribbean, and African experiences culturally related to religious practice.   Liturgical interpretations of third world and Western spiritual movements are written primarily by scholars and specialists akin to developments in politics, sociology and psychology.   While essays are analytical, the conclusions about personality and human interaction sadly drift from clear definitions.   Like Interchange and Contemplative Review, JRT seemingly addresses a narrow audience of polemics rather than an interdisciplinary audience.

Each issue features from five to seven solicited and unsolicited essays, book reviews, and announcements of conferences or publications in Afro-oriented areas.

157.   Journal of the Royal Asiatic Society of Great Britian and Ireland. DATE FOUNDED: 1823.   FREQUENCY: sa.   PRICE: 20 Pounds/yr. institutions.   PUBLISHER: Royal Asiatic Society, 56 Queen Anne Street, London W1M 9LA, England.   EDITOR: C.F. Beckingham.   ILLUSTRATIONS. INDEX.   ADVERTISEMENTS.   MANUSCRIPT SELECTION: Refereed, editorial board.   MICROFORMS: MIC.   REPRINTS: publisher.   BOOK REVIEWS: 70-80 reviews, 1-2 pp., signed.   SPECIAL ISSUES: Occasional. TARGET AUDIENCE: AC, SP.

JRASGBI is the official journal of the Asiatic Society and certainly stands as a monument in the naturalistic field of human study.   Essays deal with anthropology, archaeology, art, dramatics, economy, ethnography, history and linguistics as they apply to the near and Middle East.   Ethnographic experts, mostly Society members, provide objective discussions of theory and the welfare of political cultures.   This social criticism fosters an integrity of evidence bearing out universal and specific problems in Asian countries. Like Humboldt Journal of Social Relations, JRASGBI earns a place in social philosophy in its evaluation of major forces from capitalism to socialism.

Each issue provides a series of seven to eight major articles, many book reviews, announcements and editorials.   JRASGBI fills the hiatus created in the philosophical study of economics, politics and human equality.

158. Journal of Somatic Experience. DATE FOUNDED: 1978. FRE-
QUENCY: sa. PRICE: $39/yr. institutions, $18/yr. personal. PUBLISHER:
Human Sciences Press, Incorporated, 72 Fifth Avenue, New York, New York
10011. EDITOR: Ian J. Grand. ILLUSTRATIONS. INDEX.
ADVERTISEMENTS. CIRCULATION: 1,000. MANUSCRIPT SELECTION:
Refereed, editorial board. REPRINTS: author. BOOK REVIEWS: 2-5
reviews, 1-2 pp., signed. SPECIAL ISSUES: Occasional. INDEXED/
ABSTRACTED: PsyAb, SSCI. TARGET AUDIENCE: AC, SP. SAMPLE
COPIES: Libraries.

JSE views the human body as an essential and rich source of knowledge,
feeling and endeavor. Critical papers seek to understand the physical body's
complex interrelationship with mental and emotional dimensions. Toward this
goal, clinical case studies and philosophical debates cover such areas as
personality, health and disease, sexuality, family development, myth, dreams,
and images. Contributors are noted professionals in medicine, psychology,
philosophy, theology, and the arts. Unique examinations of body vs. psyche
serve as supplemental to papers found in Energy and Character, European
Journal of Humanistic Psychology, and Journal of Biosocial Research.
    A typical issue of JSE features five to six original articles indicative of
the interdisciplinary orientation (e.g.,"Yugoslovian notes on the body and the
mind"). These selections strengthen the dialogue so crucial in establishing a
clinical forum for creative inquiry.

159. Journal for the Scientific Study of Religion. DATE FOUNDED: 1949.
FREQUENCY: q. PRICE: $20/yr. institutions, $10/yr. student. PUBLISHER:
Lorraine D'antonio, P.O. Box U68A, University of Connecticut, Storrs,
Connecticut 06268. EDITOR: Donald Capps. ILLUSTRATIONS. INDEX.
ADVERTISEMENTS. CIRCULATION: 2,800. MANUSCRIPT SELECTION:
Refereed, editorial board. MICROFORMS: UMI. REPRINTS: publisher.
BOOK REVIEWS: 15 reviews, 1-2 pp., signed. SPECIAL ISSUES:
Occasional. INDEXED/ABSTRACTED: CathI, HumI. TARGET AUDIENCE:
AC. SAMPLE COPIES: Libraries.

JSSR is the official publication of the Society for the Scientific Study of
Religion, which aims to communicate significant research on religious
institutions and experiences. Articles explore belief systems, ontology,
conversion, and exegetical themes facing empirical religious inquiry.
Substantial and growing interest in JSSR has been due to sociologic and
anthropologic theories to help clarify American pentecostalism, the origins of
Christianity, secularization trends, and the local-cosmopolitan effect upon
morality. This new scientific vantage lends contrast to the conservative
theologies in Beacon and International Journal for Philosophy and Religion.
While still fairly encumbered by metaphors and prophetic thinking, JSSR does
try to objectify the nature of religious behavior.
    A typical issue contains seven to eight articles and several book reviews,
announcements, and news. Considering the need for hard data, JSSR
represents the closest treatise available to a science of theology.

160.   Journal for the Theory of Social Behaviour.   DATE FOUNDED: 1971.
FREQUENCY: 3/yr.   PRICE: $65/yr. institutions.   PUBLISHER: Basil
Blackwell, 108 Cowley Road, Oxford OX4 1JF, England.   EDITOR: Charles
Smith.   ILLUSTRATIONS.   INDEX.   ADVERTISEMENTS.   MANUSCRIPT
SELECTION: Refereed, editorial board.   REPRINTS: author. SPECIAL
ISSUES: 1/yr.   INDEXED/ABSTRACTED: PhilosI, PsyAb. TARGET
AUDIENCE: AC, SP. SAMPLE COPIES: Libraries. ACCEPTANCE RATE:
30%.

The primary orientation of JTSB is theoretical and methodological and only
indirectly empirical on aspects of the behavioral sciences.   Articles of high
quality   discuss   innovative   replies   to   questions   about   social   behavior,
generalization from laboratory to natural situations, and about trends in
behaviorism.   Editors discourage technical use of statistics, psychological
tests or measurement, or quantification according to nonsocial types of
scientific psychology.   Rather, papers set out to translate experiments into
the language of everyday life.   Critically examined are the assumptions and
conceptual implications for general theory.   Contributors are scholars and
practitioners.   Much like Behaviorism, JTSB strings together a net of
philosophers and psychologists for a serious exchange between intellectualism
and practical issues.
    Each issue contains seven lead articles, a discussion article (frequently a
rebuttal), and a list of books received. JTSB definitely takes a stand against
the   irrationalism   of   methodologists.   This   feature   alone   deserves   the
recognition of students and teachers.

161.   Journal of Thought. DATE FOUNDED: 1966. FREQUENCY: q.
PRICE: $12/yr. institutions. PUBLISHER: College of Education, University
of Oklahoma, Norman, Oklahoma 73019.   EDITOR: Chipman G. Stuart.
ILLUSTRATIONS.   INDEX.   ADVERTISEMENTS.   CIRCULATION: 500.
MANUSCRIPT SELECTION: Refereed, editorial board. MICROFORMS: UMI.
REPRINTS: UMI.   BOOK REVIEWS: 2-4 reviews, 1-3 pp., signed. SPECIAL
ISSUES: 1/yr. INDEXED/ABSTRACTED: ArtHumCitI, CurrContAH, LLBA,
PhilosI, SocAb, SSCI.   TARGET AUDIENCE: AC.   SAMPLE COPIES:
Libraries, individuals. ACCEPTANCE RATE: 30%.

JT is a publication devoted to encouraging scholars of diverse disciplines,
nationalities, languages and cultures to examine the significant educational
issues and problems confronting world debate.   Interdisciplinary dialogue
among scholars covers such topics as history, anthropology, Afro-American
and Eastern experiences. Essay reviews give extensive treatment to
the naturalization of individuals in the United States and abroad.   To this
extent, JT is a festschrift for the parallel study of humanities and scientific
investigation.   Authors are mostly academicians.   Editors of special issues
gladly   welcome   contributions   on   global   issues   without   overuse   of   jargon.
This commitment to clear and informative writing includes JT among such
allies as Inquiry and Isis.
    Each issue contains three distinct sections.   The first section, called
"Scribe,"   presents   a   thoughtful,   editorial   essay.   Second, "Margins of
Precision" provides two to three articles. Third, four to six regular articles
keep the reader informed on a broad range of topics. Selected book reviews
follow.

162.   Journal of Transpersonal Psychology.   DATE FOUNDED: 1969.
FREQUENCY: sa. PRICE: $18/yr. institutions, $15/yr. personal. PUBLISH-
ER: Transpersonal Institute, 345 California Avenue, Palo Alto, California
94306.   EDITOR: Miles A. Vich.   INDEX.   CIRCULATION: 2,700.
MANUSCRIPT SELECTION: Refereed, editorial board. MICROFORMS: UMI.
REPRINTS: author.   BOOK   REVIEWS: 5 reviews, 1-3 pp., signed.
INDEXED/ABSTRACTED: CurrConSocBS, PsyAB, PsyRG, SSCI. TARGET
AUDIENCE: AC, SP. ACCEPTANCE RATE: 10%.

JTP is an independent vehicle for the study and open communication of
transpersonal experiences. It accepts as its province the full range of human
awareness, especially those elements that reach across and beyond human
personality.   Transpersonal   perspectives   exercise   both   objective   and
subjective (introspective) modes of knowledge concerning education, science,
clinical and spiritual issues. JTP is widely recognized for its authoritative
word on peak experiences, species-synergy, values and states, mystical
experiences,   and   transcendence   of   self.   Authors   are   psychologists,
philosophers, and specialists in health fields.   Since its founding JTP has
addressed many general problems typically heard in European Journal of
Humanistic Psychology.
JTP's contributions to humanistic psychology continue in every issue. A
typical issue contains five major articles and book reviews, followed by the
Institute's announcements and occasionally annotations of journal articles.
Empirical papers provide an unusually fresh glimpse at theories of meditation
and collective consciousness.

163. Journal of Value Inquiry. DATE FOUNDED: 1966. FREQUENCY: q.
PRICE: $56/yr. institutions, $24/yr. personal.   PUBLISHER: Martinus
Nijhoff Publishers, P.O. Box 566, 2501 CN, the Hague, Netherlands. EDITOR:
James Wilbur.   INDEX.   ADVERTISEMENTS.   MANUSCRIPT SELECTION:
Refereed, editorial board. REPRINTS: author. BOOK REVIEWS: 3 reviews,
1-3 pp., signed. INDEXED/ABSTRACTED: PhilosI. TARGET AUDIENCE:
AC. SAMPLE COPIES: Libraries, individuals. ACCEPTANCE RATE: 20%.

JVI is an international philosophical forum devoted to the stimulation of
current research in axiology. Critical papers address themselves to questions
concerning the nature, origin, experience, and scope of values in general, as
well as to studies in ethics, legal theory, aesthetics, and methodology.
Particularly heavy coverage is given to modern theories of metaphysics, from
classical protostructures to teleological structures.   Whether JVI is
contiguous   with   Bulletin   de   Philosophie   Medievale   and   Journal   of
Philosophical Logic all depends on how axiology is defined. Contributors are
mostly analytic scholars.
Each issue of JVI contains three to four exploratory articles and three
discussion (research) articles.   JVI does accept technical writing in formal
logic which may discourage introductory readers.

164. Journal of Yoga Institute. DATE FOUNDED: 1935. FREQUENCY: m.
PRICE: $6/yr. institutions. PUBLISHER: Yoga Institute, Prabhat Colony,
Santa Cruz, East, Bombay 400 055.   EDITOR: Jayadeva Yogendra.
ILLUSTRATIONS.   ADVERTISEMENTS.   CIRCULATION: 1,000.   MANU-
SCRIPT SELECTION: Editor. BOOK REVIEWS: 1 review, 1-2 pp., signed.
TARGET AUDIENCE: GP. SAMPLE COPIES: Libraries, individuals.

JYI provides a central reference to the roots of yoga practices in Bombay. Essentially, techniques of concentration when applied to different objects and events liberate the mind from tension and counter with the perceptions of sentient beings. Methods of yoga are derived from the early writings of Shri Yogendraji and resemble self-hypnotism. Psychological articles introduce in a non-doctrinaire way the social, medical, and psychic reasons for mind-body meditation, focusing on largely the educational aspects. Authors are members of the Institute who expound on attainment of physical health. This contrasts to authors in Dharma and Dawn Magazine who force opinions over experience.

Each issue is itself a yoga essay on modern thinking and developments. Five short articles are followed by a list of educational resources available through the Institute.

165. Kabbalist. DATE FOUNDED: 1975. FREQUENCY: q. PRICE: 1.75 Pounds/yr. institutions. PUBLISHER: International Order of Kabbalists, 25, Circle Gardens, Merton Park, London SW19 3JX, England. EDITOR: J. Sturzaker. ADVERTISEMENTS. CIRCULATION: 1,000. MANUSCRIPT SELECTION: Editor. BOOK REVIEWS: 6-10 reviews, 1-2 pp. TARGET AUDIENCE: GP. ACCEPTANCE RATE: 90%.

Kabbalist is a facsimile of the early spiritual teachings about nature and minerals, all ensouled with powers that make astrology and occult science important. "Kabbalah" is the oldest mystical art linking states of subjective activity with subtle forces in the cosmos. Authors of Kabbalist are usually scholars of the International Order of Kabbalists. Critical discussion covers the phenomenon of zodiacal and planetary effects upon therapy. Toward this end, the various myths and legends from ancient Kabbalah give impetus to such approaches as gemtherapy, biotherapy, and chromotherapy. Therapeutics in Kabbalist are different from, say, Energy and Character, where healing forces may be instead attributed to "inner" vibrations.

Each issue of Kabbalist combines original notes and articles with a list of books and materials published by the Order. Noteworthy is that, for historical purposes, writings in Kabbalah reveal early techniques, species and rituals of fundamental interest to paleontologists.

166. Kinesis. DATE FOUNDED: 1968. FREQUENCY: sa. PRICE: $7.50/yr. institutions, $5/yr. personal. PUBLISHER: Department of Philosophy, Southern Illinois University, Carbondale, Illinois 62901. EDITOR: Richard Field. ADVERTISEMENTS. CIRCULATION: 200. MANUSCRIPT SELECTION: Refereed, editorial board. MICROFORMS: UMI. REPRINTS: publisher. BOOK REVIEWS: 1 review, 1-3 pp., signed. SPECIAL ISSUES: Occasional. INDEXED/ABSTRACTED: PhilosI. TARGET AUDIENCE: AC. SAMPLE COPIES: Libraries. ACCEPTANCE RATE: 25-50%.

Kinesis is specifically founded to publish papers by graduate students in all basic fields of philosophy from metaphysics to the Marxist theories on ethics and politics. Editors believe that the creative philosophical work of graduate students constitutes a substantial contribution to debate on problems basic to critical inquiry. Articles concerning education, language, and leading thinkers (Sartre, Kierkegaard, etc.) blend together the currents of modern Western scholarship. Authors thus seek to complement, not contradict, the established disciplines in both original and comprehensive articles. Like

Auslegung, *Gnosis*, and *Cornell Journal of Social Relations*, *Kinesis* succeeds in its experiment to liberate students from their subversive role in professional arenas.

The content of *Kinesis* contains three to four articles, book reviews, and notes on the contributors. Students pursuing a masters or doctorate in philosophy may wish to seriously consider this outlet for expression.

167. *Kodikas/Code: International Journal of Semantics.* DATE FOUNDED: 1979. TITLE CHANGES: *Kodikas/Code* (1979-1981). FREQUENCY: q. PRICE: 76 Deutsche Marks/yr. institutions. PUBLISHER: Gunter Narr Verlag, Stuaffenbergstr, 42, P.O. Box 2567, 7400 Tubingen 1, West Germany. EDITORS: Achim Eschbach, Ernest W.B.Hess-Luttich, Mihai Nadin, Jurgen Trabant. ILLUSTRATIONS. ADVERTISEMENTS. MANUSCRIPT SELECTION: Refereed, editorial board. REPRINTS: author. BOOK REVIEWS: 4-5 reviews, 2-3 pp., signed. SPECIAL ISSUES: Occasional. TARGET AUDIENCE: AC, SP. SAMPLE COPIES: Libraries, individuals.

KC gives particular emphasis to papers promoting research and discussion of semiotics. Semiotics relates to the constitution of signs in continuous sociologic process. Articles on semiotics analyze communication and interchange of messages among humans, other organisms, and within organisms. Principles of code changes may be based on experiments as well as other sorts of empirical evidence. This includes case studies, and investigation in the history of culture or evolution of nature. Authors are largely specialists who examine advanced topics in this field. Like *Semiotica*, KC may suffer from overspecialization of technical jargon and theory.

A regular volume or supplement selects a semiotical theme (e.g., multi-media communication) and may feature twenty to thirty articles by formidable authorities in the field.

168. *Laval Theologique et Philosophique.* DATE FOUNDED: 1945. FREQUENCY: 3/yr. PRICE: $14/yr. institutions. PUBLISHER: La Compagnie de L'Eclaireur Ltee, 206, Avenue Lambert, Beauceville, Quebec, Canada G0M 1A0. INDEX. ADVERTISEMENTS. CIRCULATION: 1,200. MANUSCRIPT SELECTION: Refereed, editorial board. MICROFORMS: UMI. REPRINTS: author. BOOK REVIEWS: 18 reviews, 1-3 pp., signed. SPECIAL ISSUES: 1/yr. INDEXED/ABSTRACTED: Info, IntZeitBibGren, PhilosI. TARGET AUDIENCE: AC. SAMPLE COPIES: Libraries, individuals. ACCEPTANCE RATE: 30%.

LTP publishes extensive research articles and reviews which chronicle items of prime interest to philosophy and theology. English and French papers exemplify advancing and defending conceptions of social, moral, and metaphysical theories. Concise and clear, LTP breaks new ground in its logical questions regarding symbolic interactionism, scientific knowledge, God and soul, and the endurance of mystical religious traditions. Polemical arguments by noted scholars throw light on the pretense and possibility of a world beyond that known, similar to articles in *Contemplative Review*, *Divus Thomas*, and *International Journal of Philosophy and Religion*.

Each issue of LTP normally contains six to seven articles including book reviews and a list of books received. It is highly recommended for foreign study in religion.

169. <u>Law and Justice</u>. DATE FOUNDED: 1962. TITLE CHANGES: <u>Quis Custodiet</u> (1962-1975). FREQUENCY: q. PRICE: 12 Pounds/yr. institutions. PUBLISHER: Edmund Plowden Trust, 51 High Street, Hampton, TW12 2SX, England. EDITOR: Michael Penty. ADVERTISEMENTS. CIRCULATION: 300. MANUSCRIPT SELECTION: Articles solicited. BOOK REVIEWS: 4-5 reviews, 1-3 pp., signed. TARGET AUDIENCE: AC. SAMPLE COPIES: Libraries, individuals.

<u>LJ</u> provides original and reprinted essays concerned with the concept of rationality, belief, and jurisprudence. Offering a wide range of perspectives, this combination of philosophy and law deepens an understanding of human action within political theory. Some historical study makes explicit the practical urgency and theoretical difficulty over the last two centuries to address social obligations, liberal equality, and ethical disclosure. Of no less interest are the compelling claims for different types of equality. Articles are written by scholars and specialists. This deliberately polemical journal may generate considerable controversy as effectively as the papers in <u>Critica</u>, <u>Human Rights Quarterly</u>, and <u>Law and Philosophy</u>.
  Contained in issues of <u>LJ</u> are four to six articles commissioned by the editors, followed by book reviews. One nice feature of <u>LJ</u> is that articles confront practical implications in areas such as industrial democracy and community control.

170. <u>Law and Philosophy</u>. DATE FOUNDED: 1982. FREQUENCY: 3/yr. PRICE: $61/yr. institutions, $22/yr. personal. PUBLISHER: D. Reidel Publishing Company, P.O. Box 322, 3300 AH Dordrecht, Netherlands. EDITOR: Alan Mabe. ILLUSTRATIONS. INDEX. ADVERTISEMENTS. MANUSCRIPT SELECTION: Refereed, editorial board. REPRINTS: author. BOOK REVIEWS: Annotated book list. SPECIAL ISSUES: Occasional. INDEXED/ABSTRACTED: PhilosI. TARGET AUDIENCE: AC. SAMPLE COPIES: Libraries.

<u>LP</u> is a forum for work in law and philosophy which is of common interest to members of both disciplines. It is open to all approaches in both fields along major legal traditions in law, civil law, or the socialist tradition. Papers exhibit reflection on the law through legal analysis but using philosophic methods. Recent trends in jurisprudence are treated in current and historical context. These contributions are written by lawyers and philosophers or specialists in political philosophy. The much-needed revival of legal discussion in philosophy fulfills the same goals as <u>Inquiry</u>, <u>Aut Aut</u> and <u>Journal of Philosophy</u>.
  A typical issue features three to five articles of a substantial nature, notes, and both a review and book note section. Extended book notes contain annotated bibliographies.

171. <u>Light</u>. DATE FOUNDED: 1881. FREQUENCY: q. PRICE: $10/yr. institutions. PUBLISHER: College of Psychic Studies, 16 Queensberry Place, London SW7 2EB, England. EDITOR: Brenda Marshall. INDEX. CIRCULATION: 2,500. MANUSCRIPT SELECTION: Refereed, editorial board. REPRINTS: author. BOOK REVIEWS: 5-6 reviews, 12 pp., signed. SPECIAL ISSUES: Occasional. TARGET AUDIENCE: AC, GP, SP. SAMPLE COPIES: Libraries, individuals.

Light exists for the reasoned and intensive examination of all aspects of spiritual and psychic exploration. Much of its material is presented in a way to attract general readership. Emphasis is greatest on personal experiences than on theory, but only experiences relating to the paranormal, survival of bodily death, mediumship, and communication. Or simply, "to understand man about the mystery of human consciousness." Advanced physics and psychology are considered the data base for reported cases of extraordinary circumstances, both confirmed and disconfirmed. Short articles clearly delve into the workings of the "inner world" and depend more on the reader's fascination than on empirical validity. By contrast, the Zetetic Scholar treats anomaly research as a scientific enterprise.

Regular issues contain ten articles including editorials and book reviews. Long and short reviews together cover several popular books on the commercial market that are often available through the College of Psychic Studies.

172. Locke Newsletter. DATE FOUNDED: 1970. FREQUENCY: a. PRICE: 4 Pounds/yr. institutions. PUBLISHER: Department of Philosophy, University of York, York, England. EDITOR: Roland Hall. ILLUSTRATIONS. ADVERTISEMENTS. CIRCULATION: 600. MANUSCRIPT SELECTION: Editor. BOOK REVIEWS: 2 reviews, 1-2 pp., signed. INDEXED/ABSTRACTED: PhilosI. TARGET AUDIENCE: AC. SAMPLE COPIES: Individuals.

LN is the most extended treatment in the literature of the historical and philosophical resonance of Locke. Among major topics discussed are empiricism, consistency and coherence of beliefs, and practical rationality. Essays on political theory begin with an interrogation of important concepts, including recognized psychological and metaphysical preconditions to, for example, materialism. In this formidable labor of exposition the authors, mostly scholars, attempt to assess how far the ideas and achievements of Locke reach into current questions about perception, social change, and ethics. LN brings together papers very simialr in style to Ethics but that are more thought-provoking in Lockian studies.

Each issue of the newsletter features short reports and news items synthesized from international trends in Locke research. Emphasis on fundamental works does presuppose the readers will have a background in Locke or related empirical thinkers.

173. Logique et Analyse. DATE FOUNDED: 1954. TITLE CHANGES: Bulletin Interieur (1954-1958). FREQUENCY: 3/yr. PRICE: 1.100 Belgium Francs/yr. institutions. PUBLISHER: Nauwelaerts Printing S.A., B 3000 Louvain, Valkerijgang, Belgium. EDITOR: M.P. Gochet. MANUSCRIPT SELECTION: Refereed, editorial board. REPRINTS: author. INDEXED/ABSTRACTED: PhilosI. TARGET AUDIENCE: AC. SAMPLE COPIES: Libraries.

LA is a unique undertaking in the exchange of formal logic. Articles focus on practical and theoretical axioms within mathematical systems that are interntionally controversial. The history of "intuitionism," for instance, really amounts to disputed extensions of Heyting's concepts, justified carefully and thoroughly in technical papers. This argument and interpretations of truth-conditional semantics are explored to study the many relations between language and reality, and causal modalities. The varieties of referential construction in LA provide a thematically unified treatment of some of the most central questions in philosophy of language. Linguistic problems examined in LA also appear in Erkenntnis, Conceptus and Journal of Philosophical Logic.

A typical issue features eight original articles in different languages. Noteworthy is that beginning students in logic may be overwhelmed by the extensive use of jargon.

174. Logos. DATE FOUNDED: 1980. FREQUENCY: a. PRICE: $7/yr. institutions. PUBLISHER: University of Santa Clara, Department of Philosophy, Santa Clara, California 95053. EDITOR: James W. Felt. INDEX. ADVERTISEMENTS. CIRCULATION: 200. MANUSCRIPT SELECTION: Refereed, editorial board. REPRINTS: author. SPECIAL ISSUES: Each issue. INDEXED/ABSTRACTED: PhilosI. TARGET AUDIENCE: AC. SAMPLE COPIES: Libraries. ACCEPTANCE RATE: 30%.

Papers in Logos examine the most pressing philosophical problems in Christianity. Neo-transcendental approaches toward scientific theory examine the intelligibility of assumptions in biomedical ethics, humanism, and ideology. Essays on theology break new ground in their abundance of information tailored for scholars and students. Christian philosophy, as derived from early Alexandrian periods, asks straightforward questions about Church rights, and the varities of a religiously pluralistic world. Authors are mainly polemicists who convey a sense of intellectual excitement, as might be found in Interchange, Cross Currents and possibly Beacon. Although Logos draws on a wide range of sources, it does not exhaust the generation of values, ideals, and actions which underlay modern Christian perspectives.

Each issue is usually thematic. Invited authors or those presenting at conferences account for five to six articles, and editorial commentary. The issue on biomedical ethics (Volume 3, 1982), for example, contains articles on abortion, parenthood, and human interdependence.

175. Magyar Filozofiai Szemle. DATE FOUNDED: 1957. FREQUENCY: 6/yr. PRICE: 162 Forints/yr. institutions. PUBLISHER: Akademiai, Kiado, 1363 Budapest, Alkotmany, Hungary. EDITOR: Ferenc L. Lendvai. INDEX. MANUSCRIPT SELECTION: Refereed, editorial board. REPRINTS: author. BOOK REVIEWS: 4 reviews, 2-3 pp., signed. TARGET AUDIENCE: AC. SAMPLE COPIES: Individuals.

MFS captures the liberal thinking displayed in modern elements of aesthetics, metaphysics, ethics, and history. This journal is for international readers seeking an effective integration of exegetics and systematic theory. MFS regards itself as a medium that investigates fundamental dimensions of human experience. Its unifying thread is the original essays which dismiss enduring paradoxes from social sciences. Authors are largely scholars who give important new information on traditions of philosophy. Clear and insightful discussion softens the domination of certain ideas and concepts used extensively by such journals as Epistemologia.

MFS publishes a selection of original critical reviews and then key evaulations of the books received. For many years MFS was neglected but there is no question about its explanatory value to professionals.

176. <u>Man and Medicine:</u> Journal of Values and Ethics. DATE FOUNDED: 1976. FREQUENCY: q. PRICE: $16.50/yr. institutions, $14/yr. personal, $9.50/yr. student. PUBLISHER: Man and Medicine, Incorporated, Columbia University, College of Physicians and Surgeons, 630 West 168th Street, New York, New York 10032. EDITOR: Michael Meyer. ILLUSTRATIONS. INDEX. ADVERTISEMENTS. MANUSCRIPT SELECTION: Refereed, editorial board. REPRINTS: author. BOOK REVIEWS: 2-3 reviews, 2-5 pp., signed. INDEXED/ABSTRACTED: PhilosI. TARGET AUDIENCE: AC, SP. SAMPLE COPIES: Libraries.

Continuing the appeal for biomedical inquiry is <u>MM</u>, a journal devoted to direct service care issues facing the philosophical establishment. Patient rights, child abuse, abortion, patient compliance, and general hospital policy are among the topics commonly seen. Central aims of the journal begin from a moral framework and derive from institutional goals of each medical profession. Contributors are frequently specialists and scholars involved in direct, objective research. This provocative search for truth puts forth a variety of social scientific principles and results in the in-depth analysis typically found in <u>Journal of Medical Ethics</u> and <u>Journal of Medicine and Philosophy.</u>
Each issue normally contains six major articles, commentaries (and replies) on previous articles, book reviews, and a list of books received. <u>MM</u> is an excellent choice for nursing and medical school libraries.

177. <u>Man and World.</u> DATE FOUNDED: 1966. FREQUENCY: q. PRICE: $58/yr. institutions, $23/yr. personal. PUBLISHER: Martinus Nijhoff Publishers, P.O. Box 566, 2501 CN, Hague, Netherlands. EDITORS: L.M. Anderson, Joseph J. Kockelmans, Calvin O. Schrag. INDEX. ADVERTISEMENTS. MANUSCRIPT SELECTION: Refereed, editorial board. REPRINTS: author. BOOK REVIEWS: 3 reviews, 1-4 pp., signed. INDEXED/ABSTRACTED: PhilosI. TARGET AUDIENCE: AC. SAMPLE COPIES: Libraries, individuals. ACCEPTANCE RATE: 15%.

<u>MW</u> seeks to elicit discussion of fundamental philosophical problems and original approaches toward a solution of them. Editors invite essays both on expressly theoretical topics and topics dealing with practical matters within the socio-political life of man. Scholarly dialogue encompasses domains of art, morality, science and religion as they relate to developments in phenomenology. Continental philosophy and the intersection between East and West move <u>MW</u> ahead of such international forums as <u>Journal of Thought,</u> <u>Journal of Mind and Behavior</u> and <u>Aut Aut.</u> <u>MW</u> also establishes closer and more immediate contact among countries of North, Central and South America through articles in French and German.
Each issue contains three thematic or key articles, followed by lengthy book reviews. Issues also contain a chronicle of the most significant events in the philosophical world of each country represented.

178. <u>Manas.</u> DATE FOUNDED: 1948. FREQUENCY: w. PRICE: $10/yr. institutions. PUBLISHER: Mana Publishing Company, P.O. Box 32112, Los Angeles, California 90032. EDITOR: Henry Geiger. CIRCULATION: 2,300. MANUSCRIPT SELECTION: Editor. MICROFORMS: UMI. REPRINTS: publisher. BOOK REVIEWS: 2 reviews, 1-2 pp. TARGET AUDIENCE: GP, SP. SAMPLE COPIES: Libraries, individuals.

Manas is an introduction to philosophy and explores pervasive features of current day human interaction. The few articles published draw heavily on past causes and explanations of free-will and determinism, crime, physicalism, moral responsibility, and emotivism. While the text is written primarily by the editor, essays by contributing scholars offer a conspectus of relatively common themes in most philosophy journals including Iyyun and Canadian Journal of Philosophy. Nonetheless, there appears a distinctly comprehensive logic to each thesis and this alone merits the specialized interest of students and philosophers.

Each issue of Manas directly adds a touch of originality to the short articles and book reviews. News and notes keep readers abreast of major trends.

179. Mankind Quarterly. DATE FOUNDED: 1960. FREQUENCY: q. PRICE: $40/yr. institutions, $20/yr. personal. PUBLISHER: Institute for the Study of Man, Suite 520, 1629 K Street North West, Washington, D.C. 20006. EDITOR: R. Lynn. ILLUSTRATIONS. INDEX. ADVERTISEMENTS. CIRCULATION: 1,200. MANUSCRIPT SELECTION: Refereed, editorial board. REPRINTS: author. BOOK REVIEWS: 8 reviews, 1-3 pp. SPECIAL ISSUES: Occasional. INDEXED/ABSTRACTED: SSCI. TARGET AUDIENCE: AC. SAMPLE COPIES: Libraries. ACCEPTANCE RATE: 25%.

MQ orients toward the techniques and philosophy for deriving intelligence and sociologic concepts from diverse theories. Particular emphasis is placed upon research and informed speculation in the areas of social psychology, human heredity, and cultural change, especially where there is widespread implications for the future of society. The clear, objective and powerful essays, mostly by experimentalists, create a series of enlightening debates well suited for the behavioral philosopher. English- speaking readers will additionally enjoy MQ's sense of operationalism. Interest in "intelligence" extends to the human condition, whereas the same topic in Artificial Intelligence might consider cybernetics.

A regular issue offers five to six original articles and book reviews. Occasional editorials describing a theme or conclusion about the state of human studies give renewed hope to the future of applied research in philosophy and anthropology.

180. Master Thoughts. DATE FOUNDED: 1972. FREQUENCY: w. PRICE: $20/yr. institutions.   PUBLISHER: Dominion Press, P.O. Box 37, San Marcos, California 92069-0025. EDITOR: A. Stuart. ILLUSTRATIONS. INDEX. CIRCULATION: 100. REPRINTS: publisher. TARGET AUDIENCE: GP.

MT is a serial on the interpretation of selected passages by Jesus from the King James version. Prophetic words are lifted in sequential order and analyzed metaphysically, beginning with the Gospel of Matthew and proceeding through all the books of the New Testament. Toward this end, the editor projects the last issue of MT in the year 2010. Since religious exegetical writing is usually theoretical, hardly any effort is made to document or verify claims. The mission of MT almost begs the question of whether every bit of painstaking analysis should distort biblical events. Translations of text are also suspicious.

MT puts forth a short installment by the editor on biblical thinking. Readers interested in this serial may find the selected quotations of personal value.

181. Mediaevel Studies. DATE FOUNDED: 1939. FREQUENCY: a. PRICE: $30/yr. institutions. PUBLISHER: Pontifical Institute of Mediaeval Studies, 59 Queenls Park Crescent East, Toronto, Ontario Canada M5S 2C4. EDITOR: Virginia Brown. ILLUSTRATIONS. INDEX. CIRCULATION: 1,000. MANUSCRIPT SELECTION: Refereed, editorial board. REPRINTS: publisher. INDEXED/ABSTRACTED: CurrContAH, CathI. TARGET AUD-IENCE: AC. ACCEPTANCE RATE: 6%.

MS publishes studies that involve archival materials or meaningfully historical records regarding medieval semantics and logic. Considered an authority, MS stimulates a driving intellectual energy full of sharp and provocative arguments to be read by nearly anyone studying the ways of ancients. Critical methods of analysis set morality, ethics, and cultural practices in the context of certain centuries, making explicit their origin of ideas. Authors are distinguished philosophers and historiographers. The dialectics in MS combine the same humanistic and synthetic aims as the Bulletin de Philosophie Medievale and Journal of Hellenic Studies.
  Authors in MS serve to restore historical research to the prominence it deserves. Each issue contains several original papers, news and announce-ments. It is unfortunate that this piece of scholarship appears only once a year.

182. Metaphilosophy. DATE FOUNDED: 1968. FREQUENCY: q. PRICE: $50.75/yr. institutions, $33.50/yr. personal. PUBLISHER: Basil Blackwell Publisher, 108 Cowley Road, Oxford, England 0X4 1JF. EDITOR: Terrell Ward Bynnm. ILLUSTRATIONS. ADVERTISEMENTS. CIRCULATION: 1,000. MANUSCRIPT SELECTION: Refereed, editorial board. MICROFORMS: BaBPub. REPRINTS: author. BOOK REVIEWS: 9 reviews, 1-4 pp., signed. SPECIAL ISSUES: Occasional. INDEXED/ ABSTRACTED: PhilosI. TARGET AUDIENCE: AC. SAMPLE COPIES: Libraries, individuals. ACCEPTANCE RATE: 10%.

Metaphilosophy publishes articles stressing consideration about philosophy or some particular school, method or field of philosophy. The intended scope is very broad and includes aspects of philosophical systems, presuppostions of philosophical ideas, and interdisciplinary study. Metaphilosophical inquiry clearly opens the pathways to essays in cybernetics, linguistics and political action theory. Articles in Metaphilosophy are generally objective and written by academicians who view the state of philosophy as evolving. As with Contemporary Philosophy, discussions offer interest for a wide audience rather than to a small circle of specialists.
  A typical issue publishes six comprehensive articles , followed by two review articles and several book reviews. Ideas and concepts assembled in Metaphilosophy have mainly pragmatic overtones for the reader's scientific ear.

183.   Method: Journal of Lonergan Studies.   DATE FOUNDED: 1983.
FREQUENCY: sa.   PRICE: $20/yr. institutions, $12/yr. personal.
PUBLISHER: Department of Philosophy, Loyola Marymount University, Los
Angeles, California 90045.   EDITOR: Mark D. Morelli.   ADVERTISEMENTS.
CIRCULATION: 200.   MANUSCRIPT SELECTION: Refereed, editorial
board.   REPRINTS: author.   BOOK REVIEWS: 6 reviews, 1-3 pp., signed.
SPECIAL ISSUES: 1/yr.   INDEXED/ABSTRACTED: PhilosI.   TARGET
AUDIENCE: AC.   SAMPLE COPIES: Libraries, individuals.

MJLS aims, first, to promote original research into the methodological
foundations of sciences and disciplines; second, to further interpretive,
historical and critical study of the philosophical, theological, and psychological writings of Bernard Lonergan; and third, to encourage study of
thinkers, past and present, who bring to light the subject of human
consciousness.   Lonergan's revered theology mirrors the tour de force of
modern dialectics; his was the development of a "generalized empirical
method."   This is a self-correcting process of learning which underpins all
philosophical (analytic) techniques.   Contributors naturally follow Lonergan's
labors in their radically polemic view of systems.   At the same time, MJLS
maintains a current flow of debate among authors, giving impetus to
advanced thinking.   The dialogue on analysis resembles that found in Journal
of Mind and Behavior, and Cognition.
  Each issue is a thorough critique of Lonergan's dynamics.   Three major
articles are followed by three to four "Dialogues," including notes and book
reviews.   In an age where philosophical methodology is specialized, MJLS
seeks to unite different approaches toward a holistic model.

184.   Midwest Quarterly.   DATE FOUNDED: 1959.   FREQUENCY: q.
PRICE: $6/yr. institutions.   PUBLISHER: Pittsburg State University,
Pittsburg, Kansas 66762.   EDITOR: James B. Schick.   INDEX.   CIRCULA-
TION: 750.   MANUSCRIPT SELECTION: Refereed, editorial board.
MICROFORMS: UMI.   REPRINTS: UMI.   BOOK REVIEWS: 2-4 reviews, 1-3
pp., signed.   SPECIAL ISSUES: Summer issue.   TARGET AUDIENCE: AC.
SAMPLE COPIES: Libraries, individuals.

Rarely is there a journal dealing with a broad range of subjects for scholars
in general.   MQ meets this need with analytic and speculative articles rather
than through pedantic essays.   Important developments in twentieth century
scholarship are woven into a rich texture of such topics as mathematics,
poetry, psychology, chemistry, biology, history, and music.   These collected
dialogues by academicians help clarify   the vagaries in contemporary
thought, in ways similar to Mankind Quarterly, Journal of Thought and
Freedom.   Within this framework, MQ considers the concept, authority, and
nature of human behavior as the instruments in current research.
  Each issue contains six major articles, five poems, and several critical book
reviews.   This reviewer finds much to recommend MQ to students in the arts
and sciences.

185. Mill Newsletter. DATE FOUNDED: 1965. FREQUENCY: sa. PRICE: free. PUBLISHER: University of Toronto Press, University of Toronto, Toronto, Ontario. EDITORS: John M. Robson, Michael Laine, Bruce L. Kinzer. ADVERTISEMENTS. CIRCULATION: 700. MANUSCRIPT SELECTION: Refereed, editorial board. REPRINTS: publisher. BOOK REVIEWS: 2 reviews, 1-2 pp., signed. INDEXED/ABSTRACTED: PhilosI. TARGET AUDIENCE: AC. SAMPLE COPIES: Libraries, individuals. ACCEPTANCE RATE: 50%.

Utilitarianism in the preserved views of John Stuart Mill (1806-1873) continues in MN. This serial gathers essays in social and legal philosophy having import on ethics, education, religion, and epistemology. By systematically analyzing practical principles of Mill, authors show the complex relations between duty of justice, individual liberty, and moral behavior. Theory and value advance interpretations of Mill's system for general readers. The evidence and assurance of each scholar's position compels readers toward a sympathetic acceptance of issues which may also appear in Free Inquiry, Journal of the History of Ideas and Law and Justice.
   Articles related to Mill's life and thinking appear among book reviews and several announcements about conferences and events. To understand why Mill's philosophy persists, readers are encouraged to peruse issues of MN.

186. Mind. DATE FOUNDED: 1876. FREQUENCY: q. PRICE: $32.50/yr. institutions, $22.50/yr. personal. PUBLISHER: Basil Blackwell Publisher, 108 Cowley Road, Oxford, England 0X4 1JF. EDITOR: D.W. Hamlyn. INDEX. ADVERTISEMENTS. MANUSCRIPT SELECTION: Refereed, editorial board. MICROFORMS: KR. REPRINTS: KR. BOOK REVIEWS: 12 reviews, 1-2 pp., signed. INDEXED/ABSTRACTED: PhilosI. TARGET AUDIENCE: AC. SAMPLE COPIES: Libraries. ACCEPTANCE RATE: 12%.

For over a century Mind has been the recognized leader of Anglo-Saxon traditions in philosophy. Articles demonstrate the kind of fresh thinking that rarely passes through scholarly journals. Informative and readable, Mind is strikingly vocal on propositions, inductive and deductive, that concern epistemology, psychology, politics, morality and history. In a strong sense it follows the classic standard of intellectual honesty and rigor, and puts readers in touch with exigent trends. Contributors are mainly polemicists who are widely known. The intensity of discussion alone parallels the arguments of Canadian Journal of Philosophy, Journal of Philosophy, Inquiry and Revue Internationale de Philosophie.
   Mind contains four leading articles and six discussion articles. The book reviews and list of books received usually follow some notices and occasional editorials. Mind has a strong claim in the role of philosophy education.

187. Modern Schoolman. DATE FOUNDED: 1925. FREQUENCY: q. PRICE: $26/yr. institutions. PUBLISHER: College of Philosophy and Letters, Saint Louis University, 3700 West Pine Boulevard, Saint Louis, Missouri 63108. EDITOR: John L. Treloar. INDEX. ADVERTISEMENTS. CIRCULATION: 1,000. MANUSCRIPT SELECTION: Refereed, editorial board. BOOK REVIEWS: 20-30 reviews, 1-2 pp., signed. INDEXED/ABSTRACTED: CathI, CurrContAH, PhilosI, RBibPhil. TARGET AUDIENCE: AC. SAMPLE COPIES: Libraries. ACCEPTANCE RATE: 27%.

MS publishes original and scholarly contributions in all fields of philosophy including aesthetics, ethics, religion, history, law, and anthropology. Meaning and value in Western thought represent the general orientation, wherein fundamental questions about knowledge are surveyed. This international library of topics accepts historical examinations of major thinkers (Sartre, Saint Augustine) as well as established axioms. The strength of MS lies in its clarity, simplicity, and ability to prod one closer to reading ideals in theory and practice. Authors are primarily scholars. While articles are pragmatic, the tendency for analytic perspectives closely identifies with articles in Journal of Critical Analysis and Process Studies.

A current issue contains three articles and book reviews. Noteworthy is that the selection of books for review provides awareness of publications in foreign languages.

188. Monist. DATE FOUNDED: 1888. (first issue, 1890). FREQUENCY: q. PRICE: $24/yr. institutions, $15/yr. personal. PUBLISHER: Hegler Institute, Box 600, La Salle, Illinois 61301. EDITOR: John Hospers. INDEX. ADVERTISEMENTS. CIRCULATION: 2,000. MANUSCRIPT SELECTION: Refereed, editorial board. MICROFORMS: UMI. REPRINTS: author. BOOK REVIEWS: 9-10 reviews, 500 words, signed. SPECIAL ISSUES: Occasional. INDEXED/ABSTRACTED: PhilosI. TARGET AUDIENCE: AC. SAMPLE COPIES: Libraries.

Monist joins the charter of celebrated periodicals devoted primarily to general philosophical inquiry. Initiated by Paul Carus, also then editor for Open Court Publishing Company, Monist has grown to become a recognized forum for independent views. Articles are substantial reviews of logic, metaphysics, existentialism, phenomenology, and extend to socio-political areas. The rare collaboration among branches of philosophy results in an in-depth study of early and modern theorization. Contributors draw from academic circles of prominence. Since debate is on occasion presented between opposing views, Monist closely shares the aims of Iyyun, Nous, and Philosophy and Rhetoric.

A typical issue of Monist feature a thematic topic and ten original articles. Following this, abstracts of relevant books are written by the book authors themselves. A list of forthcoming issues and list of books received keep readers informed of key issues. Monist most certainly makes a suitable addition to a scholar's library.

189. Morality in Media Newsletter. DATE FOUNDED: 1962. TITLE CHANGES: Operation Yorkville Newsletter (1962-1968). FREQUENCY: 8/yr. PRICE: $5/yr. institutions. PUBLISHER: Morality in Media, Incorporated, 475 Riverside Drive, New York, New York 10115. EDITOR: Evelyn Dukovic. ILLUSTRATIONS. CIRCULATION: 51,000. REPRINTS: publisher. TARGET AUDIENCE: GP. SAMPLE COPIES: Libraries, individuals.

MMN strikes out at the reprehensible cases of immorality in popular or commercial media. Pornography, obscenity, and aggressive acts of violence that stir political controversy wind up in the newsletter. In one sense MMN is a watchdog for the rapid abatement of lewd conduct. In another sense, the infiltration of "morality" into public networks threatens the very existence of freedom of speech. Both viewpoints are possible. Regular columnists apparently call for stern action by enforcement agencies. The broadcasting and international importation of indecency is as much a matter for MMN as it is for Freedom and Dignity.

Each newsletter dazzles with headline after headline, insinuating that America's media are vulgar. News clips, short columns, and notices regarding the association's lobbying efforts give the impression that the fight has only begun.

190. Movement Newspaper. DATE FOUNDED: 1974. FREQUENCY: m. PRICE: $15/yr. institutions. PUBLISHER: Movement of Spiritual Inner Awareness, P.O. Box 3935, Los Angeles, California 90051. EDITOR: Anja Leigh Russell. ILLUSTRATIONS. ADVERTISEMENTS. CIRCULATION: 6,500. MANUSCRIPT SELECTION: Editor. REPRINTS: author. BOOK REVIEWS: 2 reviews, 1-3 pp. TARGET AUDIENCE: GP. SAMPLE COPIES: Libraries, individuals.

Self-growth journals tend toward a subject matter that is frequently holistic. So might be the case with MN. This is a "new age" paper, full of uplifting articles on science fiction, personal awareness, transformational politics, cosmology, and soft religion. MN presents a narrative beginning as philosophy but which ends up as reflection of current trends in mysticism. Exclusive interviews with celebrities, swamis, and pop philosophers shape this Rolling Stones-type format into more of a mind- altering journey through sex, love, and movement expression. MN reaches a wide readership by its journalistic intention to simply entertain the public. This being the obvious goal, MN may be compared to the Kabbalist and Beacon.

Every issue moves through a spectrum of current human interest stories, from Ted Neely who played Jesus in "Jesus Christ Superstar," to inner vibrations of spiritual enhancement. The only thing that seemingly keeps MN from folding is that it does serve a useful purpose in philosophy; it parodies the esotericism in most scholarship.

191. National Forum: Phi Kappa Phi Journal. DATE FOUNDED: 1915. TITLE CHANGES: Phi Kappa Phi Journal (1915-1978). FREQUENCY: q. PRICE: $12.50/yr. institutions, $10/yr. personal. PUBLISHER: Honor Society of Phi Kappa Phi, P.O. Box 16000, Louisiana State University, Baton Rouge, Louisiana 70893. EDITOR: Stephen W. White. ILLUSTRATIONS. INDEX. CIRCULATION: 9,000. MANUSCRIPT SELECTION: Refereed, editorial board. MICROFORMS: UMI. REPRINTS: author. BOOK REVIEWS: 10-20 reviews, 1-3 pp., signed. INDEXED/ ABSTRACTED: CIJE, MC, PAIS, PhilosI, SocAb. TARGET AUDIENCE: AC, GP, SP. ACCEPTANCE RATE: 25%.

NF functions as a major forum dedicated to informing public opinion on prominent issues of the day. The journal and Phi Kappa Phi are a focal point for critical discussion on policies and trends in education, business, technology, medicine, government, law, science, art, literature, and a number of other interdisciplinary areas. Recently NF became available to the general public, thereby refining its thoughts for a wider group of professionals. Contributors are government service officials, members of the business community, and distinguished professors. Leading experts debate on world and domestic issues, from social to intellectual movements, arising from an objective base. Articles lend perspective on the same topics covered by Humanities in Society, Creativity and Innovation Network, and Free Inquiry.

A typical issue follows a central theme through thirteen short articles. Other articles and a section on "Educational Dilemmas of the 80's" string together a collection of prevalent issues. Finally, several poems are followed by book reviews. NF definitely conveys the scientific acumen so needed by philosophers in research.

192.   Nature and System: Philosophical Studies of Natural and Artificial Systems. DATE FOUNDED: 1979. FREQUENCY: q. PRICE: $14.50/yr. institutions. PUBLISHER: Nature and System, Incorporated, P.O. Box 3368, Tucson, Arizona 85722. EDITOR: Joseph L. Esposito. INDEX. ADVERTISEMENTS. CIRCULATION: 550. MANUSCRIPT SELECTION: Refereed, editorial board. REPRINTS: author. BOOK REVIEWS: 2-3 reviews, 1-2 pp., signed. INDEXED/ABSTRACTED: PhilosI. TARGET AUDIENCE: AC. SAMPLE COPIES: Libraries. ACCEPTANCE RATE: 25%.

NS is an international journal seeking to continue the theoretical spirit of philosophy of nature within a contemporary scientific context. Editors encourage the reflective investigation of philosophy as well as creative synthesis of new ideas and models. Articles also advance bold conjectures not yet well-digested in the scientific community. Authors are primarily specialists and scholars. The methodological studies harbor a sense of evolutionism, as many papers identify concepts in biology, artificial intelligence, cybernetics, semiotics, heredity, and social paradigms. Themes appear on causation, rationalism, and such individual philosophers as Hegel, Kant, Thomas and Darwin. NS' consideration of scientific problems places it among Creation/Evolution, Explorations in Knowledge and British Journal for the Philosophy of Science.
   A typical issue includes five to seven original papers geared toward "theoretical and methodological" studies. Book reviews are followed by an annual survey of science periodicals.

193.   New Ideas in Psychology. DATE FOUNDED: 1983. FREQUENCY: 3/yr. PRICE: $65/yr. institutions. PUBLISHER: Pergamon Press, Fairview Park, Elmsford, New York 10523. EDITORS: Richard Kitchener, Pierre Moessinger, John Broughton. ILLUSTRATIONS. INDEX. ADVERTISEMENTS. MANUSCRIPT SELECTION: Refereed, editorial board. REPRINTS: author. BOOK REVIEWS: 1-2 reviews, 2 pp., signed. INDEXED/ABSTRACTED: PsyAb. TARGET AUDIENCE: AC, SP. SAMPLE COPIES: Libraries, individuals. ACCEPTANCE RATE: 10%.

NIP reflects the growing dissatisfaction with fragmentation in theoretical psychology. Articles aim to integrate these fragmented ideas through new and more daring hypotheses. Particular emphasis is placed on an interdisciplinary discussion; editors view NIP as a vehicle for a rapprochement between traditions of thought that currently ignore each other. Fresh ideas may emerge from research in philosophy, from heuristic insights, or from debates and comments on conceptual problems in nearly any field of interest. This departure from usual theorizing is a start toward promising directions in uncharted territory. To the extent that NIP questions old beliefs, the outcome can only be beneficial. Contributors are mainly psychologists but may well include philosophers. Like Behaviorism, NIP welcomes diversity among philo-psychological perspectives.

Each issue contains specifically four sections. First, one to two articles appear in "How New Ideas Develop." Second, two articles appear in "Exploratory Theorizing." Third, one creative article appears in "Tentative Ideas." Fourth, two interviews feature a dialogue with well-known leaders of theoretical systems. Book reviews and editorials are at the back.

194. New Scholar. DATE FOUNDED: 1969. FREQUENCY: sa. PRICE: $32/yr. institutions, $12/yr. personal. PUBLISHER: South Hall 4607, University of California, Santa Barbara, California 93106. EDITOR: Vernon Kjonegaard. ILLUSTRATIONS. INDEX. ADVERTISEMENTS. CIRCULATION: 1,000. MANUSCRIPT SELECTION: Refereed, editorial board. MICROFORMS: UMI. REPRINTS: author. BOOK REVIEWS: 50 reviews, 1-2 pp., signed. SPECIAL ISSUES: Occasional. INDEXED/ ABSTRACTED: ABC, ChiPerI, HistAb, PsyAb, SocAb. TARGET AUDIENCE: AC. SAMPLE COPIES: Libraries. ACCEPTANCE RATE: 20%.

NS provides a multidisciplinary forum for scholars seeking a fuller understanding of the unique human condition and experience in the Americas. Articles focus on social sciences and humanities, from research to the impact of the past and contemporary events on anthropology, literary criticism, history, sociology, and psychology. Creativity shown in new methodology and interpretation adds special significance to the essays. Contributors are from scholarly disciplines and may well be seen writing for Modern Schoolman and Monist. Besides the edifying reviews, NS offers reports on major developments within areas of learning.
A typical issue contains eight to ten major articles and book reviews, including news, notes and announcements.

195. New Scholasticism. DATE FOUNDED: 1927. FREQUENCY: q. PRICE: $17/yr. institutions. PUBLISHER: Charles F. Furst, Company, 109 Market Place, Baltimore, Maryland 21202. EDITOR: Ralph M. McInerny. INDEX. ADVERTISEMENTS. CIRCULATION: 2,500. MANUSCRIPT SELECTION: Refereed, editorial board. BOOK REVIEWS: 4 reviews, 1-3 pp., signed. SPECIAL ISSUES: Occasional. INDEXED/ ABSTRACTED: PhilosI. TARGET AUDIENCE: AC. ACCEPTANCE RATE: 2%.

The long-awaited collection of philosophy essays on twentieth century scholarship is available in NS. This periodical holds an important place in the perception of modern trends, theory formation, and dynamic conflicts revealed in myths and interdisciplinary study. NS seeks the roots of European and Western experience, an enlightening compendium that foreshadows the development in specialist philosophy as well as nonspecialist professions. Articles are written by academicians and explore universal principles of morality, ethics, politics, religion, and logic. Problems and issues that surround these principles are grounded in objective debate. NS resembles the New Scholar and Monist in its detailed and illuminating examples of contemporary questions.

196. New Titles in Bioethics. DATE FOUNDED: 1975. FREQUENCY: m. PRICE: $10/yr. institutions. PUBLISHER: Center for Bioethics Library, Kennedy Institute of Ethics, Georgetown University, Washington D.C. 20057. EDITOR: Betsy Walkup. INDEX. CIRCULATION: 200. REPRINTS: publisher.

TARGET AUDIENCE: AC, SP. SAMPLE COPIES: Libraries, individuals.

NTB is a research tool for the retrieval of government documents, pamphlets, serial titles, and audiovisual aids compiled by the Center for Bioethics Library of the Kennedy Institute. This information project essentially catalogs the nation's newest publications in bioethics by consulting many bibliographic services including American Book Publishing Record, Cumulative Book Index, and Monthly Catalog of US Government Publications. As acquisitions are recorded, they are categorized according to a specific classification scheme. NTB also provides a regular up-to-date survey of discrete and out-of-print publications, or will identify major repositories around the United States. A supplement to Journal of Bioethics and Hastings Center Report, NTB provides sufficient annotation for the reader to make quick and efficient decisions.

Issues of NTB contain five to six pages with books and documents classified in numerical sequence. Regretfully, individual issues do not reprint the classification scheme and this forces readers to keep a copy of it nearby.

197. New World News. DATE FOUNDED: 1952. TITLE CHANGES: MRA Information Service (1952-1973). FREQUENCY: sa. PRICE: $20/yr. institutions. PUBLISHER: Good Road Limited, 12 Palace Street, London SW1E SJF, England. EDITORS: Kenneth Noble, Mary Lean. ILLUSTRATIONS. INDEX. CIRCULATION: 3,000. MANUSCRIPT SELECTION: Refereed, editorial board. REPRINTS: publisher. TARGET AUDIENCE: GP. SAMPLE COPIES: Libraries, individuals.

NWN is devoted primarily to reporting news of the application and outreach of social morality. Articles have a serious theoretical and philosophical angle, decrying social events in the light of religious and ethical principles. Indoctrinative columns on spiritual freedom attack different professional establishments without the vehemence found in Morality in Media, Movement Newspaper and Freedom. Rather, NWN represents a thoughtful exposition in moral judgment, uncomplicated by political dogma. Articles are written by regular columnists, scholars, and laymen. General issues link political theory to education and practice, and at the same time support current efforts toward social order.

A typical issue is barely eight pages long. Four or so feature stories are followed by announcements, editorials, and several detailed photos. One gets the impression that NWN is more a plea for cultural revolution.

198. Notre Dame Journal of Formal Logic. DATE FOUNDED: 1960. FREQUENCY: q. PRICE: $35/yr. institutions, $20/yr. personal. PUBLISH-ER: University of Notre Dame, Notre Dame, Indiana 46556. EDITORS: Penelope Maddy, Mark E. Nadel, Ernest LePore. INDEX. ADVERTISE-MENTS. CIRCULATION: 750. MANUSCRIPT SELECTION: Refereed, editorial board. REPRINTS: author. SPECIAL ISSUES: Occasional. INDEXED/ABSTRACTED: PhilosI, ZentMath. TARGET AUDIENCE: AC. SAMPLE COPIES: Libraries, individuals. ACCEPTANCE RATE: 35%.

NDJFL raises unresolved, controversial debates in the philosophy of logic. Concepts and problems concerning all areas of mathematics, history of logic and semantics, and methodology serve to define this field of enquiry. Articles by distinguished scholars attempt to clarify traditionally ambiguous questions on reference, natural language, perceptual discrimination, and theoretical rationalism. Analytic discourse is replete with technical jargon and may be too advanced for beginning students. Nonetheless, NDJFL clearly articulates methods of logic better than Synthese and Reports on Mathematical Logic simply because of its central emphasis on exploratory (tentative) models.

Each issue provides eleven stimulating articles, presented in a readable format. Arguments are well motivated and generally avoid pedantry.

199. Nous. DATE FOUNDED: 1967. FREQUENCY: q. PRICE: $32/yr. institutions, $16/yr. personal. PUBLISHER: Nous Publications, Department of Philosophy, Indiana University, Bloomington, Indiana 47405. EDITOR: Hector-Neri Castaneda. ILLUSTRATIONS. INDEX. ADVERTISEMENTS. CIRCULATION: 1,100. MANUSCRIPT SELECTION: Refereed, editorial board. MICROFORMS: UMI. REPRINTS: author. BOOK REVIEWS: 7 reviews, 2-4 pp., signed. SPECIAL ISSUES: Occasional. INDEXED/AB-STRACTED: ArtHumCitI, LLBA, PhilosI. TARGET AUDIENCE: AC. SAMPLE COPIES:Libraries. ACCEPTANCE RATE: 20%.

Nous publishes quality essays, brief discussions and symposia on philosophical problems concerning mind, language, and political and social sciences. Articles are theoretical in nature and draw on conventional methods of synthetic argument. Nous will also treat leading metaphysical issues relating to modal logic, percpetion and intentionality. Metacritical essays top the criticisms found in Metaphilosophy and Bulletin de la Societe. Its comparatively high ratio of idealistic assertion to dogma contributes to the pursuasive scholarship of discussions.

A typical issue of Nous features four to five original articles or abstracts followed by critical reviews and announcements. One outstanding advantage of Nous is its commitment to address applied as well as speculative areas of interest.

200. Objectivist Forum. DATE FOUNDED: 1980. FREQUENCY: 6/yr. Price: $20/yr. institutions. PUBLISHER: Box 5311, FDR Station, New York, New York 10150. EDITOR: Harry Binswanger. MANUSCRIPT SELECTION: Editor. REPRINTS: publisher. BOOK REVIEWS: 2 reviews, 1-5 pp., signed. TARGET AUDIENCE: GP. ACCEPTANCE RATE: 5%.

OF is published by and for advocates of "objectivism," the philosophy of Ayn Rand. Articles deliberately further the objectivist orientation as it evolved from fictional portrayals of capitalistic powers and rugged individualism. Editor Harry Binswanger faces the challenge to continue Rand's enterprise of radical philosophy now that Rand herself has died. OF may accomplish this goal; short, moving papers put to rest the illusory concepts of justice, economy, education and philosophy. Even criticism of psychology (e.g., Behaviorism) strips away the many disguises of intellectualism. While topics vary, the fundamental articulation is that true skepticism is reached beneath the cover of "fallibility." Binswanger and his consulting editor Peikoff write most of the articles, although unsolicited papers are welcome.

A typical issue features three to four short discussions which translate some current event into the language of objectivism. While Randian philosophy tends to conjur up impressions of societal recalcitrance, OF does succeed in pinning down cultural myths as cleverly as Freedom.

201. <u>Odense University Studies in Philosophy</u>. DATE FOUNDED: 1972. FREQUENCY: q. PUBLISHER: Odense University Press, Pjentedamsgae 36, DK-5000 Odense, Denmark. ILLUSTRATIONS. INDEX. MANUSCRIPT SELECTION: Refereed, editorial board. REPRINTS: publisher. TARGET AUDIENCE: AC.

202. <u>Omega: Journal of Death and Dying</u>. DATE FOUNDED: 1969. FREQUENCY: q. PRICE: $51/yr. institutions, $27/yr. personal. PUBLISH-ER: Baywood Publishing Company, 120 Marine Street, Box D, Farmingdale, New York 11735. EDITOR: Robert J. Kastenbaum. INDEX. ADVER-TISEMENTS. REPRINTS: author. INDEXED/ABSTRACTED: AbSocW, BIHEP, EM, PsyAb, SocAb. TARGET AUDIENCE: AC, SP. SAMPLE COPIES: Libraries, individuals. ACCEPTANCE RATE: 50%.

<u>Omega</u> draws significant contributions from such diverse fields as psychology, sociology, law, anthropology, medicine, education, history and literature. It emerges as the most advanced forum to achieve international recognition. Every aspect of this universal subject is explored, from terminal illness and suicide to violence, disaster and attitudes about bereavement and grief. <u>Omega</u> provides a reliable guide for clinicians, health professionals and philosophers. Writings shed a responsible and relevant light upon vitally important experiences in the life of youngsters, adults and elderly. <u>Omega</u> serves as a companion to <u>Death and Dying A to Z</u> and <u>Dreamworks</u>.
A normal issue contains ten or eleven lengthy articles and occasional notes. <u>Omega</u>'s focus on the transcending process of death is must reading for biomedical philosophers who face these issues in ethical decisions.

203. <u>One Earth</u>. FREQUENCY: bm. PRICE: 6 Pounds/yr. institutions. PUBLISHER: Findhorn Publications, Findhorn Foundation, The Park Forres, Scotland, V 36 0TZ. EDITOR: Mary Inglis. ILLUSTRATIONS: INDEX. ADVERTISEMENTS. CIRCULATION: 3,500. MANUSCRIPT SELECTION: Refereed, editorial board. REPRINTS: publisher. BOOK REVIEWS: 4-5 reviews, 1-3 pp., signed. SPECIAL ISSUES: Occasional. TARGET AUDIENCE: AC, GP. SAMPLE COPIES: Libraries.

<u>OE</u> brings perspectives from people around the world exploring the practice of "New Age" consciousness in a wide variety of fields. Most articles revolve around the life and experience of the Findhorn community. What draws scholars out of the ivory towers and into the rural community life? <u>OE</u> sensitively observes this transition in its inspirational articles on ecology, spiritualism, morality, and communal living. Goals of Findhorn communities are simple, humanistic, and generally rattle the conventions of modern society. Like <u>Man and World</u>, <u>OE</u> seeks a conservative solution to serious economic, health and religious problems. It refrains, though, from doctrines, manifestos, and pontificated resolutions.
The Findhorn magazine publishes about six original articles and book reviews per issue. News and notes and a section called "Globetrotter" announce the courageous projects of Findhorn followers.

204. <u>Owl of Minerva</u>. DATE FOUNDED: 1969. FREQUENCY: sa. PRICE: $12/yr. institutions, $10/yr. personal. PUBLISHER: Philosophy Department, Villanova University, Villanova, Pennsylvania 19085. EDITOR: Lawrence S.

Stepelevich. ILLUSTRATIONS. INDEX. ADVERTISEMENTS. CIRCULA-TION: 450. MANUSCRIPT SELECTION: Refereed, editorial board. MICROFORMS: Publisher. REPRINTS: author. BOOK REVIEWS: 4 reviews, 1-3 pp., signed. INDEXED/ABSTRACTED: PhilosI. TARGET AUDIENCE: AC.

OM is the official voice of the Hegel Society of America. Hegelianism conveys the proverbial messages of Christian philosophy as well as the critical acumen of the Enlightenment era. Hegel's reconciliation of opposing trends is visible in the depth and sincerity of articles on metaphysics, epistemology, and history. The dialectical method, theoretically transformed by Hegel, lays the basic foundation for most arguments. To those who are already familiar with Hegel's works, OM succeeds in making issues clearer. For those unfamiliar with Hegel, the translations into nonpolemical pros offer introduction. What may be lacking, however, is clear proof that Hegelianism comports to the needs of modern philosophy. Still, OM comprehends this particular philosopher in greater analysis than History and Theory.
A typical issue presents one short article and is predominately book reviews. Announcements of the Society's affairs keeps the interested reader informed of valuable opportunities to enhance Hegelian studies.

205. Oxford Literary Review. DATE FOUNDED: 1975. FREQUENCY: sa. PRICE: $18/yr. institutions, $10/yr. personal. PUBLISHER: Department of English, the University, Southhampton SO9 5NH, England. EDITORS: Geoff Bennington, Nick Royle, Ann Wordsworth, Robert Young. INDEX. ADVERTISEMENTS. CIRCULATION: 1,000. REPRINTS: author. BOOK REVIEWS: 2 reviews, 5-8 pp., signed. SPECIAL ISSUES: Occasional. INDEXED/ABSTRACTED: API, HumI. TARGET AUDIENCE: AC. SAMPLE COPIES: Libraries. ACCEPTANCE RATE: 15%.

OLR is broadly defined as a theoretical survey of readings about the post-structuralism movement in literature. Sophisticated criticism probes the need to formulate a different view of what should be involved in liter-ary education. This includes clarification of ideology, politics, textual analysis, and a speculative interest in linguistic practices. OLR editors resent being called "intellectual terrorists" because the status of their influence depends on how carefully readers understand post-structuralism. Authors, mostly scholars, generally conceive structuralism as a form of textual expression. In this sense, OLR turns toward general philosophical questions much as do Critical Inquiry and CLIO.
A typical issue contains five major articles, two book reviews, news and editorials. In a strange sense, OLR monitors the unrestrained vagaries in philosophical writing that other disciplines complain about.

206. Pacific Philosophical Quarterly. DATE FOUNDED: 1919. TITLE CHANGES: Personalist (1919-1980). FREQUENCY: q. PRICE: $30/yr. institutions, $10/yr. personal. PUBLISHER: School of Philosophy, University of Southern California, Los Angeles, California 90007. EDITORS: Harty Field, Barbara Herman, Brian Loar, Miles Morgan. ILLUSTRATIONS. INDEX. ADVERTISEMENTS. MANUSCRIPT SELECTION: Refereed, editorial board. REPRINTS: author. INDEXED/ABSTRACTED: PhilosI. TARGET AUDIENCE: AC. SAMPLE COPIES: Libraries.

The longstanding influence of Personalist, now PPQ, continues to offer theoretical essays on human character and behavior, and the circumstances inherently involved. Metacritical questions point out serious deficiencies and obscurities in modern alternatives to tradition. Polemical articles generate considerable controversy among the broad-ranging statements of intellectual thinkers, from Descartes to Hegel. Authors are mostly eminent scholars from a variety of international universities. In their serious and perceptive style, contributors establish a more productive basis for the discussion of man's values and possibilites as a rational creature than found in Journal of Mind and Behavior. However, like Mind, PPQ is written in a pleasing style, especially moving for students.

Each issue of PPQ publishes nine original articles and on occasion a special editorial.

207. Pathway to God. DATE FOUNDED: 1965. FREQUENCY: q. PRICE: 8 Rupees/yr. institutions. PUBLISHER: Academy of Comparative Philosophy and Religion. Belgaum Post: Hindwadi, Belgaum: Pin 590011 Karnataka State, India. EDITOR: K.D. Tangod. ADVERTISEMENTS. CIRCULATION: 650. MANUSCRIPT SELECTION: Refereed, editorial board. REPRINTS: publisher. BOOK REVIEWS: 3 reviews, 1-2 pp. TARGET AUDIENCE: GP. SAMPLE COPIES: Libraries.

208. Philosopher's Index. DATE FOUNDED: 1967. FREQUENCY: q. PRICE: $82/yr. institutions, $40/yr. personal. PUBLISHER: Bowling Green State University, Bowling Green, Ohio 43403. EDITOR: Richard H. Lineback. INDEX. TARGET AUDIENCE: AC. SAMPLE COPIES: Libraries.

This up-to-date index of articles from more than 300 international philosophy and interdisciplinary journals and books significantly covers the state-of-the-art progress. PI contains alphabetical listings by author and subject of original scholarly material, including bibliographies, biographies, translations, dissertations and anthologies received in the months prior to their publication. For years, PI has been the primary research tool in philosophic study, used by students and professionals alike. Special editions such as The Philosopher's Index: A Retrospective Index to U.S. Periodicals from 1940 and The Philosopher's Index: A Retrospective Index to non-U.S. English Language Publications from 1940 greatly enhance the availability of current works for the philosophical community.

Each issue provides subject and author indexes with abstracts. Selected journals in PI are in English, French, German, Spanish and Italian.

209. Philosophia (Athens). DATE FOUNDED: 1970. FREQUENCY: a. PRICE: $20/yr. institutions. PUBLISHER: Academy of Athens, Anagnostopoulou 14, Athens 136, Greece. EDITOR: Research Center for Greek Philosophy at the Academy of Athens. CIRCULATION: 500. MANUSCRIPT SELECTION: Refereed, editorial board. REPRINTS: author. BOOK REVIEWS: 10-15 reviews, 1-4 pp., signed. SPECIAL ISSUES: Occasional. INDEXED/ABSTRACTED: BulSig, PhilosI. TARGET AUDIENCE: AC. SAMPLE COPIES: Libraries. ACCEPTANCE RATE: 75%.

Philosophia makes its departure from the systematic philosophies of Greek history. Topics ranging from epistemology and morality to cosmology and Hellenic culture explore the novel intellectual methods that developed during the period. Generally known for its advances, Philosophia discovers the Greek Enlightenment through its historical , doctrines and theories. Substance, body, and soul are treated in both expository and evaluative styles, achieving the standards found in Dionysius and Journal of Hellenic Studies. Contributors are mainly specialists in Greek philosophy. Their essays, intense and thorough, translate the knowledge of the Academy of Athens into a series of well-researched arguments.

Each issue of Philosophia is largely in Greek but will include English papers. Annual editions compile twenty major articles and thirteen book reviews, plus news and notes about the Academy. Serious students of Plato, Aristotle, and Greek philosophy would welcome this journal.

210. Philosophia: A Philosophical Quarterly of Israel. DATE FOUNDED: 1971. FREQUENCY: q. PRICE: $18/yr. institutions. PUBLISHER: Bar-Ilan University, University Press, Ramat-Gan 52100, Israel. EDITOR: Asa Kasher. ILLUSTRATIONS. INDEX. ADVERTISEMENTS. CIRCULATION: 1,000. MANUSCRIPT SELECTION: Refereed, editorial board. REPRINTS: author. BOOK REVIEWS: 10 reviews, 1-4 pp., signed. SPECIAL ISSUES: Occasional. INDEXED/ABSTRACTED: PhilosI. TARGET AUDIENCE: AC. SAMPLE COPIES: Libraries, individuals. ACCEPTANCE RATE: 14%.

PPQI publishes analytic philosophy in the broadest sense. Articles, critical studies and reviews cover all fields of philosophy from ethics to epistemology, and analyze the structure and implications to establish the relevancy between natural and social sciences. Trained logicians rarely turn their attention to conceptually global interests as appear in PPQI. Arguments flourish with a special mixture of lucidity and elegance. These contributors are generally scholars from international circles of the philosophical community. Criticism of social theory thus stimulates discussion on ontology, free will, artificial intelligence, and utilitarian traditions. Like Iyyun, Dialogue and Diafora, PPQI seeks the synthesis of fundamental logic and pertinent theories open to debate.

A typical issue publishes six original essays and several book reviews. The richness and clarity of PPQI lends itself to understanding complex interpretations of formal logic.

211. Philosophia Mathematics. DATE FOUNDED: 1964. FREQUENCY: a. PRICE: $20/yr. institutions. PUBLISHER: Paideia Press, P.O. Box 8361, Norfolk, Virginia 23503. EDITOR: J. Fang. ILLUSTRATIONS. ADVERTISEMENTS. CIRCULATION: 500. MANUSCRIPT SELECTION: Refereed, editorial board. REPRINTS: author. BOOK REVIEWS: 1-5 reviews, 2 pp., signed. INDEXED/ABSTRACTED: MathR, PhilosI. TARGET AUDIENCE: AC. SAMPLE COPIES: Libraries, individuals. ACCEPTANCE RATE: 60%.

PM broadly combs the landscape of mathematical studies beyond traditional topics in logic and theory construction. Here, mathematics is viewed as an emerging sociologic discipline with relevant interests in history, education and epistemology. Essays by prominent philosophers look at the world of teachers who enter in political scholarly dialogue. PM radically departs from

Studia Logica or Journal of Philosophical Logic by its re-direction toward current identity problems in the analytic field.

PM experiences a shortage of papers because of its atypical approach to mathematics. Still, each issue manages to publish several insightful papers on often ignored matters in the field of mathematics.

212. Philosophica. DATE FOUNDED: 1963. TITLE CHANGES: Studia Philosophica Gandensia (1963-1970). FREQUENCY: sa. PRICE: $10/yr. institutions. PUBLISHER: Blandijnberg 2, B-9000 Gent, Belgium. EDITOR: Leo Apostel. ILLUSTRATIONS. ADVERTISEMENTS. CIRCULATION: 300. MANUSCRIPT SELECTION: Refereed, editorial board. REPRINTS: author. BOOK REVIEWS: 4 reviews, 1-2 pp., signed. INDEXED/ABSTRACTED: PhilosI. TARGET AUDIENCE: AC. SAMPLE COPIES: Libraries. ACCEPTANCE RATE: 25%.

Volumes of Philosophica are thematic. Philosophically relevant essays scan the definition and problems of twentieth century reasoning, methodology and philosophy of science. Critical account is given of realism, rationalism, and new perspectives in Belgian culture. Philosophica is a standard in treatments of European trends, from dialectics to hermeneutics. Contributions from scholars follow the rigor of "objective inquiry," by embodying a less liberal approach than taken by Filosofia and Grazer Philosophische. The paucity of reviews on major political movements may alter, subtly, the attraction of a broad-ranging readership.

The majority of articles are invited. Volume editors decide on appropriate topics in ethics, metaphysics, epistemology and aesthetics.

213. Philosophical Books. DATE FOUNDED: 1960. FREQUENCY: q. PRICE: $49.95/yr. institutions, $26.95/yr. personal. PUBLISHER: Basil Blackwell Publisher Limited, 108 Cowley Road, Oxford 0X4 1JF, England. EDITOR: M.A. Stewart. ADVERTISEMENTS. BOOK REVIEWS: 28-40 reviews, 2-6 pp., signed. SPECIAL ISSUES: Occasional. INDEXED/ABSTRACTED: PhilosI. TARGET AUDIENCE: AC. SAMPLE COPIES: Libraries.

PB generally compiles several contrasting reviews of recent books of most interest to modern philosophers. Profiles in theory and analysis are brought to bear upon the examined books in aesthetics, epistemology, ethics, religion, law, history, semantics, and logic. PB meets the need for prompt scholarly reviews and includes regular discussion where authors of selected titles engage in active reprisals. Like Bibliographie de la Philosophie and Erfahrungswiss Blatter, PB surveys as many titles as possible, written by foremost specialists in different philosophical areas. It would be difficult to exaggerate the value of these abstracts for the serious research professional.

A typical issue contains one lengthy discussion paper, eleven reviews, and roughly eighteen reviews of the latest publications. News and notes at the back supplement this information.

214. Philosophical Forum. DATE FOUNDED: 1969. FREQUENCY: q. PRICE: $30/yr. institutions, $12/yr. personal. PUBLISHER: Boston University, Station 247, Boston, Massachusetts 02215. EDITOR: Marx W. Wartofsky. ILLUSTRATIONS. INDEX. ADVERTISEMENTS. CIRCULATION:

2,500. MANUSCRIPT SELECTION: Refereed, editorial board. REPRINTS: author. SPECIAL ISSUES: 1/yr. INDEXED/ABSTRACTED: PhilosI. TARGET AUDIENCE: AC, GP. SAMPLE COPIES: Libraries.

PF is distinguished by its philosophical breadth of topics from humanistic pluralism to the openness of new themes and styles in applied studies. Critique and analysis of exegetical problems cover primarily religion and education. Historical problems are combined with the fresh and calculated perspectives of current thought. PF is intended for an English- speaking readership, but welcomes contributions from academicians from around the world. Essays avoid the sweeping generalizations at times apparent in Free Inquiry. Rather, arguments revolve around the same boundaries of classical theory as American Philosophical Quarterly and Monist.
  Regular and special issues contain six to ten original papers followed by book reviews. Special themes on economics, sociobiology and philosophy of women provide the basis for exploratory theories of human behavior.

215. Philosophical Inquiry. DATE FOUNDED: 1978. FREQUENCY: q. PRICE: $14/yr. institutions. PUBLISHER: P.O. Box 825, C.P. Athens, Greece. EDITOR: D.Z. Andriopoulos. ADVERTISEMENTS. CIRCULATION: 1,050. MANUSCRIPT SELECTION: Refereed, editorial board. MICROFORM: Publisher. BOOK REVIEWS: 2 reviews, 1-2 pp., signed. SPECIAL ISSUES: Occasional. INDEXED/ABSTRACTED: PhilosI. TARGET AUDIENCE: AC. SAMPLE COPIES: Libraries, individuals.

In contrast to those journals which only focus on introductory matters, PJ publishes a survey of prudentially important topics for scholars of all fields. New essays are reconciling, pruning, and elaborating the interpretation in medieval, analytic, aesthetic, and epistemiologic branches. Issues of current and seminal concern contain original, objective criticism, creating a link between history and today's central thoughts. Articles are written largely by scholars who research the many inadequacies in investigations of human behavior. The substantive dealings in logic, though without technical jargon, parallel the contents of Metaphilosophy and Pacific Philosophical Quarterly.
  Each issue is an informative study in rational belief systems. Five to seven major articles, book reviews, and occasional editorials give almost endless attention to detail.

216. Philosophical Investigations. DATE FOUNDED: 1978. FREQUENCY: q. PRICE: $49.50/yr. institutions, $24.50/yr. personal. PUBLISHER: Basil Blackwell Publisher Limited, 108 Cowley Road, Oxford OX4 1JF, England. EDITOR: D.Z. Phillips. INDEX. MANUSCRIPT SELECTION: Refereed, editorial board. REPRINTS: author. BOOK REVIEWS: 3-5 reviews, 1-3 pp., signed. SPECIAL ISSUES: Occasional. INDEXED/ ABSTRACTED: PhilosI. TARGET AUDIENCE: AC. SAMPLE ISSUES: Libraries. ACCEPTANCE RATE: 20%.

PI publishes descriptive and speculative articles following the approaches first pioneered by J.L. Austin, Gilbert Ryle and Ludwig Wittgenstein, that of construing arguments that are verified semantically. Essays provide systematic and rational accounts of language, anthropology, logic, cosmology, religion and epistemology. The origin, style, content and purpose of PI place it high among the standards of scholarly endeavors. Especially provocative are the empirical views on truth and validity put forward by a rich variety of social scientific approaches. Outstanding contributions from scholars and specialists characterize PI as a highly readable resource for the main currents in Eastern and Western thought. Principles and rules form coherent arguments similar to those in Cognition, Indian Philosophical Quarterly and Journal of Mind and Behavior.

A typical issue features six to eight discussions and a section on book reviews. This clear and orderly presentation of American philosophical tradition is excellent for advanced college students.

217. Philosophical Papers. DATE FOUNDED: 1963. TITLE CHANGES: Occasional Papers in Philosophy (1963-1967). FREQUENCY: sa. PRICE: $9/yr. institutions. PUBLISHER: Rhodes University, P.O. Box 94, Grahamstown 6140, South Africa. ADVERTISMENTS. CIRCULATION: 300. MANUSCRIPT SELECTION: Refereed, editorial board. REPRINTS: author. BOOK REVIEWS: 6-8 reviews, 1-3 pp., signed. SPECIAL ISSUES: 1/yr. INDEXED/ABSTRACTED: PhilosI. TARGET AUDIENCE: AC. SAMPLE COPIES: Libraries, individuals. ACCEPTANCE RATE: 45%.

PP is distinctively systematic in covering all central areas of philosophy from metaphysics, logic and epistemology to political and moral theory. Priority is given to papers from Southern African philosophers and on Afro-American topics. The collection of social and political issues aim to reconstitute objectively the methods of analytic reasoning. Authors argue with ruthless efficiency and detail the applied problems in Anglo-Saxon vs. African philosophy. New insights drawn from the history and sociology of science lend contrast to nonscientific challenges to religion. More vocal than Afro-American Journal of Philosophy, PP puts into focus the diverging trends among countries. Contributors are mainly scholars.

Each issue features five to seven articles and book reviews. PP also publishes a monograph series addressing thematic issues in contemporary philosophy.

218. Philosophical Quarterly. DATE FOUNDED: 1950. FREQUENCY: q. PRICE: $45/yr. institutions, $22/yr. personal. PUBLISHER: Basil Blackwell Publisher Limited, 104 Cowley Road, Oxford 0X4 1JF, England. EDITOR: Leslie Stevenson. INDEX. ADVERTISEMENTS. MANUSCRIPT SELECTION: Refereed, editorial board. MICROFORMS: UMI. REPRINTS: author. BOOK REVIEWS: 9 reviews, 1-3 pp., signed. SPECIAL ISSUES: Occasional. INDEXED/ABSTRACTED: PhilosI. TARGET AUDIENCE: AC. SAMPLE COPIES: Libraries. ACCEPTANCE RATE: 10%.

PQ originally served as the forum for the University of St. Andrews and the Scots Philosophical Club. Since that time, PQ has been a formal outlet for useful criticism in every phase of philosophic growth. The principal merits are its considerable contributions from the universities of Scotland, plus frequent contributions from American philosophers. Brilliantly written essays provide up-to-date comparisons and contrasts of leading theories, propositional arguments, and canons of social science. This critical treatment embraces virtually the entire spectrum of twentieth century thought, completely upstaging the goals of Philosophical Forum, Pacific Philosophical Quarterly and even the Journal of Philosophy.

Issues of PQ publish five to six major features, two discussion papers, critical notes and book reviews. Occasional special issues are devoted to first-order biomedical and social problems.

219. Philosophical Review. DATE FOUNDED: 1891. FREQUENCY: q. PRICE: $25/yr. institutions, $16/yr. personal. PUBLISHER: Sage School of Philosophy, 218 Goldwin Smith, Cornell University, Ithaca, New York 14853. INDEX. ADVERTISEMENTS. CIRCULATION: 3,000. MANUSCRIPT SELECTION: Refereed, editorial board. MICROFORMS: UMI. REPRINTS: author. BOOK REVIEWS: 15-12 reviews, 1-3 pp., signed. INDEXED/ABSTRACTED: BRI, PhilosI, SSCI. TARGET AUDIENCE: AC. SAMPLE COPIES: Libraries, individuals. ACCEPTANCE RATE: 5%.

This recurrent voice in the chorus of scholarly debate represents one of the first comprehensive treatments of analytic philosophy. Articles in PR offer a consistent, unified interpretation of the shape and scope of contemporary studies in logic. Esteemed authors, mostly scholars, take a fresh look at the structure of underlying dogmas and essentially translate them into critical thought-provoking statements. Major revisionist theses define for the first time the subtle concepts inherent in such topics as metaphysics, ethics, philosophy of science, epistemology, philosophy of mind, and history. The probing insights in language, for instance, forcefully defend realistic principles which keep the reader alert and thinking. PR is truly a companion to Philosophical Quarterly and International Philosophical Quarterly.
  Every issue provides two extremely long articles, three to four shorter discussions, and book reviews. Closing in on its first century, PR is a professional milestone in the global picture of philosophic development.

220. Philosophical Studies. DATE FOUNDED: 1950. FREQUENCY: 3/yr. PRICE: $128/yr. institutions, $40/yr. personal. PUBLISHER: D. Reidel Publishing Company, P.O. Box 322, 3300 AH Dordrecht, Netherlands. EDITOR: Keith Lehrer. ILLUSTRATIONS. INDEX. ADVERTISEMENTS. MANUSCRIPT SELECTION: Refereed, editorial board. REPRINTS: author. SPECIAL ISSUES: Occasional. INDEXED/ ABSTRACTED: PhilosI. TARGET AUDIENCE: AC. SAMPLE COPIES: Libraries, individuals.

PS was founded in 1950 by Herbert Feigl and Wilfrid Sellars to provide a periodical devoted to work in analytic philosophy. Editors believe in rapid publication of contributions in logic, particularly in epistemology, language, and ethics. Papers applying formal logic to fundamental problems seek clarity and precision in argument, plus a rigorous deduction of basic premises. On the basis of criticism alone, PS adopts into its metalogical methods a demanding system of science which resembles the aims of Notre Dame Journal of Formal Logic. Distinguished authors work doubly hard to render material intelligible for philosophers outside of analytic fields. Emotive and scholarly, the theoretical essays add new research to standard principles and modalities.
  Single issues contain four to six informed reviews for the diligent reader of classical argument.

221.   Philosophical Studies.   DATE FOUNDED: 1951.   FREQUENCY: a.
PRICE: $21.50/yr. institutions.   PUBLISHER: University College, Dublin
(for the National University of Ireland), Arts Building, Belfield, Dublin 4,
Ireland.   EDITOR: James D. Bastable.   CIRCULATION: 600.   MANUSCRIPT
SELECTION: Refereed, editorial board.   REPRINTS: author.   BOOK
REVIEWS: 50 reviews, 1-3 pp., signed.   INDEXED/ABSTRACTED:
ArtHumCitI, PhilosI.   TARGET AUDIENCE: AC.   SAMPLE COPIES:
Libraries. ACCEPTANCE RATE: 60%.

PS has for its aim the development and diffusion of philosophy by way of
specialized   study   without   excluding   theological,   social,   or   scientific
reflection.   It is particularly concerned with contemporary problems for the
young graduate as well as for more practical writers.   As the only review of
its kind in Ireland or Great Britain, PS publishes many facets of Irish
philosophy based on early contributions to intellectual thought.This close
examination of the introductory and complex processes of mind and nature
make PS an outstanding selection.   Authors are mainly from universities in
Ireland.   In this respect, PS accomplishes for Ireland what Iyyun and
Philosophia accomplish for Israel--a forum for scholarly debate on indigenous
philosophy.
   Each issue contains primarily articles, fifteen critical reviews, and
thirty-five book reviews.   Articles are handsomely enclosed in an attractive
dust cover.

222.   Philosophical Studies in Education.   DATE FOUNDED: 1968. TITLE
CHANGES: Ohio Valley Philosophy of Education Society Proceedings
(1968-1976).   FREQUENCY: sa.   PRICE: $8/yr. institutions, $6.50/yr.
personal. PUBLISHER: Managing Editor, 203 Education, Indiana University,
Bloomington, Indiana 47405.   EDITOR: Dennis M. Senchuk.   CIRCULATION:
250. MANUSCRIPT SELECTION: Refereed, editorial board.   MICROFORMS:
UMI.   REPRINTS: author.   INDEXED/ ABSTRACTED: PhilosI, RIE.
TARGET AUDIENCE: AC.   SAMPLE COPIES: Libraries.   ACCEPTANCE
RATE: 50%.

223.   Philosophy.   DATE FOUNDED: 1925.   FREQUENCY: q.   PRICE:
$20/yr. institutions, $10/yr. personal.   PUBLISHER: Cambridge University
Press, 32 East 57 street, New York, New York 10022.   EDITOR: Renford
Bambrough.   INDEX.   ADVERTISEMENTS.   CIRCULATION: 2,568.
MANUSCRIPT SELECTION: Editor.   MICROFORMS: EPML.   REPRINTS:
author.   BOOK REVIEWS: 10 reviews, 1-2 pp., signed.   SPECIAL ISSUES:
2/yr.   INDEXED/ABSTRACTED: CurrContAH, PhilosI.   TARGET
AUDIENCE: AC.   SAMPLE COPIES: Libraries, individuals.

Philosophy is devoted to the study of all branches of philosophy--logic,
metaphysics, epistemology, aesthetics, social and political philosophy, and
philosophies of religion, science, history, language and education. Original
articles and discussions add an important speculation to today's diverging
interests toward specialization.   From historical to contemporary, Philosophy
focuses on doctrines of monumental thinkers of the modern era.   The
assembly of facts and narrative intricately connect questions of human
personality to universal laws and principles of morality, science and
intellectual processes.   Authors are generally scholars.   Philosophy deserves
the attention of anyone concerned with mind and the nature of causation.

As such, it resembles the goals of Contemporary Philosophy and Philosophical Inquiry.

A regular issue invites unique discussion on a mixture of psychological and philosophical subjects. Contained are six lead articles, intensive reviews, booknotes, and a list of books received. A very visible distinction between Philosophy and other journals is its forward ambition toward the need for a simple and understandable text.

224. Philosophy and the Arts. DATE FOUNDED: 1975. TITLE CHANGES: Bertrand Russell Today! (1975-1980). FREQUENCY: a. PRICE: $2/yr. institutions. PUBLISHER: P.O. Box 431, Jerome Avenue Station, Bronx, New York 10467. EDITOR: Daniel Manesse. ILLUSTRATIONS. ADVERTISEMENTS. BOOK REVIEWS: 2 reviews, 1-5 pp., signed. SPECIAL ISSUES: Occasional. INDEXED/ABSTRACTED: PhilosI. TARGET AUDIENCE: AC, GP.

PA is a literary and philosophical review of current motions in the controversial areas of fiction, poetry, biography, and culture. Creative expressions in aesthetics are etched into the writings of language, politics, and ecology. PA serves both as an introduction to arts and as an application of contemporary technique in continuity with the works of metaphysical epistemology. Selected papers and poems are more dramatic than analytic. Like Aitia, Antioch Review and CLIO, PA welcomes submissions of original fiction from experts in the field. The result is an excellent exercise in fine arts appreciation.

Issues of PA may feature articles or provide excerpts from unpublished books. The current news and notes at the back definitely alert readers to the breadth of literary activity within philosophy.

225. Philosophy in Context. DATE FOUNDED: 1972. FREQUENCY: a. PRICE: $3.50/yr. institutions. PUBLISHER: Department of Philosophy, Cleveland State University, Cleveland, Ohio 44115. EDITOR: Richard M. Fox. ADVERTISEMENTS. CIRCULATION: 500. REPRINTS: publisher. SPECIAL ISSUES: Occasional. INDEXED/ABSTRACTED: PhilosI. TARGET AUDIENCE: AC, GP. SAMPLE COPIES: Libraries, individuals. ACCEPTANCE RATE: 40%.

The common notion that philosophy is unpragmatic draws diverse criticism from many of the scholarly articles in PC. PC gives consideration to realistic problems underlying the philosophy of human conduct. The nature of applied philosophy as a "pure" or traditional approach conflicts with PC's emphasis on methods and explicit goals. Essays by acclaimed specialists in psychology, anthropology, and sociology replace abstraction with scientifically verified explanations. Much like International Journal of Applied Philosophy, PC broadly asks whether people in other fields should know about philosophy.

Original papers in a regular or thematic issue vary between five and six. While clearly philosophical, essays remain devoid of complex technical jargon. This allows for daring questions about life and meaning on a level understood by most graduate students.

226. Philosophy East and West. DATE FOUNDED: 1951. FREQUENCY: q. PRICE: $18.50/yr. institutions, $15/yr. personal. PUBLISHER: University Press of Hawaii, 2840 Kolowalu Street, Honolulu, Hawaii 96822. EDITOR: Eliot Deutsch. INDEX. ADVERTISEMENTS. CIRCULATION: 1,500. MANUSCRIPT SELECTION: Editor. REPRINTS: author. BOOK REVIEWS: 5 reviews, 1-2 pp., signed. SPECIAL ISSUES: Occasional. INDEXED/ABSTRACTED: PhilosI. TARGET AUDIENCE: AC.

PEW publishes specialty articles in Asian philosophy or those seeking to illuminate distinctions between Eastern and Western philosophy. Particularly welcome are discussions on literature, science, social practices of Asian civilization, and on intercultural trends. The effects of modernity upon historically Buddhistic nations raises formal questions of adaptivity and existential identity. Such questions reinstate the need for an authoritative overview of emerging changes in the third world. Articles are written by anthropologists, paleontologists, and philosophers. Just as Journal of Chinese Philosophy concerns Oriental culture and Journal of Indian Philosophy concerns Islamic culture, so PEW concerns a synthesis of the two.
Each issue provides five major articles, one discussion paper, a feature book review, and book reviews. Following this are a list of books received, noted current periodicals, and news about research funding. PEW in so many words is an entry into the much-needed investigation of metacultural topics.

227. Philosophy and History. DATE FOUNDED: 1967. FREQUENCY: sa. PRICE: 35 Deutsche Marks/yr. institutions. PUBLISHER: Institute for Scientific Cooperation, Landhausstr, 18, 7400 Tubingen 1, West Germany. EDITOR: Jurgen H. Hohnholz. INDEX. CIRCULATION: 2,200. BOOK REVIEWS: 60 reviews, 1-3 pp., signed. TARGET AUDIENCE: AC. SAMPLE COPIES: Libraries.

228. Philosophy and Literature. DATE FOUNDED: 1976. FREQUENCY: sa. PRICE: $19.50/yr. institutions, $12/yr. personal. PUBLISHER: Johns Hopkins University Press, Baltimore, Maryland 21218. EDITOR: Denis Dutton. INDEX. ADVERTISEMENTS. CIRCULATION: 1,200. MANUSCRIPT SELECTION: Refereed, editorial board. REPRINTS: author. BOOK REVIEWS: 9-15 reviews, 1-2 pp., signed. INDEXED/ ABSTRACTED: HumI, PhilosI. TARGET AUDIENCE: AC. SAMPLE COPIES: Libraries, individuals. ACCEPTANCE RATE: 10%.

Rarely does there appear a periodical so devoted to creativity in literary investigation. PL fits this description. It fills a crucial gap between aestheticism and philosophical studies. The vitality and depth of analysis spring from the wealth of new theoretical approaches written by scholars in different fields of endeavor. In its sixth year of publication, PL brings new insights to the forefront of modern artistic criticism. Discussions explore the seemingly nebulous forms of metaphysics, intentionality, parody, and fictional portraits of humanities in general. Articles that reflect fresh thinking and diverse topics broaden the narrow horizons of classical literature, primarily Hellenic works. At the heart of PL is an untiring, calibrated focus on modern arts, perhaps in less intensity than in Midwest Quarterly and Oxford Literary Review.

Each issue contains five major articles followed by a single critical discussion and two shorter reviews. News and notes provide additional opportunities for interested readers of the arts.

229. Philosophy and Phenomenological Research. DATE FOUNDED: 1940. FREQUENCY: q. PRICE: $15/yr. institutions, $12/yr. personal. PUBLISHER: Brown University, Box 1947, Providence, Rhode Island 02912. EDITOR: Roderick M. Chisholm. ADVERTISEMENTS. MANUSCRIPT SELECTION: Refereed, editorial board. MICROFORMS: UMI. REPRINTS: author. BOOK REVIEWS: 3 reviews, 1-3 pp., signed. INDEXED/ABSTRACTED: PhilosI. TARGET AUDIENCE: AC. SAMPLE COPIES: Libraries, individuals. ACCEPTANCE RATE: 8%.

PPR is the official organ of the International Phenomenological Society. It publishes descriptive, analytical, critical, and historical articles representing the major contemporary trends in philosophy. Besides phenomenological research, essays survey areas including ethics, logic, history of philosophy, metaphysics, theory of knowledge, as well as new directions in applied philosophy. Practical criticism elegantly reveals the crucial stages in modern treatments of selfhood, transpersonalism, and study of mind. PPR provides a reference tool of prime importance for all scholars, but mostly for readers anxious to grasp the profound meanings in phenomenologic inquiry. Authors are mainly polemicists. While intending to write clearly, authors are at times hard to understand. In most other ways, PPR identifies with the same aims as Journal of the British Society for Phenomenology.
Each issue normally features about seven creative papers, three lengthy critical notes, and a list of recent publications. This journal is recommended as a supplement to books on existence and self-analysis.

230. Philosophy and Public Affairs. DATE FOUNDED: 1971. FREQUENCY: q. PRICE: $22.50/yr. institutions, $14.50/yr. personal. PUBLISHER: Princeton University Press, 41 Williams Street, Princeton, New Jersey 08540. EDITOR: Marshall Cohen. INDEX. ADVERTISEMENTS. CIRCULATION: 3,100. MANUSCRIPT SELECTION: Refereed, editorial board. MICROFORMS: UMI. REPRINTS: author. BOOK REVIEWS: 3-5 reviews, 1-2 pp., signed. SPECIAL ISSUES: Occasional ("Readers"). INDEXED/ ABSTRACTED: ABC, PhilosI. TARGET AUDIENCE: AC. SAMPLE COPIES: Libraries.

PPA promotes discussion of matters between philosophers and those in other disciplines inclined toward an objective view of freedom and human rights. Topics such as morality of war, civil disobedience, the obligations of the affluent to the starving, preferential hiring, and compensatory discrimination are thrown into question by leading scholarly thinkers. Papers clarify and examine the methods in law, political science, economics and sociology, whether as abstraction or directly investigative arguments. In this respect, PPA can fill the need for a periodical in which philosophers with different viewpoints openly debate the problems in society that concern everyone. Theories especially refrain from pedantry or pregnant assumptions about social systems. Rather, political and social factors stress easy-to-grasp ideas as found in Agora, Law and Philosophy and Man and Medicine.

PPA opens a new line of communication between specialists and academicians. Each issue provides three major papers, a correspondence and rebuttal essays, book reviews, and general news. This first-hand account of changing social patterns helps the reader consider alternative perspectives on medical and intellectual developments.

231.   Philosophy, Religion and Science (PRS) Journal.   DATE FOUNDED: 1923.   TITLE CHANGES: All-Seeing Eye (1923-1941), Horizon (1941-1959). FREQUENCY: q.   PRICE: $7.50/yr. institutions.   PUBLISHER: Philosophical Research Society, Incorporated, 3910 Los Feliz Boulevard, Los Angeles, California   90027.   EDITOR: Manly P. Hall.   ILLUSTRATIONS. CIRCULATION: 2,000.   MANUSCRIPT SELECTION: Editor. TARGET AUDIENCE: GP.   SAMPLE COPIES: Libraries.

PRS assembles the latest contributions in metaphysics and psychic research by members of the Philosophical Research Society. This nonprofit educational corporation is dedicated to the   dissemination   of   useful knowledge in fields of philosophy, comparative religion and psychology. Published are biographies, translations, research essays, and anthologies on interdisciplinary themes historically relevant to the economic and social status of science.   Contributors, mostly scholars, harbor a distinct prejudice against the progression of mankind into such technological enterprises as cybernetics and quantum physics. The expression of "mental self" seemingly opposes the contra-intuitive leaps toward materialism.   This position, while sounding spiritualistic, permeates discussions of personality and experience. Whether these aims oversimplify   PRS' purpose depends on the particular needs of the reader.   At present, readers may be the same individuals drawn to Dreamworks and Energy and Character.
  A common issue includes editorials, six feature articles, occasional replies, happenings at the Society's headquarters, and literary notes. Noteworthy are the attractive reprints of sketches from the Middle Ages.

232.   Philosophy   Research   Archives.   DATE   FOUNDED: 1975. FREQUENCY: a.   PRICE: $30/yr.   institutions, $15/yr.   personal. PUBLISHER: Philosophy   Documentation   Center, Bowling   Green   State University, Bowling Green, Ohio   43403.   EDITOR: Robert G. Turnbull. ILLUSTRATIONS.   INDEX. MANUSCRIPT SELECTION: Refereed, editorial board.   MICROFORMS: Publisher.   REPRINTS: author. INDEXED/ABSTRACTED: PhilosI. TARGET AUDIENCE: AC.   SAMPLE COPIES: Libraries.

Archival sources of publication appear in philosophy as they do in most scholarly fields. Such sources remove the   journal restrictions on page length, content, and qualifications of the author, although articles are still excellent in quality. PRA provides this rapid source of publication for English and French philosophers.   PRA is co-sponsored by the American as well as Canadian Philosophical Associations, and Philosophy Documentation Center. Published are monographs, text translations, and annotated bibliographies. The unrestricted philosophical scope offers unusual   opportunities for accpetance or re-writing of manuscripts from new philosophers.   PRA appeared originally on microfiche but switched to the printed page in March, 1983.   With some 200 or so referees on   hand, PRA is without doubt achieving its goal to attract gifted writers from diverse schools of thought.

233. <u>Philosophy and Rhetoric</u>. DATE FOUNDED: 1968. FREQUENCY: q. PRICE: $22.50/yr. institutions, $16.50/yr. personal. PUBLISHER: Pennsylvania State University Press, 215 Wagner Building, Pennsylvania State University, University Park, Pennsylvania 16802. EDITOR: Donald P. Verene. INDEX. ADVERTISEMENTS. CIRCULATION: 1,000. MANU-SCRIPT SELECTION: Refereed, editorial board. REPRINTS: author. BOOK REVIEWS: 4 reviews, 1-2 pp., signed. INDEXED/ABSTRACTED: PhilosI. TARGET AUDIENCE: AC. ACCEPTANCE RATE: 35%.

<u>PR</u> provides articulate criticism on theoretical issues between philosophy and rhetoric, historical figures and periods, and areas in human culture of psychological and sociological importance to modern thought. Philo-sophically-based arguments probe the English language in correcting conventional wisdom about the meaning of literature in twentieth century culture. Each paper tackles major protests against the distinction in linguistic theory between religion, art, and custom. This reappraisal also contains explicit reviews of denotation. Articles are prepared by scholars and specialists in different language fields.
  <u>PR</u> is worth reading for its gentle synthesis of traditionally complex topics. A typical issue provides four lead articles and two book reviews.

234. <u>Philosophy of Science</u>. DATE FOUNDED: 1933. FREQUENCY: q. PRICE: $32.50/yr. institutions. PUBLISHER: Philosophy of Science Association, 18 Morrill Hall, Department of Philosophy, Michigan State University, East Lansing, Michigan 48824. EDITOR: Robert Butts. INDEX. ADVERTISEMENTS. CIRCULATION: 2,200. MANUSCRIPT SELECTION: Refereed, editorial board. MICROFORMS: UMI. REPRINTS: author. BOOK REVIEWS: 4 reviews, 1-2 pp., signed. SPECIAL ISSUES: Occasional. INDEXED/ABSTRACTED: BioAb, BulSig, HumI, LLBA, PhilosI, PsyAb, SSCI, SocAb. TARGET AUDIENCE: AC. ACCEPTANCE RATE: 20%.

<u>PS</u> advances the specialization in biological and technological theory as related to fundamental problems in philosophy. Papers by esteemed scholars survey the structural flaws in principles, concepts, and explanatory systems regarding physics, causation, ecology, and metascience. Links between such polarities as evolutionism and creationism offer implications for society and politics. The free-flowing dialogue of <u>PS</u> encourages many more framing rules for knowledge of the individual and State. Methods and general strategy lend support to the call for a new generation of scientific philosophers. As such, articles are written primarily by philosophers and members of natural science disciplines.
  Each regular issue contains nine feature articles, several book reviews, and a list of books received. A recent special issue on "Philosophy of Biology" struck this reviewer as providing clarification on obscure and usually broad-based tenets.

235. <u>Philosophy and Social Action</u>. DATE FOUNDED: 1975. FREQUENCY: q. PRICE: $35/yr. institutions. PUBLISHER: Institute of Socio-Political Dynamics, M-120 Greater Kailash-I, New Delhi 110 048, India. EDITOR: Dhirendra Sharma. INDEX. ADVERTISEMENTS. CIRCULATION: 1,000. MANUSCRIPT SELECTION: Refereed, editorial board. REPRINTS: author. BOOK REVIEWS: 2 reviews, 1-3 pp., signed. SPECIAL ISSUES: Occasional. INDEXED/ABSTRACTED: PhilosI, SocAb. TARGET AUDIENCE: AC, GP.

SAMPLE COPIES: Libraries, individuals.

236. Philosophy and Social Criticism. DATE FOUNDED: 1978. TITLE CHANGES: Cultural Hermeneutics (1978). FREQUENCY: q. PRICE: $35/yr. institutions, $15/yr. personal, $10/yr. student. PUBLISHER: Department of Philosophy, Boston College, Chestnut Hill, Massachusetts 02167. EDITOR: David M. Rasmussen. ADVERTISEMENTS. CIRCULATION: 500. MANUSCRIPT SELECTION: Refereed, editorial board. REPRINTS: author. BOOK REVIEWS: 1 review, 1-3 pp., signed. SPECIAL ISSUES: Double issue every 2 yrs. INDEXED/ABSTRACTED: PhilosI. TARGET AUDIENCE: AC. SAMPLE COPIES: Libraries, individuals. ACCEPTANCE RATE: 30%.

It is precisely PSC's purpose to push beyond a merely theoretical explanation of social phenomena and construct newly philosophical preconditions of industrial society. Articles reflect a rising interface between politics, economics, psychology and metaphilosophy. The heuristic need to understand governments, education, and rationalized human action is satisfied. Knowledge and ideology combine to dispel misconceptions in public beliefs, as well to survey injustices in professional establishments. Contributors are largely experts in sociology, philosophy and social sciences. Their arguments share a common Anglo-Saxon bond with International Social Science Review, Human Studies, and Inquiry.

A typical issue contains six major papers, book reviews, and news and notes. This forum for open scholarly debate follows a critical-historical point of view.

237. Philosophy of the Social Sciences. DATE FOUNDED: 1971. FREQUENCY: q. PRICE: $25/yr. institutions. PUBLISHER: Wilfrid Laurier University Press, 75 University Avenue West, Waterloo, Ontario. EDITORS: J.O. Wisdom, J.N. Hattian Gadi, John O'Neill. ILLUSTRATIONS. INDEX. ADVERTISMENTS. CIRCULATION: 1,000. MANUSCRIPT SELECTION: Refereed, editorial board. MICROFORMS: Publisher. REPRINTS: author. BOOK REVIEWS: 6 reviews, 1-3 pp., signed. SPECIAL ISSUES: Occasional. INDEXED/ABSTRACTED: PhilosI, SocAb. TARGET AUDIENCE: AC. SAMPLE COPIES: Libraries, individuals. ACCEPTANCE RATE: 15%.

PSS is a bilingual collection of central empirical issues regarding meta-science. Published are articles, discussions, symposia, literature surveys, translations and review symposia of interest to the social scientist. In certain issues of PSS, topics may cover methodology, self-knowledge, and epistemic interaction. Systematically composed are accounts of valid hypotheses following the canons of logical argument. This helps establish a useful guide to scholarly research. Contributors represent a wide variety of prolific leaders in the field. Writings from different philosophic schools thus give PSS distinction from Journal of Critical Analysis and Philosophy and Social Action.

A single issue features three original, lead articles and two discussion articles followed by book reviews. Paradigms and thoughts in social science make for a well orchestrated series in formal investigation.

238. <u>Philosophy Today</u>. DATE FOUNDED: 1957. FREQUENCY: q. PRICE: $12/yr. institutions. PUBLISHER: Messenger Press, Carthagena Station, Celina, Ohio 45822. EDITOR: Robert Lechner. ILLUSTRATIONS. INDEX. ADVERTISEMENTS. CIRCULATION: 1,345. MANUSCRIPT SELECTION: Refereed, editorial board. MICROFORMS: UMI. REPRINTS: author. SPECIAL ISSUES: Occasional. INDEXED/ABSTRACTED: ArtHumCitI, CathI, PhilosI, RBibPhil. TARGET AUDIENCE: AC. SAMPLE COPIES: Libraries.

<u>PT</u> is a continental expression of emerging trends in modern philosophy. Articles are strictly surveys on phenomenology, existentialism, language, structuralism, and hermeneutics. Anglo-American philosophy provides clear introduction to Heidegger, Heraclitus, and differences between consensus and truth as sketched from a rationally justified theory of social science. <u>PT</u> taps potent thoughts from the domain of religion and psychoanalysis, mostly authored by scholars. These exploratory papers make use of classical and contemporary insights as characterized by <u>Master Thoughts</u> and <u>Interchange</u>. However, the writing in <u>PT</u> is more accessible to general readers.

Each issue covers trends and research directed to interests of scholars and teachers. Eleven lead articles are followed by a condensed index of prior issues of <u>PT</u>.

239. <u>Phoenix</u>. DATE FOUNDED: 1946. FREQUENCY: q. PRICE: $25/yr. institutions. PUBLISHER: Trinity College, Toronto, Ontario, Canada. EDITOR: M.B. Wallace. ILLUSTRATIONS. INDEX. ADVERTISEMENTS. CIRCULATION: 1,200. MANUSCRIPT SELECTION: Refereed, editorial board. REPRINTS: author. BOOK REVIEWS: 8-10 reviews, 1-2 pp., signed. TARGET AUDIENCE: AC. SAMPLE COPIES: Individuals.

240. <u>Poznan Studies in the Philosophy of the Sciences and Humanities</u>. DATE FOUNDED: 1975. FREQUENCY: sa. PUBLISHER: Editions Rodopi, BV, Keizersgracht 302-304, 1016 EX, Amsterdam, Holland. EDITORS: Piotr Buczkowski, Andrzej Klawiter, Leszek Nowak. ADVERTISEMENTS. CIRCULATION: 1,000. MANUSCRIPT SELECTION: Editor. SPECIAL ISSUES: Every issue. TARGET AUDIENCE: AC.

241. <u>Pragmatics and Beyond</u>. DATE FOUNDED: 1980. FREQUENCY: 8/yr. PRICE: $120/yr. institutions. PUBLISHER: John Benjamins Publishing Company, One Button Wood Square, Philadelphia, Pennsylvania 19130. EDITORS: Herman Parret, Jef Verschueren. MANUSCRIPT SELECTION: Refereed, editorial board. SPECIAL ISSUES: Occasional. TARGET AUDIENCE: AC.

<u>PB</u> responds to the growing number of topics epistemologically relevant to language. Articles form a new interest around conventions in linguistic study. Fundamental distinctions are made clear between syntax and semantics, between reference and natural language, and between practical and analytical principles. This new approach confronts the philosophical implications of such arguments against introspectionism and physical properties. Exploring language as method, <u>PB</u> disbands parochial postulates following the traditions of scientific analysis. Contributors are largely scholars who avoid obtruse or technical phraseology. In some respects, <u>PB</u> converts the fragmentary concepts in, for example, <u>Critical Inquiry</u>, into

incisive and reasonable models of research.

The contents of PB resemble more a newsletter than journal format. Three to five feature articles always reflect a pre-designated theme.

242. Prana Yoga Life. DATE FOUNDED: 1970. FREQUENCY: sa. PRICE: $3/yr. institutions. PUBLISHER: Prana Yoga Ashram, P.O. Box 1037, Berkeley, California 94701. EDITORS: Swami Vignanananda, Saraswathi Devi. CIRCULATION: 7,000. MANUSCRIPT SELECTION: Editors. BOOK REVIEWS: 10 reviews, 1-2 pp., signed. TARGET AUDIENCE: GP. SAMPLE COPIES: Libraries, individuals.

PYL is the bloodline to spiritual fulfillment following the teachings of Swami Sivalingam. Founder and Director of Prana Yoga Centers International, Swami-ji advocates the practical ways to physical, mental, and religious balance. The ancient science of breath control links tradition with modern efforts toward inner strength, clarity, and wisdom. Authors are usually certified yoga teachers and philosophers. This step for universal altruism essentially covers meditation and body-purification. PYL almost draws readers into a mystical trance. PYL combines the virginal history of Kabbalist with the commercialism of Dawn.

A typical issue begins with letters to the aspirants by Swami Sivalingam. Eight major articles follow and at the end are book reviews and conference notes. The bestowing of direct blessing and morality upon devotees of the Institute seriously disturbed this reviewer.

243. Prediction. DATE FOUNDED: 1936. FREQUENCY: m. PRICE: $25/yr. institutions. PUBLISHER: Link House Publications PLC, Link House, Dingwall Avenue, Croydon CR9 2TA, England. EDITOR: Jo Logan. ILLUSTRATIONS. INDEX. ADVERTISEMENTS. CIRCULATION: 35,000. MANUSCRIPT SELECTION: Editor. REPRINTS: author. BOOK REVIEWS: 7 reviews, 1-2 pp., signed. SPECIAL ISSUES: 1/yr. TARGET AUDIENCE: GP, SP. SAMPLE ISSUES: Libraries, individuals.

Prediction is England's leading popular magazine on psychical and occult subjects. Fast reading articles cover astrology, palmistry, dream interpretation, alchemy, and secrets of hidden wisdom traced to early Egyptian and Chinese origins. World events, developments in semi-scientific disciplines and the underlying philosophies of parapsychology and magic make Prediction an invaluable encyclopedia for devoted readers. Contributions are largely from freelance writers, some philosophers, and spiritualists. While enjoyable reading, the cook-book forecasting of personal goals is perhaps overconfident, impulsive, and can prove unreliable because the emotional overtones cloud the facts. Still, Prediction, like Light or Psychic Observer does serve a basic function in our sensationalistic world.

Each issue of Prediction features six main articles, interspersed with regular columns on palmistry, graphology, letters-to-the-editor, book reviews, and news and views. Britain is certainly a paradise for anyone fascinated by legend, folklore, and tales from the past. Prediction satisfies this hunger for superstition.

244. Proceedings and Addresses of the American Philosophical Association. FREQUENCY: 5/yr. PRICE: $10/yr. institutions. PUBLISHER: American Philosophical Association, Offices of the Executive Secretary, University of Delaware, Newark, Delaware 19711. EDITOR: John O'Conner. INDEX. ADVERTISEMENTS. CIRCULATION: 6,200. MICROFORMS: UMI. REPRINTS: publisher. INDEXED/ABSTRACTED: PhilosI. TARGET AUDIENCE: AC, SP.

PAAPA is the definitive statement of progress in modern American philosophy. These proceedings are a direct and detailed consideration of news, information and vital trends affecting the limits as well as developments in advanced circles of scholarly writing. Official policies and organizations are reported along with lists of teaching institutes around the nation. Featured reviews and commentaries provide useful insights on the future of philosophy and research in general. PAAPA sits in its own class of specialization.
 A regular issue contains transcripts of meetings and decisions by affiliate organizations located regionally. The "Bulletin" section furnishes a variety of historical,local and evaluative materials which broaden the formal scope of PAAPA and exorcise it from primarily esoteric philosophy.

245. Proceedings of the American Philosophical Society. DATE FOUNDED: 1838. FREQUENCY: 6/yr. PRICE: $20/yr. PUBLISHER: American Philosophical Society, 104 South Fifth Street, Washington, D.C. EDITOR: Whitfield J. Bell. ILLUSTRATIONS. INDEX. CIRCULATION: 1,400. MICROFORMS: UMI. REPRINTS: author. TARGET AUDIENCE: AC. SAMPLE COPIES: Libraries.

246. Proceedings of the Aristotelian Society. DATE FOUNDED: 1877. FREQUENCY: 3/yr. PRICE: $12/yr. institutions. PUBLISHER: Aristotelian Society, Bedford College, NW1 4NS. EDITOR: R.M. Sainsbury. INDEX. CIRCULATION: 1,800. MANUSCRIPT SELECTION: Refereed, editorial board. REPRINTS: author. INDEXED/ABSTRACTED: PhilosI. TARGET AUDIENCE: AC. SAMPLE COPIES: Libraries, individuals.

Insights and oversights of great thinkers are the best-known examples of true philosophical examination. PAS looks at neglected aspects or interprets new views in sharply focused essays on Aristotle. Papers usually read at the Society's sessions reflect the origins and development of Western traditions. PAS advances the role Aristotle plays in the conflicts and pragmatic interrelations between biology, psychology, and relativism. Authors, primarily scholars, do an admirable job of presenting Aristotle with the authority and authenticity as might be found in Journal of Hellenic Studies. It is a clearly edifying portrait of theory and central perspectives in Greco-Roman culture.
 The Society's tradition is to publish the majority of papers read at their fortnightly meetings. Each issue contains four topical papers and possibly additional papers published as supplements.

247. Process Studies. DATE FOUNDED: 1971. FREQUENCY: q. PRICE: $32/yr. institutions, $22/yr. personal, $12/yr. student. PUBLISHER: John B. Cobb Center for Process Studies, 1325 North College Avenue, Claremont, California 91711. EDITOR: Lewis S. Ford. INDEX. ADVERTISEMENTS. CIRCULATION: 1,000. MANUSCRIPT SELECTION: Refereed, editorial board. REPRINTS: author. BOOK REVIEWS: 4 reviews, 1-3 pp., signed. SPECIAL ISSUES: 2-3/yr. INDEXED/ABSTRACTED: PhilosI, RelPerI. TARGET AUDIENCE: AC. SAMPLE COPIES: Libraries. ACCEPTANCE RATE: 30%.

Process philosophy may be defined as appyling to the philosophy of Alfred North Whitehead (1861-1947) and his intellectual associates. PS seeks to explore process thought more broadly as it appears in related endeavors and to use Whitehead's conceptuality for aesthetics, mathematics, physics, biology, religion and literary criticism. This comprehensive anthology includes an organized look at logical positivism, along with twentieth century interpretations of world religions. Whitehead's fresh and stimulating approach throws into question science and unreason, the rudiments of systematic argument, and the structuralist framework. Fundamental mechanisms for social change are at the forefront of each objective essay. Contributors are mainly scholars who might publish similar ideas in Philosophy of Science and Philosophy and Social Action.
  Regular issues of PS feature four to six original papers, and four critical studies and reviews.

248. Psychic Observer. DATE FOUNDED: 1938. TITLE CHANGES: Searcher (1938-1961), Psychic Observer (1962-1973), Observer and Chimes (1974-1982). FREQUENCY: bm. PRICE: $9.50/yr. institutions. PUBLISH-ER: 5605 16th Street, North West, Washington, D.C. 20011. EDITOR: Reverend Henry J. Nagorka. ILLUSTRATIONS. INDEX. ADVERTISEMENTS. CIRCULATION: 10,000. MANUSCRIPT SELECTION: Editor. REPRINTS: publisher. BOOK REVIEWS: 4-6 reviews, 1-2 pp., signed. TARGET AUDIENCE: GP. SAMPLE COPIES: Libraries, individuals. ACCEPTANCE RATE: 10%.

PO is the journal of spiritual science. All shades of opinion concentrate on objective, progressive information in the field of parapsychology, psychotronics, metaphysics, and inner development of self. Short, easy-to-follow articles boldly assume that modern parapsychology is the key to logical interpretation of life. Insights concerning psychic acts are presented as scientific refutations of so-called "explained phenomena." PO also evokes responses to contrasting opinions on weaponry, cosmology, and concepts intriguing to both clergy and atheists. Authors essentially sculpt a radical form of anomaly research, largely based on case histories. Reported sightings of UFO's, astral projections, and death experiences supply the nourishment for creative and integrative inquiry. One wonders whether PO, like Foresight, strives for scientific answers to occult phenomena, or has become lost in its sensationalism.
  Each issue of PO contains fifteen to twenty fast-paced articles, regular departments, and unlimited classifieds of spiritual healers.

249. Psychohistory Review. DATE FOUNDED: 1972. FREQUENCY: q.
PRICE: $20/yr. institutions. PUBLISHER: Sangamon State University,
Shepard Road, Springfield, Illinois 62708. EDITOR: Charles B. Strozier.
INDEX. ADVERTISEMENTS. CIRCULATION: 700. MANUSCRIPT SELEC-
TION: Refereed, editorial board. REPRINTS: publisher. BOOK REVIEWS:
6-8 reviews, 700 words, signed. SPECIAL ISSUES: 1/yr. INDEXED/
ABSTRACTED: AmerH, HistAb, PsyAb, SocAb, USSRAcScAbJ. TARGET
AUDIENCE: AC. SAMPLE COPIES: Libraries, individuals. ACCEPTANCE
RATE: 30%.

The word "psychohistory" suffers from a terrible misconception in the
current arena of historiography. This belief is that all psychohistory is the
outright rejection of science and instead only endorses psychoanalytic
propositions. However, the real purpose of psychohistory, clearly viewed in
PR, is the "use of all forms of psychology in history." Editors of PR assume
an eclectic position toward psychohistory and welcome articles and review
essays from different schools of thought. Articles probing the personality or
cultural variables of historical figures uncover added dimensions to particular
periods of evolution. Biographies on Eric Erikson, Theodore Roosevelt and
Frank Lloyd Wright sort out the missing links in the stages of human and
cultural development. Unlike Journal of Psychohistory, PR provides a direct
service to scientific historians.
    Common issues include three lead articles, one note or comment, and
several book reviews. Announcements by the Group for the Use of
Psychology in History keep readers abreast of current research.

250. Psychological Perspectives. DATE FOUNDED: 1970. FREQUENCY:
sa. PRICE: $10/yr. institutions. PUBLISHER: C.G. Jung Institute, of Los
Angeles, 10349 West Pilo Building, Los Angeles, California 90064. EDITOR:
William   Walcott.   ILLUSTRATIONS.   INDEX.   ADVERTISEMENTS.
CIRCULATION: 1,500. MANUSCRIPT SELECTION: Refereed, editorial
board. MICROFORMS: UMI. REPRINTS: author. BOOK REVIEWS: 4
reviews, 1-3 pp., signed. SPECIAL ISSUES: Occasional. INDEXED/AB-
STRACTED: PsyAb. TARGET AUDIENCE: AC, GP, SP. SAMPLE COPIES:
Libraries. ACCEPTANCE RATE: 40%.

PP is a magazine directed entirely at those people with interest in the
psychology of Carl G. Jung (1875-1961). Finally, lay readers can enjoy the
significant insights of Jung's system without the rhetorical morass of
technical terms and meanings. Clearly written papers capture the calming
essence of Jung's thought, emphasizing his symbolism in an orderly, fruitful
way. Key selections gather the life influence of this neo-Freudian from
examined cases of treatment and theory. PP moves toward a descriptive
introduction for students. Contributors are primarily scholars and
practitioners, as is the case for another Jungian periodical, Quadrant.
    A typical issue contains five articles concerning a particular theme. Book
reviews are followed by news and information.

251. Psychological Record. DATE FOUNDED: 1937. FREQUENCY: q.
PRICE: $32/yr. institutions, $15/yr. personal, $10/yr. student. PUBLISHER:
Kenyon College, Gambier, Ohio 43022. EDITOR: Charles E.   Rice.
ILLUSTRATIONS. INDEX. ADVERTISMENTS. CIRCULATION: 1,700. MANU-
SCRIPT SELECTION: Refereed, editorial board. MICROFORMS: UMI.

REPRINTS: author. BOOK REVIEWS: 4-5 reviews, 2-4 pp., signed. SPECIAL ISSUES: Occasional. INDEXED/ABSTRACTED: BoA, CurrCon-SocBS, PsyAb. TARGET AUDIENCE: AC. SAMPLE COPIES: Libraries. ACCEPTANCE RATE: 40%.

Centuries ago it was common to assemble great thinkers in a single room for dialogue on concerned doctrines of human behavior. Today this tradition survives in PR. PR began as the only expression for behavioral sciences featuring such prominent pioneers as B.F. Skinner, and Wilfred Sellars. Even now, articles analyze the structure and implications to establish the relevancy between scientific evidence and scientific theory. Trained psychologists and philosophers collaborate on social and naturalistic investigation, but battle over particulars in theory and practice. Well-researched and original papers further explore novel intellectual methods in linguistics, psychotherapy, epistemology, interbehaviorism, and history. Authors, mostly academicians, masterfully address the questions of current applied philosophy as it evolves into a multidisciplinary field.

The special talent in PR is its advocacy of empirical research. Behaviorism follows this same path on a smaller scale. At best, the twelve articles and book reviews in each issue establish PR as invaluable for scientific awareness.

252. Public Choice. DATE FOUNDED: 1966. FREQUENCY: 6/yr. PRICE: $60/yr. institutions, $22/yr. personal, $12.50/yr. student. PUBLISHER: Martinus Nijhoff Publishers, P.O. Box 566, 2501, Hague, Netherlands. EDITOR: Gordon Tullock. ILLUSTRATIONS. INDEX. ADVERTISEMENTS. MANUSCRIPT SELECTION: Refereed, editorial board. REPRINTS: author. BOOK REVIEWS: 1-2 reviews, 1-4 pp., signed. SPECIAL ISSUES: Occasional. TARGET AUDIENCE: AC. SAMPLE COPIES: Libraries, individuals.

Now in its 40th volume, PC still constitutes the political and economical voice of consumer expression. Public support parallels the developing need for rural-urban and judicial decisions about social change. The collective dimension of services can be described with public choice theories. In PC, original and statistical reviews effectively discuss the rise and extinction of institutional networks and their many processes. Concepts of coalition, group laws, and control lend contrast to traditional mistakes in public systems. Authors reach an objective platform using reliable methods of research. While most authors are economists, their conceptual models directly draw upon the intersection of philosophy and political science. Applications to real world problems bear close resemblance to those found in International Journal of Applied Philosophy, and Humboldt Journal of Social Relations.

A typical issue contains nine original articles and a lengthy book review. Political topics in PC are essentially for philosophers of social science.

253. Quadrant: Journal of the C.G. Jung Foundation for Analytical Psychology. DATE FOUNDED: 1965. FREQUENCY: sa. PRICE: $15/yr. institutions. PUBLISHER: C.G. Jung Foundation, 28 East 39th Street, New York, New York 10016. EDITOR: Joan Carson. ILLUSTRATIONS. ADVERTISEMENTS. CIRCULATION: 2,700. MANUSCRIPT SELECTION: 2,700. REPRINTS: publisher. BOOK REVIEWS: 8 reviews, 1-2 pp., signed. TARGET AUDIENCE: AC. SAMPLE COPIES: Libraries.

Analytical psychology after Freud's death shifted toward different directions and this brought increasing awareness to Jung's system. Articles in Quadrant testify to this enduring movement as it permeates clinical and philosophical practices. Quadrant puts forth essays, reviews, and notes regarding the symbolic interpretation of dreams, mythology, and human abnormality. As in Psychological Perspectives, personality assumes a multi-essential role in the integrated self. Authors are specialists in Jungian psychology, providing emotive criticism regarding the failures of other psychologies. Such scholars face the unpleasant task of defending Jung against records (case histories) of unsatisfactory conclusions about treatment and general practicality.

254. Rassegna di Letteratura Tomistica. DATE FOUNDED: 1969. FREQUENCY: a. PRICE: 30 Lira/yr. institutions. PUBLISHER: Edizioni Domenicane, via Palmieri 19, 80100 Naples, Italy. EDITOR: P. Clemente Vansteenkiste. BOOK REVIEWS: Entire volume. TARGET AUDIENCE: AC.

255. Ratio. DATE FOUNDED: 1847. TITLE CHANGES: Abhandlungen der Fries'Schen Schule (1847-1904, 1904-1937, 1957). FREQUENCY: sa. PRICE: $55/yr. institutions, $38/yr. personal. PUBLISHER: Basil Blackwell, 108 Cowley Road, Oxford OX4 1JF, England. EDITOR: Martin Hollis. ADVERTISEMENTS. MANUSCRIPT SELECTION: Refereed, editorial board. BOOK REVIEWS: 1-2 reviews, 4-6 pp., signed. INDEXED/ABSTRACTED: PhilosI. TARGET AUDIENCE: AC. SAMPLE COPIES: Libraries.

Ratio is committed to the perennial goal of rational philosophy. Analytic essays take a resolute stand against skepticism and irrationalism while pursuing pure and applied aspects of ethics, religion, social sciences, epistemology and aesthetics. Simultaneous publications in German add to the already interdisciplinary readership. As an outgrowth of metaphilosophy, Ratio provides illustrative statements on mathematical and psychologic probabilities, systematically blending current with historical principles in logic. Objective arguments clarify the misguided problems leading to confusion. Authors of Ratio are primarily scholars. In effect, their high standard of criticism mirrors the interdisciplinary efforts seen in Analysis, Journal of Critical Analysis and Mind.
  A regular issue contains eight lead articles followed by book reviews and occasional editorial commentary. Its scientific realism is nearly immediately addictive.

256. Rationalist News. DATE FOUNDED: 1966. FREQUENCY: bm. PRICE: $5.50/yr. institutions. PUBLISHER: Rationalist Association of N.S.W., 58 Regent Street, Chippendale, N.S.W., Australia 2008. CIRCULATION: 1,000. MANUSCRIPT SELECTION: Editor. BOOK REVIEWS: 1-3 reviews, 1-2 pp., signed. TARGET AUDIENCE: AC, GP. SAMPLE COPIES: Libraries, individuals. ACCEPTANCE RATE: 90%.

257. Reformed Review. DATE FOUNDED: 1946. TITLE CHANGES: Western Seminary Bulletin (1946-1955). FREQUENCY: 3/yr. PRICE: $6/yr. institutions. PUBLISHER: Western Theological Seminary, Holland, Michigan 49423. EDITOR: M. Eugene Osterhaven. INDEX. ADVERTISEMENTS. CIRCULATION: 2,500. MANUSCRIPT SELECTION: Editor. MICROFORMS: UMI. REPRINTS: author. BOOK REVIEWS: 20 reviews, 1-2 pp., signed. INDEXED/ABSTRACTED: RelAb. TARGET AUDIENCE: AC. SAMPLE COPIES: Libraries, individuals. ACCEPTANCE RATE: 75%.

258. Religious Humanism. DATE FOUNDED: 1967. FREQUENCY: q. PRICE: $8/yr. institutions. PUBLISHER: Fellowship of Religious Humanists, P.O. Box 278 Yellow Springs, Ohio 45387. EDITORS: Paul and Lucinda Beattie. INDEX. ADVERTISEMENTS. CIRCULATION: 1,500. MANUSCRIPT SELECTION: Refereed, editorial board. MICROFORMS: UMI. REPRINTS: author. BOOK REVIEWS: 3 reviews, 1-2 pp., signed. SPECIAL ISSUES: Occasional. INDEXED/ABSTRACTED: ArtHumCitI, PhilosI, RelAb. TARGET AUDIENCE: AC, GP. SAMPLE COPIES: Libraries, individuals.

RH is generally known for its advanced, often radical suggestions in morality and human behavior. Exploratory reviews on freedom of expression, theism, and reform provide a rare mixture of lucidity and elegance. Perspectives of science critically assay the contradictions in fundamentalism as well as encourage liberalism in a "new" theology. Carefully documented reports by scholars adopt the same Maslowian goals of humanism and affinity as appear in Freedom, Humanist and especially Crucible and Scientific Atheist.
Each issue provides variety between the six to eight essays, poems, and regular departments, including book reviews. RH is an example of edifying material that is artistic and rich in interpretation.

259. Religious Studies. DATE FOUNDED: 1964. FREQUENCY: q. PRICE: $98/yr. institutions, $49/yr. personal. PUBLISHER: Cambridge University Press, Edinburgh Building, Shaftesburgy Road, Cambridge CB2 2RU, England. EDITOR: Stewart R. Sutherland. INDEX. ADVERTISEMENTS. CIRCULATION: 1,500. MANUSCRIPT SELECTION: Refereed, editorial board. REPRINTS: author. BOOK REVIEWS: 12 reviews, 1-2 pp., signed. SPECIAL ISSUES: Occasional. INDEXED/ ABSTRACTED: BritHumI, PhilosI. TARGET AUDIENCE: AC. ACCEPTANCE RATE: 15%.

RS is concerned with important problems in various fields of religious study. It sustains discussion of issues in philosophy and from psychology of religion. Emphasis is placed on identifying the historical and current (idealistic) solutions to exegetical questions about divinity, humanity, death, ontology, and the resurrection. The result is a conservative approach to doctrines in metaphysics and epistemology. Essays on spirituality and ministry crusades are heavily speculative, though scholars allude to objective evidence. In short, religious movements of modern day are represented better in RS than in other serials.
Contained in each issue are seven features and several book reviews. Periodically a debate on comparative religions kindles new findings that students and teachers may choose to pursue.

260. Reports on Mathematical Logic. DATE FOUNDED: 1965. TITLE CHANGES: Prace z Logiki (1965-1973). FREQUENCY: sa. PRICE: $8/yr. institutions. PUBLISHER: Polish Scientific Publishers, UL, Slawkowska 10, Krakow, Poland. EDITOR: Department of Logic, Jagiellonian University, Grodzka, 52, 31-044 Krakow, Poland. ILLUSTRATIONS. ADVERTISEMENTS. MANUSCRIPT SELECTION: Refereed, editorial board. REPRINTS: author. INDEXED/ABSTRACTED: MathR, PhilosI, ZentMath. TARGET AUDIENCE: AC. SAMPLE COPIES: Libraries, individuals. ACCEPTANCE RATE: 59%.

RML is chiefly devoted to propositional and predicate calculi and their models. Analytical reasoning carries through different investigations of language, ethics, metaphysics, and epistemology. Editors welcome material on neo-logistic issues but largely related to concepts and problems historically debated by Western philosophers. Algebraic formulae and several technical essays on theory and systems advance RML beyond the elementary tableau of Dafora and Philosophia. Contributors are mainly specialists in formal methods. Article format resembles that of Notre Dame Journal of Formal Logic and especially Bulletin of the Section of Logic.
A typical issue contains ten original reviews heavily embedded in symbols, terminology, and extensive syllogism. RML is perhaps a paradise for philosophers into conditional paradigms.

261. Research in Phenomenology. DATE FOUNDED: 1973. FREQUENCY: a. PRICE: $10/yr. institutions. PUBLISHER: Humanities Press, Incorporated, 450 Park Avenue South, New York, New York 10016. EDITOR: John Sallis. ADVERTISEMENTS. CIRCULATION: 1,000. MANUSCRIPT SELECTION: Refereed, editorial board. MICROFORMS: UMI. REPRINTS: author. BOOK REVIEWS: 3 reviews, 1-3 pp., signed. SPECIAL ISSUES: Occasional. INDEXED/ABSTRACTED: PhilosI. TARGET AUDIENCE: AC. SAMPLE COPIES: Libraries.

Inspired by the brilliant work of Edmond Husserl (1859-1938), RP continues the ideal, methods and concrete results of phenomenology. Theoretical research gains access to solutions within the compass of such means as existentialism, historicity, and fundamentals of twentieth century man. RP publishes creative writings by scholars which relate contemporary trends to in-depth examinations of technique and procedures. While models of research differ from Journal of Phenomenological Psychology, the general orientation is still introspectionism.
Each issue presents important currents in the study of self-hood. Five to seven articles and book reviews solidly establish a precedent for this valuable discourse on practical evidence in science.

262. Research in Philosophy and Technology. DATE FOUNDED: 1978. FREQUENCY: a. PRICE: $47.50/yr. institutions. PUBLISHER: JAI Press, 36 Sherwood Glace, Greenwich, Connecticut 06836. EDITOR: Paul T. Durbin. INDEX. MANUSCRIPT SELECTION: Refereed, editorial board. INDEXED/ABSTRACTED: HumanI. TARGET AUDIENCE: AC.

263. <u>Revelation</u>. DATE FOUNDED: 1972. FREQUENCY: 3/yr. PRICE: $6/yr. institutions. PUBLISHER: 8 Victoria Court, Victoria Road, New Brighton, Wirral, Merseyside, L4S 9UD, England. EDITOR: Peter Carman. ILLUSTRATIONS. INDEX. ADVERTISEMENTS. CIRCULATION: 250. MANUSCRIPT SELECTION: Editor. REPRINTS: publisher. BOOK REVIEWS: 7 reviews, 1-2 pp., signed. SPECIAL ISSUES: Occasional. TARGET AUDIENCE: AC, GP. SAMPLE COPIES: Libraries, individuals.

264. <u>Review of Metaphysics</u>. DATE FOUNDED: 1947. FREQUENCY: q. PRICE: $24/yr. institutions, $18/yr. personal, $9/yr. student. PUBLISHER: Philosophical Education Soceity, Incorporated, 620 Michigan Avenue, North East, Washington, D.C. EDITOR: Jude P. Dougherty. ILLUSTRATIONS. INDEX. ADVERTISEMENTS. CIRCULATION: 2,900. MANUSCRIPT SELECTION: Refereed, editorial board. MICROFORMS: UMI. REPRINTS: AMS. BOOK REVIEWS: 40 reviews, 1-2 pp., signed. SPECIAL ISSUES: Occasional. INDEXED/ABSTRACTED: ArtHumCitI, BRI, HumI, PhilosI, RBibPhil, SSI. TARGET AUDIENCE: AC. SAMPLE COPIES: Libraries, individuals. ACCEPTANCE RATE: 5%.

<u>RM</u> is devoted to the promotion of technically competent, definitive contributions to philosophical knowledge. Resolute inquiries purify the leading problems in modern studies of mankind. This anthology of original works protests the tendencies of modern reductionism, materialism, and the oversimplifications of ancient theory. Current interest in foundations of metaphysics commemorates many century-old doctrines of social science. Authors are mostly polemics from British and American universities. Current and informative, <u>RM</u> contrasts its new ideas with the more classic writings of <u>Locke Newsletter, American Philosophical Quarterly</u> and <u>Monist</u>.
  Each issue is indispensable to individuals professionally concerned with or interested in metaphysics. An issue contains six main articles, book reviews, a list of books received, and announcements.

265. <u>ReVision Journal</u>. DATE FOUNDED: 1978. FREQUENCY: sa. PRICE: $14/yr. institutions. PUBLISHER: Rudi Foundation, P.O. Box 468, Cambridge, Massachusetts 02138. EDITOR: Ken Wilber. ILLUSTRATIONS. ADVERTISEMENTS. CIRCULATION: 4,000. MANUSCRIPT SELECTION: Editor. BOOK REVIEWS: 6 reviews, 1-2 pp., signed. INDEXED/ABSTRACTED: PsyAb. TARGET AUDIENCE: AC. SAMPLE COPIES: Libraries. ACCEPTANCE RATE: 40%.

<u>RJ</u> provides interface between Western science, philosophy, psychology, and Eastern mysticism. Editors look for intellectual material that is informative and rich in speculative analyses, although general enough for laymen. Interests range from aesthetics to cosmology, with periodical essays about religion. The collective theme of "ascent to the absolute" portrays a metaphysical science based on a peculiar synthesis between Freud, Neitzsche, Heidegger and paranormality. <u>RJ</u> assembles the straightforward and popular socio-cultural stories that are striking to readers of <u>Psychic Observer</u> and <u>Light</u>.
  Topics on medicine, spirituality, science and psyche, and philosophy fill the many pages of short columns, articles and notes.

266. Revue Internationale de Philosophie. DATE FOUNDED: 1938. FREQUENCY: q. PRICE: 1,800 Belgian Francs/yr. institutions. PUBLISHER: Imprimerie Universa, rue Hoender, 24, B-9200, Wetteren, Belgium. EDITOR: Michel Meyer. ILLUSTRATIONS. INDEX. ADVERTISEMENTS. MANUSCRIPT SELECTION: Refereed, editorial board. REPRINTS: author. BOOK REVIEWS: 10 reviews, 2-5 pp., signed. SPECIAL ISSUES: Occasional. INDEXED/ABSTRACTED: ArtHumCitI, CurrContAH, PhilosI. TARGET AUDIENCE: AC.

Intensifying developments in international study of philosophy require a forum for expression. RIP serves as that forum. It is one of the leading journals covering sciences, methodology, metaphysics, epistemology, and general postulates directly influential upon writings in synthetic and analytic research. Arguments challenge the protocol of physicalism, the ancestry of factual ethics, and overall put forth solutions to many parochial assumptions of mind and nature. This logical enterprise features distinguished scholars from around the world. Their careful evaluations break new ground in areas examined by Nous, Filosofia and Grazer Philosophische Studien.
   A single issue contains eight articles and book reviews in English, French, Spanish and Italian.

267. Revue de Philosophie Ancienne. DATE FOUNDED: 1983. FREQUENCY: sa. PRICE: 1,200 Belgian Francs/yr. institutions. PUBLISHER: Ousia SC, 16 rue des Echevinus, B-1050 Bruxelles, Belgium. EDITOR: Lambros Couloubaritsis. REPRINTS: author. BOOK REVIEWS: 2 reviews, 1-4 pp., signed. SPECIAL ISSUES: 1/yr. TARGET AUDIENCE: AC.

This journal is predominately in French and publishes original treatments of ancient philosophical thinkers from Aristotle to more contemporary works on Hellenic wisdom. Topics vary along a central theme, for example, metaphysics. The historic re-creation of science and morality provides thought-provoking ideas about principles and concepts under question today. RPA moves toward a universal appreciation of early science, in particular, that of Aristotle. Essays are scholarly yet accessible to readers unfamiliar with historical philosophy. The detailed and objective focus on rhetoricians and sophists clearly establishes RPA as a journal befitting for readers who enjoy Proceedings of the Aristotelian Society, Journal of Hellenic Studies, and Dionysius.
   Each issue contains three main articles and an extensive review paper, plus book reviews.

268. Revue Philosophique. DATE FOUNDED: 1876. FREQUENCY: q. PRICE: 230 Francs/yr. institutions. PUBLISHER: Presses Universitaires de France, 12 rue Jean de Beauvais, 75005 Paris, France. EDITORS: P.M. Schuhl, Yvon Bres. ADVERTISEMENTS. CIRCULATION: 1,400. MANUSCRIPT SELECTION: Refereed, editorial board. REPRINTS: Kraus. BOOK REVIEWS: 50 reviews, 500 words, signed. SPECIAL ISSUES: 1/yr. INDEXED/ABSTRACTED: ArtHumCitI, PhilosI. TARGET AUDIENCE: AC. SAMPLE COPIES: Libraries, individuals. ACCEPTANCE RATE: 40%.

English summaries translate this unique collection of twentieth-century themes in philosophy. Themes appear on materialism, language, empiricism, aesthetics, and the fortifying beliefs of Socrates, Pascal, Hegel and Spinoza. Historic knowledge throws light upon perspectives taken for granted by modern day, Anglo-Saxon thinkers. Further, articles in RP are written primarily by teachers but are broader than usual for polemicists. While the French ideology narrows the vantage point, RP is still made the centerpiece of recent trends in theoretical philosophy.

Each issue begins with two main articles, one critical review, notes on documents, and then book reviews. French philosophy imparts a special perspective of noteworthy attention for American readers.

269. Revue Philosophique de Louvain. DATE FOUNDED: 1894. TITLE CHANGES: Revue Neo-Scolastique de Philosophie (1894-1945). FREQUENCY: q. PRICE: 1,250 Belgian Francs/yr. institutions. PUBLISHER: E. Peeters, BP 41, B-3000, Louvain, Belgium. EDITOR: Jacques Etienne. INDEX. ADVERTISEMENTS. CIRCULATION: 1,900. MANUSCRIPT SELECTION: Editor. REPRINTS: author. BOOK REVIEWS: 50 reviews, 1-3 pp., signed. INDEXED/ABSTRACTED: CathI, PhilosI. TARGET AUDIENCE: AC. SAMPLE COPIES: Libraries.

RPL publishes article summaries in French and English. One of the oldest, elite Belgian serials, RPL cross-references a wide variety of investigative topics in metaphysics, aesthetics, ethics, religion and regarding such seminal leaders as Heidegger and Aristotle. Fundamentally simple arguments point out serious deficiences and obscurities in a theory. The critical and objective style engenders raging debates among international scholars as a way of thinking about analytical methods. As such, RPL demonstrates the same confrontive integrity as Revue Internationale de Philosophie and Independent Journal of Philosophy.

Each issue publishes six lead articles followed by book reviews and notes. Awareness of Belgian writings significantly broadens the Western orientation of most American philosophers.

270. Revue des Sciences Philosophiques et Theologiques. DATE FOUNDED; 1907. FREQUENCY: q. PRICE: 326 Francs/yr. institutions. PUBLISHER: Bernard Quelquejeu 20 rue des Tanneries, 75013 Paris, France. EDITOR: Libraire Philosophique. INDEX. CIRCULATION: 1,400. MANUSCRIPT SELECTION: Refereed, editorial board. REPRINTS: author. BOOK REVIEWS: 2-3 reviews, 2-7 pp., signed. INDEXED/ABSTRACTED: OldTAb, PhilosI. TARGET AUDIENCE: AC. SAMPLE COPIES: Libraries.

271. Rhetoric Society Quarterly. DATE FOUNDED: 1968. FREQUENCY: q. PRICE: $6/yr. institutions. PUBLISHER: Rhetoric Society of America, Department of Philosophy, St. Cloud State University, St.Cloud, Minnesota 5630. EDITOR: George E. Yoos. ADVERTISEMENTS. CIRCULATION: 700. MANUSCRIPT SELECTION: Refereed, editorial board. REPRINTS: author. BOOK REVIEWS: 2-5 reviews, 1-3 pp., signed. SPECIAL ISSUES: 1/yr. TARGET AUDIENCE: AC. SAMPLE COPIES: Libraries, individuals. ACCEPTANCE RATE: 20%.

272. Rivista di Psicologia dell'Arte. DATE FOUNDED: 1979. FRE-
QUENCY: sa. PRICE: $20/yr. institutions. PUBLISHER: Jartrakor
Edizioni, 20 via dei Pianellazi, Rome 00186, Italy. EDITOR: Sergis
Lombardo. ILLUSTRATIONS. INDEX. CIRCULATION: 1,500. MANU-
SCRIPT SELECTION: Refereed, editorial board. REPRINTS: author. BOOK
REVIEWS: 1-2 reviews, 2 pp., signed. TARGET AUDIENCE: AC, GP.
ACCEPTANCE RATE: 70%.

English summaries allow readers to appreciate the scientific competence of
RPA. This journal extends aesthetic maturity to regions beyond traditional
psychology of perception. Psychoanalytic interpretations are given of
imagination, and mechanisms of personality. Probing questions unravel the
mysteries of implicit patterns, processes, and causes centered on the
complex power and limits of knowledge. This hybrid of epistemology and
psychotherapy advances the latest form of art therapy but is distinctly
philosophical in its universal statements about mind and nature. Authors
are primarily psychologists and philosophers. Stylistically attractive, RPA
describes with great care and precision the breadth of ideas found in Journal
of Aesthetics and Art Criticism.
  A typical issue of RPA contains four lengthy articles, book reviews, and
special editorials. The beautiful illustrations illuminate ideas for the general
reading audience.

273. Russell: Journal of the Bertrand Russell Archives. DATE FOUNDED:
1971. FREQUENCY: sa. PRICE: $15/yr. institutions, $8.50/yr. personal.
PUBLISHER: McMaster University Library Press, Hamilton, Ontario L8S
4LG, Canada. EDITOR: Kenneth Blackwell. ILLUSTRATIONS. INDEX.
ADVERTISEMENTS. CIRCULATION: 700. MANUSCRIPT SELECTION:
Refereed, editorial board. BOOK REVIEWS: 3 reviews, 1-3 pp., signed.
INDEXED/ABSTRACTED: ArtHumCitI, PhilosI. TARGET AUDIENCE: AC.
SAMPLE COPIES: Libraries, individuals.

274. St. Louis Journal of Philosophy. DATE FOUNDED: 1982. FREQUEN-
CY: sa. PRICE: $7/yr. institutions, $6/yr. personal. PUBLISHER:
Department of Philosophy, St. Louis University, St. Louis, Missouri 63103.
EDITORS: Graduate Association in Philosophy. ILLUSTRATIONS.
ADVERTISEMENTS. REPRINTS: author. BOOK REVIEWS: 2 reviews, 2
pp., signed. SPECIAL ISSUES: Occasional. TARGET AUDIENCE: AC.
SAMPLE COPIES: Libraries, individuals.

SLJP plays a continuous role in the publication of younger philosophers.
Papers in any area of philosophy are considered, without bias toward
recognized schools or theoretical orientation. Nearly every article offers a
systematic and detailed exposition of the problems and solutions for many
pressing philosophical questions. Student authors are sensitive to the
uncertainties of orthodox principles in logic, metaphysics, phenomenology,
history and epistemology. Examined are new arguments based on more
speculative than empirical evidence, but convincing in terms of structure and
execution. SLJP joins the ranks of such high quality serials as Auslegung and
Gnosis by its furtherance of student participation.

Each issue publishes three to five articles categorized into three sections: Articles, treatises, and reviews. Book notes and announcements communicate useful directions for young philosophers aspiring toward a university appointment.

275. <u>Saiva Siddhanta</u>. DATE FOUNDED: 1966. FREQUENCY: q. PRICE: $5/yr. institutions. PUBLISHER: K. Ramalingam, Tamil Manam, East Park Road, Sherroy Nager, Madras 60030, India. EDITOR: V.A. Devasemapathi. ILLUSTRATIONS. INDEX. ADVERTISEMENTS. CIRCULATION: 600. MANUSCRIPT SELECTION: Editor. REPRINTS: publisher. BOOK REVIEWS: 2 reviews, 1-2 pp., signed. TARGET AUDIENCE: GP. SAMPLE COPIES: Libraries, individuals.

276. <u>Salesianum</u>. DATE FOUNDED: 1938. FREQUENCY: q. PRICE: $28/yr. institutions. PUBLISHER: Piazza Atenee Salesiano 00139, Rome, Italy. INDEX. CIRCULATION: 700. MANUSCRIPT SELECTION: Editor. BOOK REVIEWS: 100 reviews, 250-300 words, signed. INDEXED/ ABSTRACTED: IntBibZeit. TARGET AUDIENCE: AC. SAMPLE COPIES: Libraries, individuals.

277. <u>Sapienza</u>. DATE FOUNDED: 1948. FREQUENCY: q. PRICE: $16/yr. institutions. PUBLISHER: Vicoletto S. Pietro a Maiella, 4, 80134 Naples, Italy. EDITORS: Dominican Fathers. INDEX. ADVERTISEMENTS. CIRCULATION: 800. MANUSCRIPT SELECTION: Refereed, editorial board. BOOK REVIEWS: 2-5 reviews, 750 words. SPECIAL ISSUES: 1/yr. INDEXED/ABSTRACTED: OldTAb. TARGET AUDIENCE: AC. SAMPLE COPIES: Libraries.

278. <u>Schopenhauer-Jahrbuch</u>. DATE FOUNDED: 1912. FREQUENCY: a. PRICE: 45 Deutsche Marks/yr. institutions, 15 Deutsche Marks/yr. student. PUBLISHER: Waldemar Kramer, Bornheimer Landwehr 57a, 6000 Frankfurt/Main 60, West Germany. EDITOR: Wolfgang Schirmacher. CIRCULATION: 1,000. MANUSCRIPT SELECTION: Editor. REPRINTS: author. BOOK REVIEWS: 10 reviews, 1-3 pp., signed. INDEXED/AB-STRACTED: PhilosI. TARGET AUDIENCE: AC, GP. ACCEPTANCE RATE: 50%.

Critiques of monumental thinkers usually attract an international patronage because of the many unanswered questions about theory and practice. <u>SJ</u> establishes such a platform for questions regarding the intercultural theories of Arthur Schopenhauer (1788-1860), pessimist and metaphysician. This remarkable collection of excerpts and analysis re-states the primary significance of European (German) philosophy during the nineteenth century. Topics related to Schopenhauer, his life and contributions, are published in German, English, and French by esteemed members of the International Schopenhauer-Geselleschaft, the largest philosophical society in Germany. Contributors first present their papers at various meetings and lecture series sponsored by the Gesellschaft. Like most dedicatory journals, <u>SJ</u> includes diverse reactions from individuals of all branches of philosophy and social sciences.

The volume pays tremendous respect to Shopenhauer's progressive insights. A series of original articles follows with an up-to-date bibliography of literature on Schopenhauer.

279. Science and Nature. DATE FOUNDED: 1978. FREQUENCY: a. PRICE: $12/yr. institutions, $5/yr. personal. PUBLISHER: Dialectics Workshop, 53 Hickory Hill, Tappan, New York 10983. EDITOR: Lester Talkington. ILLUSTRATIONS. ADVERTISEMENTS. CIRCULATION: 600. MANUSCRIPT SELECTION: Refereed, editorial board. REPRINTS: publisher. BOOK REVIEWS: 7 reviews, 1-2 pp., signed. TARGET AUDIENCE: AC. SAMPLE COPIES: Libraries, individuals.

What is the role of ideology in the natural sciences? SN proposes a simple and atechnical answer to this question. Elaborations of theory, practice, and implications in physical, biological and formal (mathematical and logical) sciences are interconnected in this dialectic journal. SN demonstrates historical and sociologic problems within the Marxist world view and helps further the development of materialism and epistemology. Basic concepts in Marxist philosophy furnish overwhelming evidence for the laws of unity, struggle of opposites and differences between contradiction and causation. Taking this Marxist position sharpens the rivalry with such journals as Creation Research Society Quarterly, as well as Creation/Evolution. The Marxist thinking alone identifies contributors as political scientists and philosophers concerned with issues of government.
Experienced theorists will appreciate the concise and persuasive premises. Each issue of SN features about eleven articles under a different classification. Such classification as "Feedback," "Theory of Knowledge," "Philosophy Tutorial," and " Dynamics' Downfall" poke fun at the capitalistic trends toward militarization and computerization.

280. Science of Science. DATE FOUNDED: 1980. FREQUENCY: q. PRICE: $70/yr. institutions, $22/yr. personal. PUBLISHER: D. Reidel Publishing Company, P.O. Box 322, 3300 AH Dordrecht, Netherlands. EDITORS: Ignacy Malecki, Bohadan Walentynowicz. ILLUSTRATIONS. INDEX. ADVERTISEMENTS. MANUSCRIPT SELECTION: Refereed, editorial board. REPRINTS: author. SPECIAL ISSUES: Occasional. TARGET AUDIENCE: AC. SAMPLE COPIES: Libraries.

SS is an international journal of studies on scientific reasoning and the scientific enterprise. Full-length papers communicate on all major areas of science, broadly embracing natural and social sciences. SS serves as a systematic fund of statements, propositions, hypotheses, and research activity. Scientists from primarily socialist countries contribute objective examinations of policy, research design, technology, creativity, and organizational networks. Just as Aut Aut dissects political factors, so SS dissects the crucial scientific factors in twentieth century materialism.
SS publishes three to five corsucating articles on skeptical science, followed by book notes. Secrets of the Socialist system are divulged on a level understandable to introductory students.

281. Scientia. DATE FOUNDED: 1907. FREQUENCY: 3/yr. PRICE:
$54/yr. institutions. PUBLISHER: Revista Scientia Editrice-via Guastalla a,
20122 Milano, Italy. EDITOR: N. Conetti. ILLUSTRATIONS. INDEX.
ADVERTISEMENTS. CIRCULATION: 4,000. MANUSCRIPT SELECTION:
Editor. REPRINTS: author. BOOK REVIEWS: 20 reviews, 1-3 pp. SPECIAL
ISSUES: 2/yr. INDEXED/ABSTRACTED: PhilosI. TARGET AUDIENCE: AC.

Scientia is a means of communication between specialists in various
disciplines that promote a synthetic vision and critical examination of
problems in science. On the basis of these premises the disciplines range
from history of science to mathematics, astronomy, physics, chemistry,
biology and all its allied fields including behavioral psychology. Critical
papers are written by scientists and technicians for a highly qualified (not
technical) audience. However, these papers are all solicited by the editor.
For 75 years Scientia has remained faithful to the driving aims of new
philosophical movements. As in Research in Philosophy and Technology and
Philosophy of Science, the particular accelerators in Scientia are its
scientific theorizing and multiplicative impact on informed readers.
  Each issue contains articles in the author's original language and then
translated into Italian or English. Four major articles are followed by book
reviews and a list of books received.

282. Seeker Magazine. DATE FOUNDED: 1969. TITLE CHANGES: New
Focus (1969-1971), Seeker Newsletter (1972-1981). FREQUENCY: sa. PRICE:
$10/yr. institutions. PUBLISHER: P.O. Box 7601, San Diego, California
92107. EDITORS: Diane K. Pike, Arleen Lorrance. ILLUSTRATIONS.
CIRCULATION: 1,000. MANUSCRIPT SELECTION: Editors. TARGET
AUDIENCE: GP. SAMPLE COPIES: Libraries, individuals. ACCEPTANCE
RATE: 50%.

India's flowing influence of spiritual self-growth moves at a rapid pace
through pages of SM. This popularized tribunal of Indian philosophy, ecology,
communal living, and inner awareness takes an everyday look at what goes
on in India. American columnists retrospect their experiences and new
realizations of India's religious naturalism. Unresolved conflicts about death,
mysticism, and the psyche in general are put into proper focus. Articles
even condemn the Guru-attraction in fundamentalistic Indian groups. Thus
SM dispells the false and stereotypic myths of Eastern religion, defining the
role of divinity in more practical terms. In contrast to Dawn and Dharma,
SM offers a refreshing glimpse at the Indian life-style infrequently seen
through the eyes of American seekers.
  SM fills its pages with short articles by regular columnists. Reported
stories and reviews of such governmental officials as Indira Gandhi make SM
more of a sociologic than an exclusively philosophic magazine.

283. Seikyo Times. DATE FOUNDED: 1965. FREQUENCY: m. PRICE:
$36/yr. PUBLISHER: 525 Wilshire Boulevard, Santa Monica, California
90401. EDITOR: George M. Williams. ILLUSTRATIONS. INDEX.
ADVERTISEMENTS. MANUSCRIPT SELECTION: Refereed, editorial board.
REPRINTS: publisher. TARGET AUDIENCE: GP, SP. SAMPLE COPIES:
Libraries.

ST is the definitive synthesis of subjects related to Nichiren Shoshu Buddhism and the activities of the Soka Gakkai International. This evolving peace movement since Daishonin's death in 1282 is a tribute to both priesthood and laity who lead a pilgrimage toward cultural humanity. The result is a leading international society which convenes at the Head Temple Taiseki-ji for special religious and festival ceremonies. The commemorative photos in each article tell almost a legendary story of the individuals who fought for peace. ST is an inviting escape from the battlegrounds of any military society. While less probing than Philosophy and Social Action, it does cover the prevailing conditions for human rights.

A regular issue contains ten spiritually-moving articles on current international activities of the Soka Gakkai International (SGI). The column called "Around the World" provides a small sample of readers' reactions to the flourishing SGI movement.

284. Self-Knowledge. DATE FOUNDED: 1948. FREQUENCY: q. PRICE: 4 Pounds/yr. institutions. PUBLISHER: 29, Chepstow Villas, London West 1142, England. EDITOR: Shanti-shan. ILLUSTRATIONS. INDEX. CIRCULATION: 1,000. MANUSCRIPT SELECTION: Refereed, editorial board. TARGET AUDIENCE: GP. SAMPLE COPIES: Libraries, individuals.

Yoga traditions encompass a history of psychologic and philosophic methods and rituals embedded in spiritual devotion. SK continues this outlook through the ancient teachings of Adhyatma Yoga. The highest spiritual wisdom experienced by the Seers of Truth in ancient times has been passed down to the present day through an unbroken line of sages. The metaphysical teachings promote a nondualistic explanation of the universe. In fact, its practical side governs clear guidance about man's moral acts. However, SK insists it is an educational and not a theoretical journal; instruction includes a belief in God, practical uses of Yoga and an altruistic service to mankind. Whether readers feel this "instruction" is atheoretical may depend on how "education" is defined. For reference, consider Prana Yoga Life and Energy and Character.

Every issue offers new spiritual lessons in eight articles. The essential goal of SK, differing slightly from other serials, is to enable the pupil the discovery of his own nature--rather than that of somebody else's.

285. Self-Realization. DATE FOUNDED: 1925. TITLE CHANGES: East-West (1925-1934), Inner Culture (1934-1944), East-West (1944-1948). FREQUENCY: q. PRICE: $2.40/yr. institutions. PUBLISHER: Self-Realization Fellowship, 3880 San Rafael Avenue, Los Angeles, California 90065. EDITOR: Jane Brush. ILLUSTRATIONS. INDEX. ADVERTISEMENTS. CIRCULATION: 22,000. MANUSCRIPT SELECTION: Refereed, editorial board. BOOK REVIEWS: 1 review, 1-2 pp. TARGET AUDIENCE: AC, GP, SP. SAMPLE COPIES: Libraries.

SR is dedicated to the investigation of practical methods of harmonizing the physical, mental, and spiritual aspects of man's "being" through universal laws of life. Articles explain that all true religious philosophies derive from perception of truth and expansion of consciousness. Special attention is given to the religious geniuses of the Hindu tradition and Christianity, as well as to teachings of Paramahansa Yogananda. Yoga meditation moves toward the same attainment of "oneness" as do methods in Self-Knowledge.

A typical issue contains eight short papers on various topics regarding service, devotion, knowledge, and meditation.   Hinduistic metaphysics persists in the commentary on God, proper diet, right living, and cosmic energy.

286.   Semiotext.   DATE FOUNDED: 1974.   FREQUENCY: 3/yr. PRICE: $24/yr. institutions, $12/yr. personal, $10/yr. student.   PUBLISHER: Polymorph Press, 522 Philosophy Hall, Columbia University, New York, New York   10027.   EDITOR: Sylvere Lotringer.   ILLUSTRATIONS. INDEX. ADVERTISEMENTS.   CIRCULATION: 10,000.   MANUSCRIPT SELECTION: Refereed,   editorial   board.   SPECIAL   ISSUES: Occasional.   TARGET AUDIENCE: AC.

Semiotext contributes to the idealistic debate about nature and functions of cultural politics.   Critical essays examine how far inherited images of authority and social regimes derive from aristocratic and traditional order. These carefully constructed arguments by scholars illuminate the mistaken assumptions in such views as Marxist philosophy, and historically significant events such as the rise of Nazism.   It is seldom that one serial covers so global a topic as macropolitical influences in the modern world and beyond. Semiotext greets readers with the same aims as found in Das Arguments and Philosophy and Public Affairs.
   Semiotext provides an excellent and timely review of political concepts in three to six original articles.   Special issues on polysexuality, Nietzsche, and anti-Oedipus theories mix general with esoteric knowledge.

287.   Semiotica.   DATE FOUNDED: 1969.   FREQUENCY: 2 double issues/yr.   PRICE: $208/yr. institutions, $104/yr. personal.   PUBLISHER: Mouton Publishers, 200 Saw Mill River Road, Hawthorne, New York, 10532. EDITOR: Thomas A. Sebeok.   ILLUSTRATIONS.   INDEX.   ADVER-TISEMENTS.   MANUSCRIPT SELECTION: Refereed, editorial board. REPRINTS: author. BOOK REVIEWS: 1-2 reviews, 2 pp., signed. SPECIAL ISSUES: Occasional.   TARGET   AUDIENCE: AC.   SAMPLE   COPIES: Libraries. ACCEPTANCE RATE: 33%.

Semiotica is the organ of the International Association of Semiotic Studies, founded in 1969.   Articles in English and French develop semiotic concepts within the lines of the scientific approach commonly found in Kodikas/Code. Recognized scholars critically evaluate the structure of language and verbal communication as indicative of cultural and historical shifts in symbolic interaction.   Factors in generating conversation, semiosis and metaphor support the driving interest in semiotic research.   New theories speculate on ape language, abstractions, and meaning in general.
   A regular issue contains six pragmatic articles and book reviews. The essential reason for Semiotica, apart from disciplinary interest, is to declare independence from other synthetic treatments of linguistic behavior.

288.   Sigmund Freud House Bulletin.   DATE FOUNDED: 1975. FREQUENCY: sa.   PRICE: $15/yr. institutions.   PUBLISHER: Sigmund Freud Society, 1090 Vienna Beiggasse 19 Austria.   EDITOR: The Society. MANUSCRIPT SELECTION: Refereed, editorial board. REPRINTS: author. BOOK REVIEWS: 1-2 reviews, 1-3 pp., signed. TARGET AUDIENCE: AC,

GP.SAMPLE COPIES: Libraries, individuals.

289. Signs: Journal of Women in Culture and Society. DATE FOUNDED:
1975. FREQUENCY: q. PRICE: $24/yr. institutions, $16/yr. personal,
$14.40/yr. student. PUBLISHER: University of Chicago Press, 11030 Langley
Avenue, Chicago, Illinois 60628. EDITOR: Catharine R. Stimpson.
ILLUSTRATIONS. INDEX. ADVERTISEMENTS. MANUSCRIPT SELECTION:
Refereed, editorial board. REPRINTS: author. BOOK REVIEWS: 2-4
reviews, 1-2 pp., signed. SPECIAL ISSUES: Occasional. TARGET AU-
DIENCE: AC. SAMPLE COPIES: Libraries.

Signs establishes itself internationally as one of the most respectable journals
devoted to the discussion of scholarship about women.   Original research,
contemplative essays and commentary bridge the humanities and social
sciences by examining the status of women and religion, and national
development and the workplace.   Past special issues have concentrated on
single themes about women and sexuality, and implications for a liberal
culture.   In this way, Signs foreshadows the emerging existentialism of the
woman's role in Western civilization.   Like Hypatia, topics on feminism
challenge traditions with alternative solutions to modern needs. Contributors
are mainly female scholars and specialists in political science and philosophy.
The highly successful articles undoubtedly reflect the supportive readership.
   Current issues contain four to five original papers, book reviews, and a
unique section entitled "The New Scholarship: Review Essays" which focuses
on a particular discipline.

290. Social Theory and Practice. DATE FOUNDED: 1970. FREQUENCY:
3/yr.   PRICE: $27/yr. institutions, $12/yr. personal. PUBLISHER: Department of Philosophy, Florida State University, Tallahassee, Florida   32306.
EDITOR: Peter C. Dalton. INDEX. ADVERTISEMENTS. CIRCULATION:
600. MANUSCRIPT SELECTION: Refereed, editorial board. MICROFORMS:
UMI.   REPRINTS: UMI. BOOK REVIEWS: 1-2 reviews/volume, 1-4 pp.,
signed.   SPECIAL ISSUES: Occasional. INDEXED/ABSTRACTED: ABC,
AbCrP, CIJE, LLBA, PhilosI, RBibPhil, SSCI, SocAB. TARGET AUDIENCE:
AC. SAMPLE COPIES: Libraries, individuals. ACCEPTANCE RATE: 10%.

STP is intended to provide a forum for discussion of important and controversial issues in social, political, legal, economic, educational and moral
philosophy.   Critical studies of classical or contemporary social philosophy
contain serious theoretical arguments on pornography, feminism, rational
action and utilitarianism.   Constructive inquiry generally engages the reader
to question the social forces over the course of history, from the Holocaust to
the "new middle class." STP deals at all levels with the logic of philosophical
implications to understand social behavior.   Articles by philosophers share the
same format as Modern Schoolman and Philosophy and Social Action.
   A typical issue publishes five feature articles, occasional book reviews, and
a list of books received.   The articles go to great effort to minimize jargon.

291. <u>Sophia: A Journal in Philosophical Theology</u>. DATE FOUNDED: 1962. FREQUENCY: 3/yr. PRICE: $7.50/yr. institutions. PUBLISHER: School of Humanities, Deakin University, Victoria 3217, Australia. EDITOR: M.J. Charlesworth. CIRCULATION: 750. MANUSCRIPT SELECTION: Editor. REPRINTS: author. TARGET AUDIENCE: AC. SAMPLE COPIES: Libraries, individuals. ACCEPTANCE RATE: 50%.

<u>Sophia</u> asks religious questions at the risk of controversy. Papers provide rational clarification of essentially pragmatic puzzles facing theologians. Metaphilosophical at times, <u>Sophia</u> sets out to treat beliefs and actions of mankind against a backdrop of divine worshop. The emphasis upon principles of mystic science supports this unique approach to the ancient problems in sociology, epistemology, and history. Interesting claims about materialism and celestial phenomena move at a quicker pace than articles in <u>Religious Studies</u> and <u>Laval Theologique et Philosophique</u>.
   <u>Sophia</u> publishes four lead articles encased in what almost looks like a brochure.

292. <u>Southern Journal of Philosophy</u>. DATE FOUNDED: 1963. FREQUENCY: q. PRICE: $14/yr. institutions. PUBLISHER: Department of Philosophy, Memphis State University, Memphis, Tennessee 38152. EDITOR: Nancy D. Simco. INDEX. ADVERTISEMENTS. CIRCULATION: 1,200. MANUSCRIPT SELECTION: Refereed, editorial board. MICROFORMS: UMI. REPRINTS: author. BOOK REVIEWS: 1 review, 1-3 pp., signed. SPECIAL ISSUES: 1/yr. INDEXED/ABSTRACTED: ArtHumCitI, CurrContAH, PhilosI. TARGET AUDIENCE: AC. SAMPLE COPIES: Libraries, individuals. ACCEPTANCE RATE: 8%.

So much of the best contemporary philosophy appears in a growing proliferation of journals. At times journals find it difficult to keep track of this progress. <u>SJP</u> claims exception to this rule by its candor and international contribution to general branches of social science. Sharp essays try to reconcile personal experiences of the social world with representations of that world, especially in relation to psychology and history. The critical arguments are anchored in solid logical foundations resembling <u>Filosofia</u>, <u>Chroniques des Philosophie</u> and <u>Philosophical Forum</u>.
   A typical issue contains ten full-length articles, book reviews, and announcements of relevant conferences and events. Conceptually, <u>SJP</u> champions the need for a single resource on up-to-date trends in philosophy.

293. <u>Southwestern Philosophical Society</u> (newsletter). DATE FOUNDED: 1936. FREQUENCY: q. PRICE: $15/yr. institutions. PUBLISHER: Southwestern Philosophical Society, North Texas State University, Department of Philosophy, Denton, Texas 76203. EDITOR: Max Oelschlaeger. CIRCULATION: 300. BOOK REVIEWS: 1 review, 700 words, signed. TARGET AUDIENCE: AC.

294. <u>Soviet Studies in Philosophy</u>. DATE FOUNDED: 1962. FREQUENCY: q. PRICE: $170/yr. institutions, $44/yr. personal. PUBLISHER: M.E. Sharpe, Incorporated, 80 Business Park Drive, Armonk, New York 10504. EDITOR: John Somerville. INDEX. ADVERTISEMENTS. MANUSCRIPT SELECTION: Refereed, editorial board. INDEXED/ABSTRACTED:

CurrContAH, PhilosI.   TARGET AUDIENCE: AC.   SAMPLE COPIES:
Libraries, individuals.

Rarely does a journal contain unabridged translation of articles chiefly from
Soviet publications. Excerpts from Chinese texts are available in Chinese
Studies in Philosophy and of course history and religion journals quote
selected passages from the Bible. But the task to bring Soviet ideas onto
American shores requires the elegance and careful scrutiny only found in SSP.
This journal advances scientific-philosophical theory as espoused by Soviet
thinkers in their original sources. Social determinants of political objectivity,
individual ideals, and concepts in epistemology derive largely from socialism.
This bias moves the reader to understand internal frustration in Soviet
establishments.   The so-called Communistic underpinning so boldly felt in
Science of Science and Science and Nature are inconsequential in many of the
translations.
   Each issue of SSP presents six reprinted or original papers from a selection
of esteemed Soviet journals, for example, Filosofski Nauki and Vestnik
Moskovskogo Universitela seriia filosofii.

295.   Soziale Welt: Zeitschrift fur Soziatwissenschaftliche Forschung und
Praxis.   DATE FOUNDED: 1949.   FREQUENCY: q. PRICE: 72 Deutsche
Marks/yr. institutions.   PUBLISHER: Verlag Otto Schwartz and Company,
Annastr 7, 3400 Gottingen, West Germany.   EDITORS: Heinz Hartmann,
Ulrich Beck.   ILLUSTRATIONS.   INDEX.   ADVERTISEMENTS.   CIRCULA-
TION: 1,200.   MANUSCRIPT SELECTION: Editor.   REPRINTS: author.
SPECIAL ISSUES: Occasional.   TARGET AUDIENCE: AC.   ACCEPTANCE
RATE: 20%.

296.   Speculum.   DATE FOUNDED: 1926.   FREQUENCY: q. PRICE: $50/yr.
institutions.   PUBLISHER: Medieval Academy, 1430 Massachusetts Avenue,
Cambridge,   Massachusetts   02138.   EDITOR: Luke H. Wenger.
ILLUSTRATIONS.   INDEX.   ADVERTISEMENTS.   CIRCULATION: 5,625.
MANUSCRIPT SELECTION: Refereed, editorial board. MICROFORMS: UMI.
REPRINTS: author.   BOOK REVIEWS: 50 reviews, 1-2 pp., signed. SPECIAL
ISSUES: Occasional.   TARGET AUDIENCE: AC.   ACCEPTANCE RATE:
12%.

297.   Spectrum.   DATE FOUNDED: 1969.   FREQUENCY: q. PRICE: $15/yr.
institutions.   PUBLISHER: Association of Adventist Forums, Box 5330,
Takoma Park, Maryland   20912.   EDITOR: Roy Branson.   INDEX.
CIRCULATION: 7,000.   REPRINTS: publisher.   BOOK REVIEWS: 2 reviews,
1-3 pp., signed. TARGET AUDIENCE: AC, GP. SAMPLE COPIES: Libraries.

Spectrum is a journal established to encourage Seventh-day Adventist
participation in the discussion of contemporary issues from a Christian
viewpoint, and to look without prejudice at intellectual and cultural growth.
Statements of fact emanate from Adventist history, church organizations, and
debates between religion and science.   Spectrum kindles a noncommital
attitude toward philosophical judgments about man's loss of liberty and belief
in traditional doctrines.   At the same time, special theme papers are
inherently evangelical.   The roster of goals and objectives pursued by
Adventists clearly fuel emotions against the scientific and atheistic

communities. In this way, Spectrum conveys a message similar to Creation Research Society Quarterly and Contemplative Review.

Spectrum publishes three lead articles, seven short papers under a special section, reports, responses and book reviews. For those sympathetic to the Adventist movement, Spectrum is quite an accommodation.

298. Stromata. DATE FOUNDED: 1944. FREQUENCY: q. PRICE: $20/yr. institutions. PUBLISHER: Facultades Filosofia y Teologia, Casilla 10, 1663-San Miguel, Argentina. EDITOR: Miquel Anjel Fiorito. INDEX. ADVERTISEMENTS. CIRCULATION: 1,000. MANUSCRIPT SELECTION: Refereed, editorial board. REPRINTS: author. BOOK REVIEWS: 30 reviews, 1-2 pp., signed. INDEXED/ABSTRACTED: PhilosI. TARGET AUDIENCE: AC. SAMPLE COPIES: Libraries. ACCEPTANCE RATE: 50%.

299. Studia Estetyczne. DATE FOUNDED: 1960. TITLE CHANGES: Estetyka (1960-1963). FREQUENCY: a. PRICE: 90 Zloty/yr. institutions. PUBLISHER: Panstwowe Wydaunictine Waukowe, Gindown 10, 00-251 Warsaw, Poland. EDITOR: Staw Kizemien-Gjak. ILLUSTRATIONS. INDEX. CIRCULATION: 600. MANUSCRIPT SELECTION: Editor. REPRINTS: author. BOOK REVIEWS: 10 reviews, 1-3 pp., signed. INDEXED/ABSTRACTED: PhilosI. TARGET AUDIENCE: AC. SAMPLE COPIES: Libraries, individuals. ACCEPTANCE RATE: 90%.

300. Studia Filozoficzne. DATE FOUNDED: 1957. TITLE CHANGES: Mysl Filozoficzna (1957-1958). FREQUENCY: m. PRICE: 960 Zloty/yr. institutions. PUBLISHER: Institute of Philosophy and Sociology, Committee of Philosophical Sciences, Polish Academy of Science, Polish Scientific Publishers, Nowy Swiat 49, 00-042 Warsaw, Poland. EDITOR: Michal Hempolinski. INDEX. CIRCULATION: 3,500. MANUSCRIPT SELECTION: Refereed, editorial board. BOOK REVIEWS: 3-4 reviews, 1-3 pp., signed. SPECIAL ISSUES: 1-2/yr. INDEXED/ABSTRACTED: PhilosI. TARGET AUDIENCE: AC. SAMPLE COPIES: Libraries, individuals. ACCEPTANCE RATE: 75%.

SF is the central Polish philosophical journal. It synthesizes a dozen or so journals in Poland proper. Issues provide a surprisingly prolific exchange with Western philosophers on aesthetics, epistemology, ethics, morality, history, and social sciences. The scientific level of papers is decisive and matches the caliber of most American periodicals. The special double issues are available in English and Russian. Articles essentially survey the burgeoning ideas in Marxism in relation to culturalization. Under pressure to reach international readers, SF explores in-depth problems of contemporary revolutions, the visions of individual freedom, and Polish religions. SF is much like a Newsweek of modern Polish thought written for academic and possibly general audiences.

SF provides twelve main articles and book reviews. Every article is appended with an English summary.

301. Studia Leibmitiana Sonderhefte. DATE FOUNDED: 1969. FREQUEN-CY: sa. PUBLISHER: Franz Steiner Verlag, 6MBH, 62 Wiesbaden, Friedrich-str 24, West Germany. EDITORS: Gottfried Wienhelm Leibniz Society. ILLUSTRATIONS. INDEX. MANUSCRIPT SELECTION: Refereed, editorial

board.   REPRINTS: publisher.   SPECIAL ISSUES: Occasional.   TARGET
AUDIENCE: AC.

302.   Studia Logica.   DATE FOUNDED: 1953.   FREQUENCY: q. PRICE:
$60/yr. institutions.   PUBLISHER: North-Holland Publishing Company, P.O.
Box 103, 1000 AC Amsterdam, Netherlands.   EDITOR: Polish Academy of
Sciences,Institute of Philosophy and Sociology.   ILLUSTRATIONS. INDEX.
ADVERTISEMENTS.   MANUSCRIPT SELECTION: Refereed, editorial board.
REPRINTS: author. BOOK REVIEWS: 10 reviews, 1-3 pp., signed. SPECIAL
ISSUES: Occasional.   INDEXED/ABSTRACTED: MathR, PhilosI, RZ.
TARGET AUDIENCE: AC.   SAMPLE COPIES: Libraries, individuals.
ACCEPTANCE RATE: 60%.

SL is an interdisciplinary forum for technical and mathematical dialogue in
contemporary logic and especially in linguistics. Analytic methods dominate
the penetrating resolutions between standard, nonstandard and idealistic
postulates underlying theories in algebra, physics, and systems. Formal systems
provide principles and valid reasoning, mostly by philosophers, on subjects also
found in Reports on Mathematical Logic, Philosophical Review and Notre
Dame Journal of Formal Logic.
 SL contains five major articles, book reviews and a list of books received.
At best, SL closes the international gap between Anglo-Saxon and Polish philosophies.

303.   Studia Universitatis Babes-Bolyai, Series Philosophia.   DATE FOUNDED:
1956.   FREQUENCY: a. PRICE: $30/yr. institutions.   PUBLISHER: Babes-
Bolyai Universus, R-3400 CLUJ-Napoca, Romania.   EDITOR: Ion Vlad.
CIRCULATION: 400. MANUSCRIPT SELECTION: Refereed, editorial board.
BOOK REVIEWS: 2-3 reviews, 700 words, signed. TARGET AUDIENCE: AC.
SAMPLE COPIES: Libraries.

304.   Studies in Formative Spirituality.   DATE FOUNDED: 1980.   TITLE
CHANGES: Humanitas (1980).   FREQUENCY: 3/yr. PRICE: $14/yr.
PUBLISHER: Institute of Formative Spirituality, Duquesne University,
Pittsburgh, Pennsylvania 15282.   EDITOR: Adrian van Kaam.   INDEX.
CIRCULATION: 3,000. MANUSCRIPT SELECTION: Refereed, editorial
board.   MICRFORMS: UMI. REPRINTS: author. BOOK REVIEWS: 6
summaries, 20 annotations, 1-5 pp. INDEXED/ABSTRACTED: CathI, RelAb.
TARGET AUDIENCE: AC. SAMPLE COPIES: Libraries.

This unique journal is designed to integrate the transcendent, functional and
socio-historical dimensions of human and Christian formation. SFS' purpose is
to provide a discipline-related approach to important issues of dynamic
spiritual growth from   the point of view of science and its auxilliary
disciplines. Contemporary experts in "formative spirituality" contribute
thematic articles, translations from foreign journals, and   summaries of
selected works.   SFS offers a systematic, objective look at philosophical,
psychological and religious growth characteristic of Cross Currents and
Energy and Character.
 A typical issue enumerates on international trends regarding ascetical and
mystical theology, medicine, psychiatry, and social sciences. Four to six
articles are followed by a glossary of the Science of Foundational Formative

Spirituality, a selected topical bibliography of new books.

305. Studies in Language. DATE FOUNDED: 1977. FREQUENCY: 3/yr.
PRICE: $52/yr. institutions. PUBLISHER: John Benjamins Publishing
Company, One Buttonwood Square, Philadelphia, Pennsylvania 19130.
EDITOR: John W.M. Verhaar. BOOK REVIEWS: 4 reviews, 1-5 pp., signed.
SPECIAL ISSUES: Occasional. TARGET AUDIENCE: AC. SAMPLE COPIES:
Libraries.

306. Studies in Philosophy and the History of Philosophy. DATE FOUNDED:
1961. FREQUENCY: a. Price: $25/yr. institutions. PUBLISHER: Catholic
University of America Press, Catholic University, Washington D.C. 20064.
EDITOR: Jude P. Dougherty. INDEX. CIRCULATION: 1,200. MANUSCRIPT
SELECTION: Refereed, editorial board. TARGET AUDIENCE: AC.

307. Studies in Soviet Thought. DATE FOUNDED: 1961. FREQUENCY: q.
PRICE: $340/yr. institutions, $110/yr. personal. PUBLISHER: D. Reidel
Publishing Company, P.O. Box 3300 Dordrecht, Netherlands. EDITORS:
Thomas J. Blakely, Guido Jung, NIkolaus Lobkowicz. ILLUSTRATIONS.
INDEX. ADVERTISEMENTS. MANUSCRIPT SELECTION: Refereed, editorial
board. BOOK REVIEWS: 2 reviews, 2 pp., signed. SPECIAL ISSUES:
Occasional. TARGET AUDIENCE: AC. SAMPLE COPIES: Libraries.

SST serves as an international medium for the publication of critical
observations and writings on Soviet philosophy. A companion to Soviet
Studies in Philosophy, articles focus primarily on recent Soviet thought
dealing with pre- and post-revolutionary developments. The systematization
of socialist government and implications for the central Marxist theories
provide stimulating ideas for the advanced reader. SST offers the best
collection of challenging and generally well-executed criticism of political
interactions to better understand current and projected changes in the Soviet
Union.
   Each issue publishes three to five research papers, short notes, comments,
reports, critical reviews, and discussions, followed by book reviews.

308. Symbol. DATE FOUNDED: 1983. FREQUENCY: q. PRICE: $10/yr.
institutions. PUBLISHER: Geomantic Research, 142 Pheasant Rise, Bar Hill,
Cambridge CB3 8SD, England. EDITOR: Nigel Pennick. ILLUSTRATIONS.
ADVERTISEMENTS. CIRCULATION: 200. MANUSCRIPT SELECTION:
Editor. BOOK REVIEWS: 6 reviews, 1-3 pp., signed. TARGET AUDIENCE:
AC. SAMPLE COPIES: Libraries.

309. Synthese. DATE FOUNDED: 1936. FREQUENCY: 3/yr. PRICE:
$281/yr. institutions, $88/yr. personal. PUBLISHER: D. Reidel Publishing
Company, P.O. Box 322, 3300 AH Dordrecht, Netherlands. EDITOR: Jaakks
Hintikka. ILLUSTRATIONS. INDEX. ADVERTISEMENTS. MANUSCRIPT
SELECTION: Refereed, editorial board. REPRINTS: author. SPECIAL
ISSUES: Occasional. INDEXED/ABSTRACTED: PhilosI. TARGET AUDIENCE:
AC. SAMPLE COPIES: Libraries.

Outstanding essays come to grips with the notion of knowledge and logic. This well-seasoned journal constitutes a forum for topics on methodology, and philosophy of science. Articles in Synthese define and describe problems of scientific discovery, of scientific inference, and of induction and probability. The equivocal roles of mathematics and causation find new solutions through discussions on linguistics and symbolic logic. This fresh philosophizing answers questions basic to the human conduct, but without burdensome jargon. Further, Synthese acts as a testing ground for newly formulated concepts, principles, and behavioral systems. In ways similar to Nous, Journal of Philosophy and Ratio, Synthese argues for an applied sense of empiricism.

Philosophical and scientific ideas appear among five to six original articles. Synthese provides readers with many opportunities to enjoy academic debate on transcultural themes.

310. Teaching Philosophy. DATE FOUNDED: 1975. FREQUENCY: q. PRICE: $27/yr. institutions, $15/yr. personal. PUBLISHER: Philosophy Documentation Center, Bowling Green State University, Bowling Green, Ohio 45221. EDITOR: Arnold Wilson. ILLUSTRATIONS. INDEX. ADVERTISEMENTS. CIRCULATION: 1,040. MANUSCRIPT SELECTION: Refereed, editorial board. REPRINTS: author. BOOK REVIEWS: 20 reviews, 1-2 pp., signed. SPECIAL ISSUES: Occasional. INDEXED/ABSTRACTED: PhilosI. TARGET AUDIENCE: AC. SAMPLE COPIES: Libraries, individuals. ACCEPTANCE RATE: 20%.

Today's philosophers typically enter their classroom careers with little or no teaching preparation. TP rushes to this need with tangible and effective methods of philosophy instruction. Editorial policy restricts foundational and philosophic inquiry to problems of pedagogy. This includes theoretical models, innovative learning strategy, and evaluations of new books and audio-visual equipment. TP bravely reports on experimental and interdisciplinary course curricula related to such current trends as "philosophy for children" and elementary logic in student counseling. Methods of critical thinking resemble those found in Australian Logic Teachers Journal and Educational Philosophy and Theory.

A regular issue features five lead articles, two review essays, and a list of new publications. College and university teachers are seriously at a loss without this resource periodical.

311. Telos: A Journal of Critical Social Thought. DATE FOUNDED: 1968. FREQUENCY: q. PRICE: $40/yr. institutions, $20/yr. personal. PUBLISHER: Telos Press Limited, Box 3111, St. Louis, Missouri 63130. EDITOR: Paul Piccone. INDEX. ADVERTISEMENTS. CIRCULATION: 4,000. MANUSCRIPT SELECTION: Refereed, editorial board. REPRINTS: author. BOOK REVIEWS: 4-8 reviews, 1-3 pp., signed. SPECIAL ISSUES: Occasional. INDEXED/ABSTRACTED: PhilosI. TARGET AUDIENCE: AC. SAMPLE COPIES: Libraries. ACCEPTANCE RATE: 5%.

312. Teosofi i Norden. DATE FOUNDED: 1890. TITLE CHANGES: Teosofisk Tidskrift (1890-1960). FREQUENCY: q. PRICE: 35 Swiss Crowns/yr. institutions. PUBLISHER: Theosophical Society in Sweden, Karlavagen 44, S-114 49, Stockolm, Sweden. EDITORS: B. Melander, Hilda Frazer. ILLUSTRATIONS. INDEX. ADVERTISEMENTS. CIRCULATION: 1,200. MANUSCRIPT

SELECTION: Refereed, editorial board. REPRINTS: author. BOOK REVIEWS: 2-4 reviews,1-3 pp., signed. TARGET AUDIENCE: AC. SAMPLE COPIES: Libraries, individuals.

313. Theologia 21. DATE FOUNDED: 1970. TITLE CHANGES: Immorality Newsletter (1970-1976). FREQUENCY: 5/yr. PRICE: $20/yr. institutions. PUBLISHER: Dominion Press, P.O. Box 37, San Marcos, California 92069-0025. EDITOR: A. Stuart Otto. ILLUSTRATIONS. INDEX. CIRCULATION: 500. MICROFORMS: UMI. REPRINTS: publisher. TARGET AUDIENCE: AC.

Theologia 21 is sharply critical of twentieth century theology. Speculative questions about Christianity are not connected to any denomination. Rather, Theologia 21 follows a metaphysical Bible interpretation, focusing on general religious applications to life and experiences of mankind. Similar to Master Thoughts, this material harbors the same exhortative views of Eastern and Western culture as an evangelical magazine. Thus, each skeptical evaluation contains a remedy for neglected directions in current theology.
This enlarged newsletter fits in a handsome vinyl binder and contains sixteen to thirty pages per year. Occasional charts and diagrams help illustrate the configuration of abstract and polemical arguments.

314. Theologie und Philosophie. DATE FOUNDED: 1926. TITLE CHANGES: Scholastik (1926-1962). FREQUENCY: q. PRICE: 142 Deutsche Marks/yr. institutions. PUBLISHER: Verlag-Herder, Hermann-Herder Street, 4 7800 Freiburg/BR, West Germany. EDITOR: Hermann Josef Sieben. INDEX. CIRCULATION: 800. MANUSCRIPT SELECTION: Refereed, editorial board. BOOK REVIEWS: 50-60 reviews, 1-2 pp., signed. INDEXED/ ABSTRACTED: BulSig, CathI, PhilosI, RelAb. TARGET AUDIENCE: AC. SAMPLE COPIES: Individuals. ACCEPTANCE RATE: 50%.

315. Theoretical Medicine. DATE FOUNDED: 1980. TITLE CHANGES: Metamedicine (1980-1983). FREQUENCY: q. PRICE: $64.50/yr. institutions, $24/yr. personal. PUBLISHER: D. Reidel Publishing Company, P.O. Box 322, 3300 AH Dordrecht, Netherlands. EDITOR: Kazem Sadegh-Zadeh. ILLUSTRATIONS. INDEX. ADVERTISEMENTS. MANUSCRIPT SELECTION: Refereed, editorial board. REPRINTS: author. INDEXED/ABSTRACTED: PhilosI. TARGET AUDIENCE: AC, SP. SAMPLE COPIES: Libraries.

TM continues its interdisciplinary focus on heuristic approaches and the developing new methods in medical and allied health sciences. Special points of interest include the application to medicine of advanced theories in philosophy of science, logic, and mathematics. The study of axiomatic problems bear upon modal language, knowledge acquisition, and theory formation. Clinical judgments are another area involving morality and ethics. This analysis of structure and dynamics in medicine by specialists helps to clarify the interplay between social and scientific institutions. TM thus perceives its mission along the same paths as Journal of Medical Ethics, Journal of Medicine and Philosophy, and National Forum.
Since 1982, TM has published several thematic issues devoted to special topics, with a guest editor responsible for each. This series of provocative papers belongs in the professional's library.

316. Theosophical Movement. DATE FOUNDED: 1930. FREQUENCY: m. PRICE: $7/yr. institutions. PUBLISHER: Theosophy Company Private Limited, 40 New Marine Lines, Bombay 400020, India. EDITOR: M. Daster. INDEX. CIRCULATION: 1,000. MANUSCRIPT SELECTION: Editor. TARGET AUDIENCE: AC. SAMPLE COPIES: Libraries, individuals.

317. Theosophist. DATE FOUNDED: 1879. FREQUENCY: m. PRICE: $16/yr. institutions. PUBLISHER: K. Ramanathan, Manager, Theosophical Publishing House, Adyar, Madras, India. EDITOR: Radha S. Burnier. ILLUSTRATIONS. INDEX. ADVERTISEMENTS. CIRCULATION: 1,600. MANUSCRIPT SELECTION: Editor. BOOK REVIEWS: 3 reviews, 1-3 pp., signed. SPECIAL ISSUES: Occasional. TARGET AUDIENCE: AC, GP. SAMPLE COPIES: Libraries, individuals. ACCEPTANCE RATE: 75%.

This journal promotes the three objectives of the Theosophical Society: (1) universal brotherhood, (2) comparative study of religion, philosophy and science, and (3) investigation of unexplained laws of nature and the powers latent in man. Since its inception in 1875, the Society has spread its teaching by correspondence and controversy against Lamaism and Christianism. Toward these ends, Theosophist publishes such illustrative anecdotes as, for instance, authenticated historical cases, which largely turn the minds of phenomenalists into useful and suggestive channels. The realization of "brotherhood" echoes in short, uplifting pieces on religion, philosophy, and doctrines of social science. Articles resemble those in Theosophy regarding the science of spirit.
   A typical issue features seventeen short articles followed by letters to the editor and an international directory. This century-old magazine is the official voice of universal arcane philosophy.

318. Theosophy. DATE FOUNDED: 1909. FREQUENCY: m. PRICE: $10/yr. institutions. PUBLISHER: Theosophy Company, 245 West 33rd Street, Los Angeles, California 90007. EDITOR: A. Bivins. CIRCULATION: 1,000. MANUSCRIPT SELECTION: Refereed, editorial board. REPRINTS: author. BOOK REVIEWS: 2 reviews, 2 pp. TARGET AUDIENCE: AC, GP. SAMPLE COPIES: Libraries, individuals.

Theosophy solves the enduring riddles of occultism and problems of world religions. It is established in alliance with Theosophist to study ancient and modern aims of humanity. Inspection of world scriptures is broken down psychologically into realistic concepts. Theosophical articles also attempt to define "soul," as apart from "spirit." Distinct attention is paid to freeing the Western mind from prejudices imposed by inherited religions. The views of contributors, mostly members of the Movement, pivot around this approach.
   Each issue of Theosophy publishes four main articles, and then a section called "Letters, Questions, Comment." "On the Lookout" is a panoramic view of international events supporting theosophy.

319. Thinking: Journal of Philosophy for Children. DATE FOUNDED: 1979. FREQUENCY: q. PRICE: $20/yr. institutions, $12/yr. personal. PUBLISHER: The First Mountain Foundation, P.O. Box 196, Montclair, New Jersey 07042. EDITOR: Matthew Lipman. ILLUSTRATIONS. INDEX. ADVERTISEMENTS. CIRCULATION: 1,000. MANUSCRIPT SELECTION: Refereed, editorial

board. REPRINTS: author. BOOK REVIEWS: 3-6 reviews/yr., 1-2 pp., signed. INDEXED/ABSTRACTED: PhilosI. TARGET AUDIENCE: AC, SP. ACCEPTANCE RATE: 80%.

Today's public school systems are the training grounds for many programs in elementary logic especially designed for children to learn basic philosophy. This focus, largely begun by Matthew Lipman, cultivates opportunities for philosophy in primary and secondary education. Thinking responds to this belief in a thorough-going evaluation of childhood reasoning and systematic suggestions for simplified philosophy. Papers report direct applications of books, audio-visual and other methods using logic and ethical concepts in reading groups, classroom discussions, and in school-wide projects. Presenting philosophic questions and possible solutions hopes to prepare children for adult situations. Still, contributors to Thinking feel the oppressing criticism of parents and school officials that morality and ethics are outside the school's responsibility. The unprecedented explosion of interest in philosophy for children explains growing attraction to Thinking as a major resource.

Issues of Thinking contain different departments including "Thinking in Stories," " Education," "Reflections," "Philosophy for Children; a bibliography," and recent adoptions of philosophy programs. Announcements follow about the perpetual growth of this field.

320. Thomist. DATE FOUNDED: 1939. FREQUENCY: q. PRICE: $10/yr. institutions. PUBLISHER: Dominican Fathers, Province of St. Joseph, 487 Michigan Avenue, Washington D.C. 20017. EDITOR: Joseph A. Dinoi. INDEX. ADVERTISEMENTS. CIRCULATION: 1,150. MANUSCRIPT SELECTION: Refereed, editorial board. REPRINTS: author. BOOK REVIEWS: 8-10 reviews, 1-4 pp., signed. INDEXED/ABSTRACTED: CathI, JProCIn, PhilosI, RBibPhil, RelAb. TARGET AUDIENCE: AC. SAMPLE COPIES: Libraries, individuals.

Thomist addresses itself to the philosophical and theological questions of the day as derived from works of Thomas Aquinas. Critical, speculative essays carry on a running dialogue between early traditional ways and the inherited career of Thomistic philosophy as contained in spiritual and cultural society. Thomist is one of the few journals in English which undertakes to confront intellectual assumptions in classic and modern theories. Contributors are mostly scholars who gather notes on Kant, Lonergan, Rahner, Popper and others regarding epistemology, metaphysics, and religion. Like Divus Thomas and Method, Thomist offers a new direction for scientifically understanding mysticism, ontology and deontology.

Articles in Thomist show how natural laws fit into numerous theories on the developing mind. Five major articles, book reviews, and a list of books received achieve this goal.

321. Thought. DATE FOUNDED: 1927. FREQUENCY: q. PRICE: $15/yr. institutions. PUBLISHER: Fordham, University, Bronx, New York 10458. EDITOR: G. Richard Dimler. ADVERTISEMENTS. CIRCULATION: 1,500. MANUSCRIPT SELECTION: Refereed, editorial board. REPRINTS: author. SPECIAL ISSUES: 2/yr. INDEXED/ABSTRACTED: AbEnSt, ArtHumCitI, BulSig, CathI, InAmPerV, PhilosI. TARGET AUDIENCE: AC. SAMPLE COPIES: Libraries, individuals. ACCEPTANCE RATE: 25%.

Thought comes at a time when ideas in philosophy, theology, and humanities are disassociated. Articles put an end to this disassociation in their world-wide orientation toward eclectic Christian thought. Important currents cover political affairs, history, Catholic reform, literature, and the investigation of ecumenism in new religions. The humanistic focus further corners Platonic-Aristotelian concepts of reason, wisdom, and intuition and present-day trends engulfed in technocracy. Eminent scholars stage continuous debate on the realistic nature of social science. Articles pose less risk to "freedom" than those found in Dignity and Interchange.

Thought publishes four lucid articles, three feature reviews, and a series of essays classified into religious thought, philosophy, science, literature and literary criticism, and history.

322. Tijdschrift voor Philosophie. DATE FOUNDED: 1939. FREQUENCY: q. PRICE: $78/yr. institutions. PUBLISHER: VZW, Kardinaal Mercierplein 2, B-3000 Leuven, Belgium. EDITOR: S. Ijsseling. INDEX. CIRCULATION: 700. MANUSCRIPT SELECTION: Refereed, editorial board. BOOK REVIEWS: 75 reviews, 500 words, signed. INDEXED/ABSTRACTED: LLBA, PhilosI. TARGET AUDIENCE: AC. SAMPLE COPIES: Libraries, individuals. ACCEPTANCE RATE: 50%.

323. Topoi. DATE FOUNDED: 1982. FREQUENCY: sa. PRICE: $36/yr. institutions, $18/yr. personal. PUBLISHER: D. Reidel Publishing Company, P.O. Box 322, 3300 AH Dordrecht, Netherlands. EDITORS: Ermanno Bencivenga, Enrico M. Forni. ILLUSTRATIONS. INDEX. ADVERTISEMENTS. MANUSCRIPT SELECTION: Refereed, editorial board. REPRINTS: author. SPECIAL ISSUES: Occasional. INDEXED/ABSTRACTED: PhilosI. TARGET AUDIENCE: AC. SAMPLE COPIES: Libraries.

Topoi is a new journal covering philosophical theory and history of philosophy. Timely reviews illustrate the growth of principal matters related to logic, epistemology, semiology, perception, and methodology. Analytic pieces rationalize behaviors in political and social context, whereas theoretical articles discuss the interpretation of such dynamics as psyche, milieu and personality. The global scope of Topoi puts forth fundamental questions about educational philosophy, including current issues of morality in policy- making. Where possible, authors focus on a single theme or examine classic thinkers. The significantly expanded subject matter of Topoi rivals such complete serials as Synthese and Philosophy in Context.

324. Tradition. DATE FOUNDED: 1961. FREQUENCY: q. PRICE: $48/yr. institutions. PUBLISHER: Human Sciences Press, 72 Fifth Avenue, New York, New York 10011. EDITOR: Rabbi Shalom Carmy. INDEX. ADVERTISEMENTS. CIRCULATION: 2,000. MANUSCRIPT SELECTION: Refereed, editorial board. MICROFORMS: UMI. REPRINTS: author. SPECIAL ISSUES: Occasional. INDEXED/ABSTRACTED: ArtHumCitI, IJewPer, OldTAb, PsyAb, PhilosI, RelAb. TARGET AUDIENCE: AC. SAMPLE COPIES: Libraries, individuals.

Tradition is widely recognized as the most articulate medium of contemporary orthodox Jewish thought. This journal serves an important role for rabbis, scholars and laymen. Articles draw from a variety of fields, from ethics to modern philosophy concerning Jewish law and literary criticism. The common denominator is that each essay aims to enunciate orthodox Jewish lifestyles in contrast to conservatism (Conservative Judaism). The current viability of orthodox traditions signify its strongly rooted history in theology. Contributors are distinguished authorities primarily from Israeli and North American universities. For them, religion in the twentieth century becomes an application of faith, ritualism, and overt philosophical beliefs.

Each issue of Tradition provides six original essays on eclectic topics, a survey of recent Halakhic periodical literature, book reviews, and a communication. This journal is a publication of the Rabbinical Council of America and consequently represents the summit of Jewish thought.

325. Transactions of the Charles S. Pierce Society. DATE FOUNDED: 1965. FREQUENCY: q. PRICE: $27/yr. institutions, $18/yr. personal. PUBLISHER: Peter Hare, Philosophy Department, Baldy Hall, State University of New York, Buffalo, Buffalo, New York 14260. EDITORS: Richard Robin, Peter Hare. INDEX. ADVERTISEMENTS. CIRCULATION: 500. MANUSCRIPT SELECTION: Refereed, editorial board. BOOK REVIEWS: 3 reviews, 1-3 pp., signed. INDEXED/ABSTRACTED: ArtHumCitI, PhilosI. TARGET AUDIENCE: AC. ACCEPTANCE RATE: 50%.

TCPS is concerned with the philosophical works of Charles S. Pierce (1834-1914) and other leading thinkers in the history of American pragmatism. Papers trace the development and influence of Pierce's theories through sixty years of his prolific career. Functionally philosophic principles are evaluated in continental perspective. Significant essays also communicate problems in interpreting Pierce and whether his work withstands the criticism from other naturalistic schools of philosophy (e.g., functionalism). The metaphysical and epistemological schema are brought out in an unusually informative style, delightful to read. Contributors are mainly scholars whose topics resemble the contents of Pragmatics and Beyond.

A regular issue leads off with five main articles, and then follows with book reviews. The re-birth of Pierce's pragmatism evokes an almost compelling instinct toward this journal.

326. Truth Seeker. DATE FOUNDED: 1873. FREQUENCY: m. PRICE: $6/yr. institution. PUBLISHER: Truth Seeker ,Coropration, P.O. Box 2832, San Diego, California 92112. EDITOR: James H. Johnson. INDEX. CIRCULATION: 600. MANUSCRIPT SELECTION: Editor. TARGET AUDIENCE: AC, GP. SAMPLE COPIES: Libraries.

327. Ultimate Reality and Meaning. DATE FOUNDED: 1978. FREQUENCY: q. PRICE: $40/yr. institutions, $22/yr. personal. PUBLISHER: University of Toronto Press, Journals Department, 5201 Dufferin Street, Donsview, Ontario M3H 5T8, Canada. EDITOR: Tibor Horvath. INDEX. ADVERTISEMENTS. CIRCULATION: 500. MANUSCRIPT SELECTION: Refereed, editorial board. REPRINTS: publisher. BOOK REVIEWS: 3-4 reviews, 1-4 pp., signed. INDEXED/ABSTRACTED: ArtHumCitI, CurrContAH, IntBibZeit, LLBA, PhilosI, RelAB, SocAb. TARGET AUDIENCE: AC. SAMPLE COPIES: Libraries, individuals. ACCEPTANCE RATE: 65%.

URM is the official organ of the Institute of Encyclopedia of Ultimate Reality and Meaning, an association of teachers and experts in scientific and social research. Each volume includes studies of the most difficult philosophical systems in anthropology, psychology, religion, aesthetics, and natural science. Authors are usually invited to write critical reviews on American historical thoughts, personalism, or other antecedental systems. In general, themes are based on the principle of analytical decisions. Studies regarding axioms or as global as the history of mankind shed new light upon the heuristic expectations of modern science. This growing scholarly journal now enters its sixth year of publication, following the rigor of Journal of Critical Analysis, Philosophical Forum and Philosophical Review.

Studies in the philosophy of "understanding" are at the forefront of each volume. Issues contain three main articles, reviews, and evaluations of articles. Articles in the section "Method and Systematic Reflections" are of particular interest to young philosophers.

328. Viewpoint Aquarius. DATE FOUNDED: 1972. FREQUENCY: m. PRICE: $15/yr. institutions. PUBLISHER: Box 97, Camberley, Surrey, GU15 2LH, England. EDITORS: Rex Dutta, Jean Coulsting. MANUSCRIPT SELECTION: Editors. REPRINTS: publisher. BOOK REVIEWS: 2 reviews, 1-2 pp., signed. SPECIAL ISSUES: Occasional. TARGET AUDIENCE: GP. ACCEPTANCE RATE: 50%.

329. Vivarium. DATE FOUNDED: 1962. FREQUENCY: sa. PRICE: 60 Guilders/yr. institutions. PUBLISHER: E.J. Brill, P.O. Box 9000, 2300 PA Leiden, Netherlands. EDITORS: C.J. de Vogel, L.M. de Rijk, H.A.G. Braakhuis, F.F. Blok, J. Ijsewijn, C.H. Kneepkens. INDEX. ADVERTISEMENTS. CIRCULATION: 450. MANUSCRIPT SELECTION: Refereed, editorial board. BOOK REVIEWS: 2 reviews, 750 words, signed. INDEXED/ABSTRACTED: PhilosI. TARGET AUDIENCE: AC. SAMPLE COPIES: Libraries, individuals. ACCEPTANCE RATE: 40%.

Vivarium is devoted to the profane side of medieval philosophy and the intellectual life of the Middle Ages and Renaissance. The journal's scope encompasses theories of language (rhetoric), the quadrivium, and philosophies of Latin and new-Latin literature. Logical underpinnings place the examined aspects of each essay in an analytical framework. There they are historically transformed to medieval periods when religion and metaphysics were dominant themes. In this way, Vivarium becomes a valid reference for historians by historiographers. Unlike Speculum or Bulletin de Philosophie Medievale, Vivarium confines discussion to history of ideas.

Issues of Vivarium contain five lengthy articles, book reviews, and a list of books received. Special attention is paid to relationships between history and domains of social learning.

330. This World. DATE FOUNDED: 1982. FREQUENCY: 3/yr. PRICE: $16/yr. institutions. PUBLISHER: Institute for Educational Affairs, 210 East 86th Street, 6th Floor, New York, New York 10028. EDITOR: Michael A. Scully. CIRCULATION: 3,000. MANUSCRIPT SELECTION: Editor. BOOK REVIEWS: 6 reviews, 2 pp., signed. TARGET AUDIENCE: AC. SAMPLE COPIES: Libraries. ACCEPTANCE RATE: 10%.

TW integrates philosophy and egalitarianism with a look at shapers of modern cultural thought. Economics, politics, and American industrial traditions lose their amorphous sense of power to careful, objective criticisms of social problems. Topics on consumerism, commercialism, and materialism reveal the contradictions that make man incomplete and unhappy. Daring essays focus on "emulation" and whether civilization has muddled along, more or less, a victim of indignity. Articles by scholars literally evaluate the evolution of religion, history of ideas, and social sciences from ancient periods to the contemporary age of progress. The ambitions of TW twin the aims of Thought and Midwest Quarterly.

 TW publishes editorials, seven featured articles under different headings, and sections on "Another Look" and "Bookshelf." The gulf between international countries of late has drawn the attention of many concerned commentators. TW benefits readers who desire resolutions to this chasm.

331. World Order. DATE FOUNDED: 1966. FREQUENCY: q. PRICE: $10/yr. institutions. PUBLISHER: National Spiritual Assembly of the Bahaiis of the United States. 536 Sheridan Road, Wilmette, Florida 60091. EDITOR: Firuz Kazemzadeh. ILLUSTRATIONS. INDEX. CIRCULATION: 5,000. MANUSCRIPT SELECTION: Refereed, editorial board. MICROFORMS: UMI. BOOK REVIEWS: 1 review, 2 pp., signed. SPECIAL ISSUES: Occasional. INDEXED/ABSTRACTED: InAmPerV. TARGET AUDIENCE: AC, GP, SP.

332. World Tribune. DATE FOUNDED: 1964. FREQUENCY: w. PRICE: $36/yr. institutions. PUBLISHER: 525 Wilshire Boulevard, Santa Monica, California 90401. EDITOR: George M. Williams. ILLUSTRATIONS. INDEX. ADVERTISEMENTS. CIRCULATION: 60,000. MANUSCRIPT SELECTION: Refereed, editorial board. SPECIAL ISSUES: m. TARGET AUDIENCE: GP. SAMPLE COPIES: Libraries.

333. Yoga: Magazine for the Universal Religion. DATE FOUNDED: 1958. FREQUENCY: q. PRICE: 50 Krones/yr. institutions. PUBLISHER: N.U. Yoga Ashrama, Gylling, DK-8300 Odder, Denmark. EDITOR: Swami Sanatanananda. ILLUSTRATIONS. CIRCULATION: 1,000. MANUSCRIPT SELECTION: Editor. REPRINTS: publisher. BOOK REVIEWS: 1-2 reviews, 500 words. SPECIAL ISSUES: Occasional. TARGET AUDIENCE: GP, SP. SAMPLE COPIES: Libraries, individuals.

Yoga publishes empirical topics on the universal religion founded by Swami Narayanananda. The application of yoga methods places man within a symbolic system linking consciousness and physical oneness. Contributors to this cause have supposedly attained the highest level of spiritual evolution (Nirvikalpa Samadhi, or transcendental state). Through their shared experiences, readers learn attitudes about psychology and medicine, both being instruments in aesthetics and meditation. Theories of "inner wisdom" and healing by faith, however, digress from Yoga's otherwise practical accounts of personal self-growth. The informally written essays closely resemble articles in Journal of Yoga Institute and Self-Knowledge.

 Each issue contains six short articles and book reviews, followed by news and notes of national yoga courses.

334. Zetetic Scholar. DATE FOUNDED: 1978. FREQUENCY: sa. PRICE: $18/yr. institutions, $12/yr. personal. PUBLISHER: Department of Sociology, Eastern Michigan University, Ypsilanti, Michigan 48197. EDITOR: Marcello Truzzi. ILLUSTRATIONS. CIRCULATION: 600. MANUSCRIPT SELECTION: Editor.   BOOK   REVIEWS: 60   reviews,   500   words,   signed. INDEXED/ABSTRACTED: SocAb.   TARGET   AUDIENCE: AC,   SP. ACCEPTANCE RATE: 60%.

Historically, the institutionalization of paranormal study has been anathemic for most serious scientists. ZS, however, breaks this tradition in dealing with all aspects of the acceptance and rejection of claims about anomalies. ZS is the official publication for the Center for Scientific Anomalies Research, an interdisciplinary recognized consortium of psychologists, philosophers, and sociologists exploring the facts and falsehoods of unexplained phenomena. Much of ZS explicitly confronts the crass dogmatism in quasi-scientific reports of psychic experiences. Then, too, proponents and critics alike may support valid observation in either laboratory or case studies.   Dialogue between such noted experts as Richard Kammann, James Randi, Hans Eysenck and Thomas Sebeok enhance the status of objectivity. ZS far surpasses in quality and scholarship any other anomalies journal thus far listed in this analytical guide. It is clearly the exceptional model of analysis in legitimate psychic research.
A single issue contains eight main articles, book reviews, and an extensive bibliographic list of books and materials published in the field. ZS will entice even the most radical opponent of paranormal study.

335.   Zygon: Journal of Religion and Science. DATE FOUNDED: 1966. FREQUENCY: q.   PRICE: $18/yr. institutions, $14/yr. personal, $10/yr. student. PUBLISHER: University of Chicago Press, 11030 Langley Avenue, Chicago, Illinois   60628.   EDITOR: Ralph W. Burhoe.   ILLUSTRATIONS. INDEX. ADVERTISEMENTS. MANUSCRIPT SELECTION: Refereed, editorial board. REPRINTS: author. BOOK REVIEWS: 1-5 reviews, 1-3 pp., signed. SPECIAL ISSUES: Occasional. INDEXED/ABSTRACTED: ArtHumCitI, CathI, PhilosI. TARGET AUDIENCE: AC. SAMPLE COPIES: Libraries.

Zygon is a gathering of   intellects.   It represents a unique attempt to revitalize religious wisdom by means of new scientific understandings in such diverse areas as ethics and genetics, cognition and faith, science and supernatural, purpose and destiny, and the universality of mind and matter. Contributors include distinguished scientists and humanists who unify the facts and values for rational arguments. The journal also provides a platform for the Institute on Religion in an Age of Science, and the Center for Advanced Study in Religion and Science.   Both organizations pursue the synthesis of biological   and   cultural   philosophies   in   an   age   of   disjointed   theories. Fragments of different thought develop a range of themes complementary to Journal for the   Scientific   Study of Religion,   Philosophy, Religion and Science, and Process Studies.
Each issue features three to five original essays, book reviews, and general notes about activities in the sponsoring organizations. Zygon opens a window for the Western scholar into the important currents of speculative ontology.

GEOGRAPHICAL INDEX

References are to item entry numbers, not page numbers.

SUBJECT INDEX

References are to item entry numbers, not page numbers.

ABOUT THE COMPILER

DOUGLAS H. RUBEN is a psychologist with advanced training in philosophy from Wayne State University and Western Michigan University. He serves on the editorial boards of *NCA Catalyst* and *Interbehaviorist* and is guest reviewer for several journals. He has published over fifteen books and fifty articles on the philosophy of science and clinical psychology, including such bibliographies as *Progress in Assertiveness* and *Drug Abuse and the Elderly*. His other current works include *Reassessment in Psychology: The Interbehavioral Alternative, New Ideas in Therapy*, and *Sixty Seconds to Success*. He is currently completing *Psychology Journals and Serials* for Greenwood Press.